Library of
Davidson College

PELICAN BOOKS

THE MISERY OF CHRISTIANITY

Dr Joachim Kahl was born in 1941. He graduated at the University of Marburg in the faculty of Protestant theology, with a thesis on philosophy and Christology in the thought of Friedrich Gogarten. After leaving the Church in 1967 he began a second course of studies at the University of Frankfurt, specializing in philosophy, sociology and political science.

JOACHIM KAHL

The Misery of Christianity

OR

*A Plea for a
Humanity without God*

WITH A PREFACE BY
Gerhard Szczesny

TRANSLATED BY
N. D. Smith

PENGUIN BOOKS

Penguin Books Ltd, Harmondsworth, Middlesex, England
Penguin Books Australia Ltd, Ringwood, Victoria, Australia

Das Elend des Christentums first published in Hamburg 1968
This translation published in Pelican Books 1971
Copyright © Rowohlt Taschenbuch Verlag GmbH, 1968
Translation © N. D. Smith, 1971

The Scripture quotations in this publication are
from the Revised Standard Version of the Bible,
copyrighted 1946 and 1952 by the Division of
Christian Education of the National Council of
Churches of Christ in the U.S.A., and used by
permission

Made and printed in Great Britain by
Hazell, Watson & Viney Ltd
Aylesbury, Bucks

Set in Monotype Plantin

This book is sold subject to the condition
that it shall not, by way of trade or otherwise,
be lent, re-sold, hired out, or otherwise circulated
without the publisher's prior consent in any form o
binding or cover other than that in which it is
published and without a similar condition
including this condition being imposed
on the subsequent purchaser

TO
ANNEGRET KAHL AND
RÜTGER SCHÄFER

My grateful thanks to my friends at Marburg
and Frankfurt for their helpful criticism

J. K.

Have the courage to use your own intellect – KANT

The criticism of religion is the presupposition of all criticism – MARX

Contents

Foreword to the English edition ... 9

Preface by Gerhard Szczesny ... 15

Introduction ... 19

1. What is Christian? ... 25

    The Balance-Sheet of Church History: Anarchy in Ethics ... 27
    The Church as a Slave-Owner
    The Persecution of the Pagans
    The Persecution of the Jews
    The Persecution of Christian 'Heretics'
    The Defamation of Sexuality and of Women
    Possible Objections are Refuted

    The Impossibility of Knowing the Historical Jesus ... 101

    The Balance-Sheet of the History of Theology: Chaos in Dogma ... 121
    The New Testament
    The Early Church
    The Middle Ages
    The Reformation
    The Modern Age
    Today

2. Irrationality in Theology ... 143

    The Two Structural Principles of Theology: Adherence to Authority and Maximum Content ... 144
    Rudolf Bultmann's Concept of Theology
    Gerhard Ebeling's Concept of Theology

CONTENTS

The Demythologization Programme – A Romantic Attempt to Vindicate the Honour of the Christian Faith   156

The Procedure: The 'Hermeneutical' Brainwashing of Unpopular Ideas and Texts

The Result (Expressed in a Friendly Way): Much Ado About Nothing

3. Post-Christian Perspectives – Religious Freedom   178

   The Concept of Religious Freedom   178
   The Separation of State and Churches   183
   The Separation of Universities and Churches   186
   The Separation of Schools and Churches   190

4. The Christian West – Ideology and Reality   193

   Bibliography   200
   Glossary   214

Foreword to the English edition

ARGUMENTS against Christianity have been produced since before the days of Marcus Aurelius and there are Christian apologists who pre-date Athenagoras.[1] Since those days the millions of words poured out by writers attacking or defending Christianity seem to have done little to alter the fact that the Churches are still with us, still powerful, rich and persuasive. One needs, therefore, some justification for publishing yet another blast against the Christian religion. Clearly with a phenomenon as varied and as complex as Christianity the last word cannot be said; it will be a matter for future generations to discover whether it can continue to grow and to adapt itself as it has in the past, or whether it will decline either into a small esoteric cult or into a quaint folk custom. But in the meantime we are faced with Churches which still offer themselves not simply as the answer to our problems in some future life (indeed modern theology is becoming less and less interested in the 'hereafter'), but as a way to solve our immediate social problems. Christianity, despite some half-hearted claims to the contrary, is a real political force in the sense that it offers principles by which we are to regulate our life structures, our societies; these principles have been elaborated by theologians and by ecclesiastical social thinkers to the point where they are identifiable as coherent social ideologies. However, unlike most political parties, the rationale of their ideologies (some would say their ideology) is total. Once people have accepted the Christian view, once they begin to organize along Christian lines, then there is

---

1. Athenagoras was a Greek Christian of the second century, of whose life nothing is known. Of the two main works attributed to him, one is entitled *Intercession for the Christians* and is addressed to Marcus Aurelius, the other is called *On the Resurrection of the Dead*.

no appeal to an external rationality. Criticism, even of a minor kind, is heresy, and rejection of even part of Christian 'truth' is liable to carry with it exclusion from the society which embodies it. It is because Christianity is making fresh bids for attention, many of them mutually contradictory, as the solution to the ideological mess in which much of the world finds itself that yet another critique is needed.

Joachim Kahl has offered a total, root and branch attack; for him, light and shade mean only a relative difference in iniquity. His contention is not that Christianity has failed the ideals of its founders, but that those ideals are themselves so corrupt that first Christianity, then Christendom, and finally the liberal capitalism which it spawns, are bound to reflect that corruption. In this view, the blemishes in the Church referred to by Pope John XXIII or by the World Council of Churches are not the unhappy anomalies they are often held to be, but flow naturally from a Christian world picture. Kahl reminds us again of the familiar horrors: the Crusades, the Inquisition, Luther's support for the bloody suppression of the peasants' rebellion, Catholic and Protestant witch-burning, Anglican persecution of Catholics, Catholic persecution of all non-Catholics, Christians of all kinds killing Jews, engaging in slavery and so on. In short he demands that we look again at all those things Christians normally claim are not essential to the spirit of Christianity and were perpetrated by wicked and misguided men whose religious insight was at fault or whose cupidity overcame their principles. He demands also that we see this claim as false and recognize that the misery Christianity has visited on the world is not accidental or incidental but a direct consequence of an ideology that compels those who hold it towards a struggle for power. He is concerned to make the point that, at least since the Carolingian renaissance, Christianity has been the ideology of the western ruling classes.

However, it is not enough just to rake up past offences and use them to build an anti-Christian polemic – instead it is important to see what is happening now. It is clear, even to the most obtuse, that the diversity of view to be found within western secular society is reflected or repeated within the ecclesiastical structures. In a sense this is hardly surprising, for the people who make up the latter are also an integral part of the former. This being so there are obvious dangers in supposing that Christianity can be made to conform to a single analytical pattern, a mistake made as often by its defenders as by its critics. Kahl devotes a good deal of space to analysing both the institutions and the ideology of the Churches in order to discover what kind of philosophical and political insights the apparently purely ecclesial and theological positions embody. This is, of course, only one of the many possible approaches and it is thick with traps for the incautious – it is worth pointing out the two most important of them. First it is necessary to be very clear about the connection between formulations of belief and patterns of moral behaviour. In general it is a more reliable guide to a man's belief or to the beliefs of a group, a society, to look at what he *does*, or they *do*. Change does not occur evenly at the same pace in structures, infra-structures and individuals. But because it does occur it is essential not to be ensnared by the other part of the difficulty, which is the temptation to interpret words, concepts, and total belief structures, univocally. This may be done either horizontally, within differing contemporary cultures, or vertically, through differing historical moments. To take a relatively simple example: it is at least misleading to treat 'family' as if it meant the same thing to an inhabitant of the Ruwenzori Mountains as it does to an inhabitant of Selly Oak. It is equally misleading to suppose that it meant the same thing in A.D. 71, A.D. 971 or A.D. 1971. Therefore when Christian ideologies talk of the 'sanctity of the family', although they may not always realize it, what they must mean is *this* particular family with all the socio-political choices such a belief entails. It is this that Kahl comes close to missing, for not only does he treat Christianity as if it embodied a unity of belief through time and space but also as if it embodied a uniformity of religious concept.

In this book the author launches a massive broadside at Christianity, not only at the conceptual level but also historically and socially. For Kahl, Christianity is totally and unrelievedly disastrous; but it seems to me that there is another side to the coin. It is to be seen in the person of Camillo Torres, the Colombian priest who joined the guerrillas because his Christianity compelled him to do more than preach to the hungry. He was excommunicated for his pains, but his death has turned him into a martyr for the Christian left and the Church now chooses to forget that she ever rejected him. We may see this other side of the coin too in the heroic work of Dom Helder Camara, Archbishop of Olinda and Recife, who has fought a magnificent battle against the tyrants of Brazil; we may see it in the priests, nuns and laymen of Brazil who have been tortured for their part in the fight – a fight to which they have been committed by their understanding of the meaning of Christian love. We may see it in those Protestants who resisted Hitler when all others in Germany had accepted him: such men as Bonhoeffer are not to be dismissed lightly. Much of the growing demand for social change, for greater justice for all men, is also being voiced at higher levels in the Churches. Pope John XXIII was the first to give it a voice in the Roman Church, even if a somewhat hesitant one, in his second Vatican Council. The World Council of Churches has increasingly adopted a tone critical of the social, military and economic activities of the great western powers. Calls for social revolution are being heard with increasing frequency wherever Christians gather, particularly in the large international conferences. Talks are taking place more and more often between the Churches and their traditional enemies, the Communist parties – we may smile a little at the spectacle of one great orthodoxy chatting to another but at least on the Christian side this represents a genuine desire to see change in the human condition.

Alongside this slow switch in direction we find the theologians. These are the men whose work is most likely to set the pattern of future Christian thinking, for it is their function to spell out the ideological currents present in the Churches. Recently they have been interpreting the movements of revolutionary change growing throughout the world as belonging to the central core of Christianity. This in itself would be comparatively unimportant were it not for the fact that the claim is increasingly being accompanied by the assertion that Christianity is really the only genuinely revolutionary movement.[2] The danger of this is obvious. Theologians of this kind interpret class conflict and revolutionary consciousness according to the attitudes and understanding of the Christian liberal west. There is no space here to analyse their mistakes, but because they commonly misinterpret what is happening, because they do not know what, for example, class-consciousness and solidarity mean, because they fail to understand what is involved in exploitation and what is meant by building revolutionary opposition, they tend to reinforce the kind of mistake that leads ultimately to the blocking of the very social change for which they are hoping.

But despite the hesitations and mistakes it remains that there is enough evidence of genuine change within Christianity for it to be impossible to disregard it. It is Kahl's contention that ultimately Christianity cannot change, that it must finally eject its revolutionaries and decide to support western liberal capitalism. Many of his examples are German; the institutions to which he points do not always exist in other countries – but the parallels do, and his analysis can be lifted wholesale without the slightest difficulty and fitted into the British or, indeed, any European or American social picture. For Kahl the 'misery of Christianity' exists precisely because the religion itself is one produced by western culture just as it in its turn has helped to create and modify that culture. The weakness in his case seems to me to be due to his looking not at people but at the system in which they find themselves, for ultimately it remains that people are more creative than the institutions which they build. The question raised by this book, and hence its importance, is whether that creativity can only appear if people break free of the institution and its ideology or whether they can so transform that ideology as to make it humanly acceptable. For those who are no longer Christians and for those who never were, Kahl's

2. See the work of Jürgen Moltmann and, more particularly, of Herbert McCabe, OP. The latter's book, *Law, Love and Language*, London, 1968, is a very advanced example of the way in which this claim is worked out.

FOREWORD TO THE ENGLISH EDITION

message is clear; we cannot afford to treat Christianity as the harmless foible of a declining few, for it is once again emerging as a serious ideology and making fresh claims to convert the world in new and more effective ways. For Christians too the demand he makes is clear: if they are to be taken seriously as part of the movement of world revolution then they must explicitly and publicly repudiate that fatal involvement with the forces of repression and, above all, they must show how they can humanize their own institutions and bring their representatives and leaders to a sense of human responsibility. Kahl does not believe this to be possible; men like McCabe and Robinson believe that it is. The weaknesses of Kahl's analysis are clear – I have pointed to some of them – yet his charge remains valid. What this book calls upon Christians to do is to make themselves humanly and socially credible.

NEIL MIDDLETON

Preface

THE author of this book, a man who surely must know, attacks Christianity – its dogmas, its ethics and its institutions. His attack is violent and sometimes furious.

He takes Christianity seriously, then.

Can anyone take it seriously nowadays? Apart from the struggles for the last remaining positions of power in society that are still being fought by Christianity in retreat, does any aspect of Christianity bother anyone at all now? Does it still have any influence on our lives? Are members of the general public, including educated people, seriously interested in the conflict between the fundamentalists and the demythologizers? Hardly at all. The present 'chaos in dogma', as the author of this book calls it, would seem to be about as important or as unimportant, not only to the non-Christian but also to the great majority of Christians who pay their church tax,[1] as the recurrent reports of the Loch Ness monster. If there is such a thing, that is all right. If there is not, that is all right too.

Apart from those who are directly involved in the battle of dogmas, Christians are no longer expected to leap to the defence of this or that theology. What most people have long since become accustomed to expect from them – and what they too, as Christians, apparently expect from themselves – is something quite different. They are expected, for example, to be against libertinism or for the pill, to regard authority and order as given by God, to be awarded the Order of Lenin or to give their blessing to the American involvement in Vietnam. Joachim Kahl has

---

1. All adult German Christians are obliged by law to pay a church tax, which is generally automatically deducted from their earnings like income tax – *Translator*. See the section on 'The Separation of State and Churches' below, p. 183 ff.

impressive things to say in this book about what he calls the Christian 'anarchy in ethics'. And it is good for us to be reminded by him of the morality practised by Christians, of the atrocities which have been committed throughout history in the name of the religion of love of one's fellow-men and which were appalling even to the contemporaries of Hitler and Stalin. The breakdown of Christian morality does not, of course, in any way disprove the possible truth of the Christian faith. Nor does it prove it. Anyone who feels that the statement of accounts that follows is too crudely on the debit side as far as Christianity is concerned should study the section on 'The Balance-Sheet of Church History' very carefully – the pagans and the heretics have many pamphlets (which include their exaggerations and their injustices) to their credit.

To summarize this section, 'Anarchy in Ethics' – when they are preaching morality or engaging in politics, Christians ought, in a word, to leave their faith out of it. It does not help anyone to understand any more clearly the positions they assume nor does it in any way contribute to a justification of those positions. All that it does is to inflate purely worldly decisions, which are bound also to affect and do in fact always affect those who are similarly involved in history but have a different faith or none at all, to the size of cosmic events.

All this is extremely exasperating, especially to Christians, quarrelling as they are, constantly, among themselves. But what can still anger, even now, those who do *not* believe?

Joachim Kahl leaves us in no doubt. They are angered by Christian presumption and dishonesty. The spiritual, moral and political claims still made even nowadays by official Christianity are in fact groundless. It is common knowledge that those who really believe in one form or another of Christianity constitute only a tiny minority. Despite this, there seems to be no end to the grandiose discussion of the fact that the Federal Republic and the whole of the western world ought to be Christian. Yet no one believes that the Apostolic and the Nicene Creeds mean anything any more or have any effect at all in the philosophical, literary or artistic fields or even in life itself. They ceased to mean anything many years ago. All the same, theology still goes on fancying itself in the role of spiritual director.

Even worse than the presumption and dishonesty of Christians is the fact that those who are not Christians put up with that attitude on the part of those who are. Young people still grow up to adulthood taking this great lie for granted and accepting without question the purely decorative use of professions of faith and creeds and the concealment of petty activity or no activity at all behind great words. They belong to one or another religious movement or church group through no choice of their own but simply because they were baptized into it, and they continue as members of that religious movement simply so that they can have that peace which religion is said to provide.

This brings us to the heart of the trouble. Since it is apparently impossible for people to decide to get rid once and for all of what they no longer believe in, it is also impossible for anyone to see clearly whether the questions which Christianity set out to answer a long time ago still remain valid questions for us today. It is not until the debris of dogmas, formulations and concepts left behind as a legacy to us by a burnt-out Christianity has been cleared away that we shall be able to discover what is hidden underneath. Many people think we shall find nothing at all. Others believe that we shall find the last remnant of truth and reality waiting to be conquered by reason. It is, however, just possible that neither of these will be revealed – on the one hand, nothing or, on the other, a new field of knowledge waiting to be opened up to science and politics – but, instead, a sphere which has for a long time been hidden from our sight. What is this sphere? It is the area of those questions which man has always been privileged to ask even if he can never answer them, but only express them again and again in different ways.

If this were the result of the great clearing-up operation, then biblical faith would no doubt be brought to light again in it – we would rediscover a *re*mythologized Christianity, changed back into cryptograms, parables and images, one of the many stories in which men express their hopes and their suffering.

This is not, of course, something that the reader will find

explicitly stated in Joachim Kahl's book. All the same, I am sure that it would not be going against the author's intention and his own opinion to remember every now and then, while reading his book, that Feuerbach's thesis about theology, the secret of which is anthropology, can also be interpreted in favour of religion.

Munich, August 1968　　　　　　　　　　GERHARD SZCZESNY

Introduction

'FOR Germany, the critique of religion is essentially over.' This is what Karl Marx wrote in his *Critique of Hegel's Philosophy of Law* more than a century ago. Anyone who sets out to challenge Christianity today certainly has to abandon any dreams he may have of his own originality. Can anyone say anything fundamentally new after the long process of disenchantment of religion that has been carried out through the centuries by Celsius and Porphyry, the writers of the French and English Enlightenment, Reimarus, Feuerbach, Marx, Nietzsche, Overbeck and Freud? Only the very ignorant can echo the meaningless statement that all this is ancient history and has long ago been refuted by the counter-criticism of theologians.

The need to criticize Christianity and theology once again arises from the simple fact that they have continued to exist. Despite the havoc caused in the preserves of religion by the authors and movements I have mentioned, they continue to exist. So the light of reason must once again be turned on the present representatives of religion, who are benefiting from the universal tendency to forget. The appearance of justification must be removed from the current reproach that the critic of religion is disposed to imitate the scholarship and the distortions of the past.

This book is a public answer to an appeal made to me by Dorothee Sölle, the Cologne theologian, who was 'representative' of many of my erstwhile travelling companions. After I had told her of my intention to leave the Church, she wrote me a letter entreating me to read Bert Brecht's 'But who is the party?' and enclosing the poem, which is addressed to a man who has left:

> Show us the way that we must go and we
> will go that way like you, but
> do not go the right way without us.
> Without us, that way
> would be wrong.
> Do not part company with us!
> We may go astray and you may be right so
> do not part company with us ...

The right way is the non-Christian way – a way that has been analysed critically and atheistically, for example by Herbert Marcuse and his younger contemporary, Max Horkheimer.

My aim in writing this book is quite modest. I have confined myself to expressing a few ideas that have occurred to me and to throwing a few sidelights on the subject of religion and humanity because I suspect that these may act as suitable agents in alienating readers from Chsritianity by bringing about a diffused sense of uneasiness in the minds of a number of them.

This book is really nothing more or less than a pamphlet. I cannot conceal my polemical intention in writing it, nor do I wish to. It is the result of a long-lasting attack of compulsive intellectual washing. The middle-class prejudice that rational criticism can only be properly expressed if one is removed from the heat of the conflict is not one which I share. I have not written this book, as Tacitus said in his *Annals*, 'without anger and without study', but with anger and with study. In the course of writing it, study preceded anger, which came about almost as a matter of course. Anyone who has never become indignant about Christianity has never really known it.

Although a great deal of what is said in this book is fragmentary and, because it is a pamphlet, much of what it contains is in the form of slogans, it does – or at least I hope it does – deal with all the essential aspects of Christian faith. But I must hasten to extinguish too high hopes – the reader will not find, in the pages which follow, an all-embracing historical and social analysis of Christianity. I do not wish to replace studies of this kind, but rather to stimulate the reader to turn to them.

INTRODUCTION

What objection will my opponents in the Church raise to this?

They will say, no doubt, that my break with theology is the result of my reaching an impasse, which is understandable in view of the chaotic situation in which Protestant theology is placed nowadays at university level. They will also say that it is both rash and presumptuous for so young a person to say no, quite flatly, to such a complex phenomenon as Christianity. My answer to this is simple. If young pastors are allowed to be the best judges, after seven years spent studying theology, of what they have agreed to do, then I too should also be allowed to be the best judge of what I can no longer agree to do.

I have learnt a great deal from Franz Overbeck's writings – so much that his personal fate terrifies me. At the end of his long period as Professor of Theology at Basle, he admitted: 'I can honestly say that Christianity has cost me my life. To such an extent that, although I never possessed it and only became a theologian as a result of a "misunderstanding", I have taken the whole of my life to get rid of it.'[1] Does this situation have to be perpetuated? Christianity has already cheated too many people out of their lives. That is why I want to get rid of it, right away.

What I have written will probably make theologians suspect even more strongly that I have never really known what the Christian faith is. Applying what Gerhard Ebeling has said to me, that is, that 'the man who deliberately chooses to reject the gospel has not, in the last resort, really understood it',[2] it will be said, no doubt, that I have understood faith wrongly, regarding it as a kind of quiz game, and that I have spoken about faith as a blind man speaks about colour. I have only two things to say in my own defence against this trick, invariably used to ward off unwelcome criticism.

The first is a subjective, personal defence. I led youth groups, helped with children's services and gave sermons regularly and

1. Quoted by Nigg, *Franz Overbeck*, p. 67.
2. Ebeling, 'Hauptprobleme ...', p. 125. (Where titles have been abbreviated in footnotes, see Bibliography – *Translator*.)

voluntarily for more than eight years. I did not engage in these and similar church activities without deep inner commitment – in other words, 'faith'.

The second is an objective defence. A non-Christian can certainly understand the gospel, take it seriously and reject it. It cannot be denied that the criticism of many free-thinkers and confirmed atheists is full of platitudes and ignorance – there are many such passages, for example, in the writings of Bertrand Russell. But must it inevitably be so? Really crushing criticism does not always suspect every theologian of being an obscurantist or that base clerical deception and striving after power is lurking everywhere in Christianity. On the contrary, the true critic of Christianity takes the gospel precisely at its word and examines whether it has really brought 'peace on earth and good will among men' and whether Jesus Christ has really given rest to those 'who labour and are heavily laden' and has made 'all things new'.

This sociological method of criticism measures the phenomena to be investigated by the yardstick of their own claims. In carrying out concrete individual analyses, it insists on making a distinction between the real content and its ideological veil. Religion is in this way not broken open from outside, but, so to speak, understood from within and subjected to immanent criticism from the point of view of its own problems and needs. It is, in other words, beaten on its own territory, if not with its own weapons. In this process of getting to the truth, immanent criticism ultimately changes into a kind of criticism which blows up the Christian framework of relationships and lays bare the ideological limitations of the conceptual structure of theology. In this way, for example, 'care for the salvation of mankind' can be transformed into a strategical and tactical plan to emancipate society.

To conclude this introduction, I have decided to add a few provisional remarks about the situation in which Christianity finds itself today. These will supplement the list of contents and give the reader some indication as to what he may expect from my book.

INTRODUCTION

It would be premature at the moment and too much of a simplification to say that Christianity is now no more than a corpse which can only be given a semblance of life if interested politicians, theologians and church functionaries supply it with oxygen. Nonetheless, it is very difficult indeed to ignore the increasing loss of substance and of function in Christianity. The more the Christian mythology has lost its power to console, to motivate and to convince, the more important has become the culture industry in society. The frustrations of a heartless and inhuman functional society are made bearable now, not by religious illusions, but predominantly by the stupefying flood of products from an omnipresent entertainment industry.

All the same, very few individuals have so far succeeded, within capitalist society, in freeing themselves completely from the enchantment of the traditional religious rituals and mysteries. It is, of course, true that most people no longer take a regular and active part in the affairs of the Church. On the other hand, however, they do not leave it and they still hope, perhaps consciously, perhaps only unconsciously, to derive some benefit from the Church. These expectations range from the wish to have certain special occasions in life, such as marriage and the birth of children, marked by church solemnities, to the desire to safeguard the western world from communism. In the first case the pastor is seen as a reverend master of ceremonies; in the second, the Church is regarded as the protectress of the Holy Grail, the guardian of morals and order. This pious humbug represents the subjective defeat of a social order which condemns people to impotence and which allows them to grasp hold of anything at all that promises them some kind of security.

What a feeling of consolation and safety belonging to a worldwide and centuries old organization like the Church gives to weak and damaged individuals! Seen from the point of view of social psychology, what we have here is the phenomenon of unburdening, in which we spare ourselves the need to reflect anew and make fresh decisions. This attitude is encouraged and justified by the traditionally thoughtless practice of identifying Christianity with humanity, as the current lip-service to the presumably lofty ethics of the Sermon on the Mount demonstrates.

How do established theologians react to the loss of substance and of function in Christianity that has taken place in the lives of the great mass of people over the past two centuries? If they do not cling defiantly to the old dogmas and ostensibly repudiate the spirit of the age – if, in other words, they are not rigid confessionalists, fundamentalists or anti-modernists – then they usually behave impartially and are open to the world. They make use of contemporary scientific knowledge and are able to express clever opinions about most modern questions. But they do waste a great deal of time and energy in attempting – usually dishonestly and always subject to authority – to verify that some modern datum or movement is basically biblical and soundly Christian. These modern questions include, for example, the problem of contemporary man's view of the world, the equality of women, sexual ethics, and the autonomy of reason. For the rest, their studies are usually a weak infusion of various disciplines, made serviceable and Christian. This is very clear, for instance, from the sociological, psychological and philosophical analyses of Paul Tillich or Jürgen Moltmann.

No theology, however modern or revolutionary it may appear to be, has anything new to say in reply to an advanced critical and atheistic theory. The very opposite is true. At the most, it can only confirm the opinion of Franz Overbeck, that theology is a parasite eating at a table which others have set.

I

What is Christian?

EVERYONE who has, up to now, attempted to criticize Christianity has had to endure the reproach that he was fighting against a caricature – that his picture of Christianity was either carelessly or malevolently distorted, one-sided and prejudiced. True Christianity, it has always been claimed, was quite different and was not affected by criticism.

If the critic of Christianity is to strip this piece of Christian apologetics once and for all time of its semblance of legitimacy, he must forgo the privilege of attempting to define the essence of Christianity himself and follow the theologians, who say, quite simply, 'We are the ones who establish what Christianity is'.

The method of taking what Christians themselves define as Christian as one's point of departure would, however, seem to lead us into a state of embarrassment that cannot be overcome – Christians themselves do not know what is Christian. What some Christians regard as God's most holy will, others condemn as the way of the devil.

With which Christian denomination should the non-Christian critic concern himself? If he is to be quite fair, he cannot really ignore any group. He is therefore bound, in his criticism, to concern himself with all the Christian groups and admit that there is no Christianity as such, but only a great number of Christianities. Looked at from the point of view of comparative religion, Christianity is a syncretistic religion. From the point of view of the critic of ideology, Christian theology is an accumulation of empty formulae which can be filled with whatever content you like. It is impossible to criticize Christianity as such materially, because there is no Christianity as such and never has been. There is no uniform Christian concept of God and there-is, for example, no one Christian attitude towards war. There is absolutely no agreement within Christian circles about what is Christian.

My aim here is to criticize Christianity as a whole. Must I therefore try to prove each Christianity individually wrong? Is there nothing that all Christians share? Is there not a certain unity and some connection with the Fathers of the Church? As I shall show in some detail, this unity does not exist in the content of Christian ideas and statements, but it does exist in their structure. What unites the systematic writings of Rudolf Bultmann, for example, with the pamphlets of the Jehovah's Witnesses, and what the Greek Fathers of the Church share with Martin Niemöller, is the same basic structure of their statements. Every Christian appeals to authority and offers the maximum content. Every theological affirmation is irrational in some aspect and always breaks off reflection at a certain point.

To this extent, it is possible to speak of Christianity as such and of theology as such and to burst them wide open at the point where they are united.

In using the word 'Christian' here and throughout this book, then, I mean all people, without distinction, who call themselves by that name and who want to be regarded as such, including those who are outside the framework of the great churches and are called, by those churches, members of sects or heretics. If I am to make a scientific analysis, I am bound to do this. In a certain sense, too, Christianity as a whole will gain because of my decision to treat it in this way – those who belong to minority groups and the 'lone wolves' do at least give Christianity a touch of humanity. The members of the smaller groups do not, of course, regard themselves as heretics, but as the true Christians. The person who is standing outside the Christian framework must take this into account and should try not to fall a victim to the superstition of the great number – a superstition which the great churches do all they can to encourage.

WHAT IS CHRISTIAN?

The Balance-Sheet of Church History: Anarchy in Ethics

Christian politicians are in the habit nowadays of evoking, with excessive emotion, the 'great social and moral values of Christianity' which, they claim, 'cannot be abandoned' and which alone can preserve us from the evil arch-enemy from the East. Similarly, Christian theologians are in the habit of tracing almost all the advances made in history – including, for example, the emergence of the natural sciences – back to an 'ultimately Christian origin'.

In view of this blindness to history and the modern tendency towards an ahistorical consciousness, it would perhaps be as well to present the reader with the very extensive catalogue of sins that have been committed throughout history by the churches. I shall not, of course, simply compile an arbitrary and disconnected list of atrocities – although there has been no lack of these in the history of Christianity. On the contrary, I will present these sins systematically and let history itself pronounce judgement on the Christian faith.

Unlike the teaching of many theologians, who, understandably enough, are at pains to render the history of the Church quite harmless and rob it of all evidence that would prove the anti-Christian case, it is clear from the writings of Franz Overbeck that the history of Christianity is the best school for atheism.[1] What, then, does it really mean, we may ask, that the religion which peddles the love of one's fellow-men has, from its earliest beginnings right up to the present day, tolerated, encouraged and even committed the most inhuman atrocities in the name of God, in the name of Jesus Christ and in the name of the Bible? What does it really imply – the fact that Christians have been able and are still able to perpetrate the most shocking brutalities again and again with a clear conscience and a detailed theological alibi?

1. Overbeck, *Christentum und Kultur*, p. 265.

THE CHURCH AS A SLAVE-OWNER[2]

For as far back as it is possible to trace the history of mankind, there have always been two groups of people in society – the rulers and the ruled, the masters and the servants, the rich and the poor, the exploiters and the exploited. This class structure, which was expressed most clearly in the ancient world in the slave economy, was taken over unquestioningly by Christianity as a pure datum.

Doubts were expressed from time to time in the pre-Christian and non-Christian ancient world – but not in the Old Testament – as to whether slavery was really lawful, and it was even possible, in certain Greek utopias, for a society without slavery to exist, at least in the minds of men. Under the influence of the Stoic philosophers, moreover, the Roman slave laws were made more liberal and more humane. On the other hand, nothing of this kind is discernible in the New Testament.

The New Testament has many harsh things to say against illicit sexual intercourse, against homosexuality and against the wearing of long hair by women. It does not, however, denounce or forbid the exploitation of the many as living tools by the few, or their being bought and sold like so much merchandise. Nowhere does it even express the thought that though slavery is objectionable it could not be abolished at the time because of the prevailing positions of power. It affirms the very opposite.

The parables which Jesus told according to the gospels presuppose slavery. Far from criticizing it, they glorify it as a model of the relationship between God and man – Matt. xviii, 23 ff. ('Therefore the kingdom of heaven may be compared to a king who wished to settle accounts with his servants'); xxv, 14 ff.; Mark xiii, 34; Luke xii, 42 ff.; xvii, 7 ff.

Paul, too, not only accepted slavery as a matter of course, but

2. For the material provided in this section, I have relied a great deal not only on the full histories of the Church compiled by Heussi, Loewenich and Schmidt, but also, particularly, on Deschner, Dobschütz, Heer, Knoll, Kupisch, Overbeck, and Wendland, in whose books all the facts that I have given can be verified.

even affirmed it explicitly. He sent Onesimus, the runaway slave whom he had converted, back to his Christian master, Philemon (see the letter to Philemon). It is moreover quite clear from the apostle's own words that he was not concerned with the emancipation of slaves: 'Everyone should remain in the state in which he was called. Were you a slave when you were called? Never mind. But if you can gain your freedom, make use of your present condition instead. For he who was called in the Lord as a slave is a freedman of the Lord. Likewise, he who was free when called is a slave of Christ' (1 Cor. vii, 20-22). Most Christian readers of the Bible are hardly conscious of the monstrous cynicism underlying these words. By means of a verbal trick worthy of a crooked horsedealer – giving a double meaning to the two concepts slave and freedman – those who are already oppressed are completely taken in. By virtue of the religious fiction that they are really freedmen of Christ, these factual slaves are persuaded that they ought to be indifferent to their lack of freedom. Paul at the same time also renames the slave-owner the slave of Christ and thus draws a veil over the existing injustice of slavery, which is justified as God's will.

The great contempt for human nature which characterizes the whole of the New Testament is manifested above all in the so-called household codes – those lists of 'moral' precepts for slaves, slave-owners, women and citizens. This is what Paul had to say to slaves in his household codes: submit yourselves voluntarily to your masters in a spirit of humble obedience, 'so that the name of God and the teaching may not be defamed' (1 Tim. vi, 1), 'so that in everything they [slaves] may adorn the doctrine of God our Saviour' (Tit. ii, 10), 'as slaves of Christ, doing the will of God from the heart, rendering service with a good will as to the Lord and not to men' (Eph. vi, 6 f.), 'knowing that from the Lord you will receive the inheritance as your reward' (Col. iii, 24).

I have given all these quotations to prove that early Christianity was guilty of being the agent of a repressive society. Already, established positions of power were enveloped in divine glory and social restraints were reinforced in the minds and wills of men by religious commandments – what was obtained by violence and extortion was really the result of free personal decision. Submission to human domination was glorified as an act of submission to God. Man's psychological apparatus for punishing himself – his bad conscience – was used to regulate all his impulses and he came to think that what was violently imposed from outside was the consequence of his own free will. Existing suffering was overcome by the power of religion and ontologized, never criticized.

The New Testament is a manifesto of inhumanity. It is mass deception planned on a large scale. It makes people stupid instead of making them aware of their own objective interests.

The fatal ideological function carried out by the main theme of the New Testament, the innocent suffering and death of Jesus, is clear from a passage in the first letter of Peter (ii, 18 ff.). Referring to Jesus' passion, the author calls upon slaves to be obedient even to bad masters and to allow themselves to be punished even if they are innocent. The true aspect of the *theologia crucis* or theology of the cross, so highly esteemed by Protestants especially, is all too clearly revealed here – the suffering of Christ serves as an alibi and as an illusion of consolation for the innocent suffering of other men.

What, after all, is the cross of Jesus Christ? It is nothing but the sum total of a sado-masochistic glorification of pain. If it is possible to extract any meaning at all from an instrument of torture such as the cross, then this can only be done by considering, not the cross of Jesus, but the crosses along the Via Latina between Rome and Capua, from which six thousand slaves, the revolutionary supporters of Spartacus, were hung after their defeat in the slave war in 71 B.C. Their blood at least flowed for something meaningful – for human happiness – even though it flowed in vain.

The early Church retained the New Testament attitude to slavery. The idea of the religious equality of all men before God, which was common to other ancient religions as well as Christianity, in no sense led to that of the political and social equality of all men. The idea of real emancipation was always rejected

WHAT IS CHRISTIAN?

whenever it made an appearance. Bishop Ignatius of Antioch forbade Christian slaves to demand their redemption at the expense of the local church. Slaves were instructed, in the letter of Barnabas, to revere their owners as the 'likeness of God'. Tertullian, the Father of the Church, tried to convince slaves that freedom and servitude in the world were meaningless sham – mere appearance compared with true freedom in Christ, who liberated men from the servitude of sin. Man could not be deprived more drastically of everything that he desired for his happiness. The dualistic anthropology underlying all these standpoints is particularly well brought out in Lactantius's statement: 'Since we measure all human things, not with the yardstick of the body, but with that of the spirit, our slaves, although they are differently situated from ourselves as far as the body is concerned, are nonetheless not our slaves – we regard them as our brothers in the spirit and as our fellow-slaves in religion and call them this.'[3] In a word, the early Church never envisaged any real abolition of slavery in this life. If certain Christian landowners did occasionally give individual slaves their freedom, they did not do so because they recognized that these men had a right to political and social freedom, but because they felt constrained to perform a 'good work' for the salvation of their own souls.

From the very beginning, Christian preaching stabilized the practice of slavery. Augustine showed what an excellent oil the new religion was for the machinery of the masters in society when he called on those who were not slaves to give thanks because Christ and his Church did not make free men of slaves, but good slaves of bad slaves.

The Church's adaptation to the social and political power structure of the state – an unhesitating act of opportunism – took place at last in the fourth century. As the exponents of the Roman feudal class, the emperors raised Christianity to the level of the state religion. Constantine began this process in

---

3. Quoted and translated from Overbeck's article on the Church's relationship with slavery in the Roman Empire, 'Über das Verhältnis der alten Kirche zur Sklaverei im römischen Reiche', p. 194.

A.D. 313 and it was completed in 380 by Gratian and Theodosius.

Members of the aristocracy and of the higher clergy quickly began to become entangled with each other in their functions and privileges in society. Valuable realms were bestowed upon bishops – many noblemen made sure of eternal salvation by giving great estates to the Church, which, after very few years, became the richest landowner with the greatest number of slaves in the Empire. Like all exploiters, the Church made unsparing use of her power, with the result that the position of the slaves who had been transferred to her ownership deteriorated rapidly. The non-Christian ancient world had conceived the idea of man's inviolable right to freedom. Not so Christianity, which created an unassailable right to the absence of freedom. The emancipation of the Church's slaves was declared to be impossible in principle, since it was not the clergy but God himself who had control of the rights of ownership, and property could only be disposed of by the masters. (This was legally laid down in Gratian's Decree, the *Decretum Gratiani*, which appeared shortly after 1140, with reference to monastic slaves.)

The frequent attempt on the part of modern apologists to find, at least in embryo, the presence of the 'individual's right to self-determination' in the Church's attitude to slavery is bound to fail. It was above all in the monastic life that a mockery was made of freedom. 'The state in the ancient world did not deny the slave any personal right which the monastic rule did not also deny to the monk and, by making complete obedience to the abbot and the rule, accompanied by the total destruction of one's personal will, the supreme monastic virtue, only the nature of slavery could be changed for the slave when he entered the monastery.'[4]

Slavery continued throughout the whole of the Christian Middle Ages and was defended by leading scholastic theologians such as Thomas Aquinas, Albert the Great and Duns Scotus. Thomas accepted Aristotle's view that the slave was an 'inspired tool of his master' and a 'non-member of society'. Popes and

4. ibid., p. 215.

bishops, prelates and superiors of monasteries had control of thousands of male and female slaves who had the task of cultivating the enormous farm lands. Those who ran away were relentlessly pursued, caught and brought back. As *fugitivi*, an iron ring with Christian symbols was then put round their necks. Canon law treated all slaves as objects and classified them under the heading 'church property' (human material). They were not, of course, admitted to the offices of the Church. Slavery was also declared to be an ecclesiastical disciplinary measure. In 655, the Synod of Toledo declared that all the children of priests were to be treated as slaves. This declaration was repeated at Pavia in 1022 and included later, round about the year 1140, in Gratian's Decree. In 1179, at the Third Lateran Council, all those who opposed the Roman papacy were threatened with slavery. Even though the punishments could not be carried out, the popes imposed slavery on Venice in 1309, 1482 and 1506, on Florence in 1376, and on the whole of England in 1508.

The slave trade was given a new lease of life at the end of the Middle Ages by the Spanish and Portuguese conquests and colonization in the New World. In his bull of 1454, *Romanus Pontifex*, Pope Nicholas V gave his blessing to the practice of enslaving all conquered peoples. In 1487, Innocent VIII accepted, as a gift from Isabella of Spain, a large number of slaves from Malaga. In 1493, Alexander VI divided the world between Spain and Portugal and sanctioned the normal practice of forced labour, declaring it to be quite lawful. In 1548, Paul III granted to all men and to all members of the clergy the right to keep slaves. Papal galleys set out to catch men and many fervent prayers of thanksgiving rose up to heaven whenever a rich catch of 'tools with souls' was made.

Christian theologians seriously discussed the 'problem' of whether a pocket mirror was a just price for a negro. The Jesuit college in the Congo owned twelve thousand slaves in 1666 and the popes rejoiced in their services until the end of the eighteenth century in the Papal States. Even as late as 1864, there were slaves in the service of the Church – owned by the Benedictines in Brazil.

From the very beginning, Protestantism followed the same course, after Luther had justified serfdom and slavery theologically. The missionaries gave theological approval to the slave trade and it was consequently practised with a clear conscience by the Protestant states until far into the nineteenth century. Even now, in the twentieth century, the Christian Ethiopians go out hunting for human beings and sell their plunder on the slave market.

The brief survey of slavery in the Christian world which I have just given shows clearly not only that Christianity failed pitifully to rise to the social problem of the nineteenth century (this is something that discerning theologians at least are prepared to admit nowadays), but also that it came to terms, very early on, with the powers which were economically dominant in society. Up to the fourth century, the Church simply clung to the existing power structures in society, playing the subordinate part of their ideological handmaiden. Later on, however, the higher clergy themselves plundered the mass of the people, especially the peasants. The Church was completely integrated into the medieval feudal system. The leading positions in the Church were occupied exclusively by noblemen, usually the second sons of ruling families – the eldest son or *primogenitus* inherited the father's rights, while the second son or *secundogenitus* entered holy orders and was given the office of bishop or abbot. Abbots were often required to produce evidence of nobility going back over several generations. The reigning prince acted as patron and supervised the distribution of benefices among the clergy, with the inevitable result that members of his own family received the best livings.

Thanks to constant wars of conquest and to a carefully devised system of taxation, by the close of the Middle Ages the papacy had managed to become the most prosperous financial power in Europe by a process of strictly legal robbery. Pope John XXII (1316–1334), for example, spent his revenue in the following way: 63·7% on his wars, 12·7% on officials' salaries, 7·16% on alms, which included expenditure on new church buildings and missions, 3·35% on clothing, 0·17% on ornaments and finery, 2·9% on buildings, 2·5% on his kitchen and cellar and 4% on his friends and relations.[5]

Lack of space prevents me from discussing the attitude of Luther. It is, in any case, well known that he was hostile to the peasants and that he – and indeed the whole Protestant world which followed him – justified the existing privileged class structure of society with religious arguments. I will therefore go on at once to review briefly the position occupied by the churches in the capitalist system of the nineteenth century.

The indescribable misery which capitalism caused among the great masses of the people at that time cannot, of course, be adequately conveyed here in a few lines.

In 1840, the average length of life of a worker in Liverpool was fifteen years. Fifty-seven per cent of working-class children in Manchester died before reaching the age of five. It was common for nine- and ten-year-olds to work for twenty-four and thirty-six hours without a break. At night-time, they were driven to work and kept awake with whips. Public petitions were drawn up in 1860 urging the reduction of working hours to eighteen per day. Children of three and four worked standing on chairs in the lace factories. They often had less room in the straw-plaiting factories than a dog in its kennel. Naked and half-naked four- and five-year olds crawled, together with grown men and women, hanging on to chains through the narrow, hot galleries of the coal mines. Anyone who complained was dismissed at once and, as a 'marked man', would not find fresh employment. People lay down to die in ditches and were covered with earth where they lay. They received practically no education at all – apart from religious instruction.[6]

There is no record of the churches having protested against these conditions. The first law in Germany forbidding the employment of children below the age of nine in factories (1839) was, typically enough, passed at the insistence of the military authorities, who had been struck by the physical unfitness of those recruits who had previously been employed in industry.

At long last, the churches tried to help – offering faint-hearted

5. Figures taken from Schmidt, *Grundriss der Kirchengeschichte*, p. 256 f.
6. Deschner, *Das Jahrhundert der Barbarei*, p. 38.

THE MISERY OF CHRISTIANITY

and frugal assistance. Where a surgical operation was called for, they stuck on plasters. Appeals were made to the generosity and spirit of patronage of the Christian aristocrats and factory owners, but these did not get to the root of the trouble. Even reformers like Wichern and Ketteler tended to rely on patriarchal ideas and to fob off the oppressed with pitiful alms. Above all, the infamous capitalist system continued to be regarded as the result of God's will.

What is the situation today? The complicity between Christianity and capitalism has not changed fundamentally. In her official task of ministering to people's needs, the Church binds up a few wounds with her right hand, which she helps to open again with her left, by giving ideological support to a false world order. While good but gullible parish voluntary workers collect donations for Christian Aid or CAFOD, the great American concerns, managed almost entirely by devout Christians, continue to carry out their policy of neo-colonization and of increasing existing misery in the Third World. They do this unchallenged and under the aegis of the government chiefs in the White House, all of whom are practising Christians. It is true that, in Latin America, there are members of the Catholic Church, priests, who have joined the side of the exploited masses. But in so doing they are not primarily motivated by a burning desire to be politically at one with those who are striving towards the social emancipation of the 'damned of this earth'. They are aiming, in a spirit of opportunism, to keep the people faithful to the Catholic religion they have inherited. If a socialist revolution seemed inevitable, the Church would at least side with the victorious power and do everything possible to prevent the new society from moving towards atheism.

But how has it been possible for the Church to succeed, throughout the centuries and up to the present day, in lulling the outlaws into a sense of security and giving the oppressors an easy conscience? This can best be explained by a brief presentation of the most important aspects of the Christian ideology.

The first theme that we must consider is the Christian *teach-*

ing about God in the narrower sense, in other words, the doctrine of creation. This affirms that, despite man's fall through sin, God founded and established a basically good world – as the first chapter of the Bible puts it, 'God saw everything that he had made, and behold, it was very good'. From this affirmation has come the liturgical call to men and women, God's creatures, to praise and thank God unceasingly. This has in turn helped to draw a veil over the misery in their lives. How many Christian hymns call on us to 'praise the Lord' who has given us life, health and prosperity, who guides our ways and rules the world, and who helps us in our deepest need? The myth of God's welfare state, which was reduced to secular terms in the nineteenth-century philosophical movement known as idealism, to the view that everything that was real was also good, and has now, in the twentieth century, been ultimately watered down to a resigned belief in what Bollnow has called 'a world which is, in the last resort, whole', has long bound people, as it were by an oath, to the existing power structures. If people have to be thankful for something, they can hardly criticize it.

In this way, concrete social and political positions of power have been and still are being strengthened in the will of God. This idea is generally conveyed, in the case of the Catholic Church, by the so-called doctrine of the natural law ('it is of its very nature so') or, in the case of Protestantism, by the doctrine of the orders of creation. It was, for example, possible for the monarchy ('Emperor by God's grace') on the one hand and slavery on the other to be justified by religious arguments based on these doctrines for almost two thousand years.

Whenever men become dissatisfied with their state in life (as they sometimes do during or after a war), Christian theologians are still not at a loss and can use the doctrine of creation with shallow rhetoric. 'How unsearchable are God's judgements and how inscrutable are his ways! Who can presume to argue with him? My dear child, you must not doubt.' This is the Church's infallible way of silencing all criticism and all protest – further evidence of the inevitable Christian practice of wrapping the causes of human evil and distress (which are usually far from

THE MISERY OF CHRISTIANITY

unsearchable) in mystery and frustrating any attempt to get rid of them.

This smokescreen is made thicker by the Christian use of the *doctrine of sin*, according to which all conflicts between men and all abuses are a consequence of man's disobedience to God's holy commandments. What is really the far-reaching result of an irrational social order which mutilates and deforms its members is placed fairly and squarely on the shoulders of the victims.

Since Adam's fall, all human beings have been living in a 'state of corruption'. They are evil – the different Christian denominations are not in agreement among themselves about the degree of human evil – and must therefore be punished and restrained. God has therefore decreed, as a disciplinary measure, that there should be inferior and superior social orders, and it is from these that the ruling class and the slave class have been derived. This situation will last until the end of the world and cannot be done away with because of the fact that evil is inherent in man. Any attempt to put an end to this state of things is regarded as sacrilege and fanaticism and can only be condemned.

Every Sunday, people are chastised in sermons in which they are told that they are sinners, worthless and cringing creatures without freedom. In fact they are, as such, extremely useful to the social élite, the ruling classes, who can only survive and prosper as long as the great masses of the people remain helpless and lacking in self-confidence.

So that the great mass of men may never hit on the idea of taking their history into their own hands in a conscious attempt to develop their own creative possibilities, the *Christological teaching* of the churches tells them explicitly that they are not capable of doing this. The decisive problems of human existence (in a word, man's salvation) cannot be solved by men themselves, but only by the redeemer whom God has sent to men as an act of pure grace.

Jesus Christ does not, of course, redeem men simply from material misery. He brings what are said to be higher gifts and shows clearly that social justice and political freedom are not essential, but are simply of this world and carnal. The man who is redeemed in Christ can safely remain a slave in this world.

The value of the redemption shared by those who believe in Christ has to be proved in their imitation of Christ. It is by following in the footsteps of their redeemer that they show whether or not they have inwardly overcome the world and have willingly taken up their cross. True human freedom is, in practice, to be found in man's ability to suffer humbly. How can the redeemed believer even want to live better than the Lord, who suffered and yet was innocent? We, on the other hand, are guilty and richly deserve all the suffering we meet in this world.

It is also quite clear from the so-called *doctrine of grace* that all Christian teaching aims to keep men in a state of immaturity. Man is always dependent on God's grace – as Christ said in John's gospel (xv, 5), 'Apart from me you can do nothing'. Since this divine grace is not encountered in a vacuum, but only in concrete social and human situations, it is of necessity tied to certain human beings. This is why, for example, kings and emperors were, and princes of the Church are still, addressed as 'Your Grace'.

Anyone who really believes that human beings are thus totally dependent on grace must also think of them as outlaws, in other words, as people who have no rights at all even to the most basic of human needs. Luther wrote, with cynical clarity, in his commentary on the first article of faith:

> I believe that God has created me together with all creatures, has given me body and soul, eyes, ears and limbs, reason and every sense and still preserves these, that he has also given me clothes and shoes, food and drink, house and home, wife and children, fields, cattle and all things, that he also supplies me abundantly and every day with nourishment and every physical need, shields me against all adversity and protects and guards me from all evil and that he does *all this* in a spirit of purely paternal and divine goodness and mercy *without any merit and worthiness on my part*.[7]

Anyone who really thinks like that is in fact handing people over

7. Quoted from Luther's commentaries on the creed, *Bekenntnisschriften*, p. 510 ff.; my italics.

to the mercy of their more powerful brothers. The concept of grace is the ideological product of a lawless society.

A brief glance at Christian *anthropology* produces the same results. The socially conditioned impotence of the great mass of people to organize and express their needs and abilities independently and rationally is reinforced by the mystifying doctrine that man is created. What are the norms of behaviour that are suitable for a creature? Humility, servility, self-sacrifice, obedience, patience, gratitude, placing oneself completely at God's mercy, relying on God and not on one's own strength, regarding oneself as the fortunate recipient of gifts, submitting all one's desires to the will of God, believing, against all appearances, in God's love and faithfulness, forgetfulness of self. The aim of these 'virtues' is to stifle all personal initiative, the courage of one's convictions and the desire for emancipation, and to give these the bad name of 'pride', a high-ranking capital sin. For centuries, the Church has, in her preaching, produced and cultivated an attitude of subjection and a feeling of inferiority by consistently blessing those 'who labour and are heavily laden' instead of calling on them to deprive their oppressors of their power.

All these infamies are finally confirmed and endorsed with the seals of eternity in Christian *eschatology*. The first general aim of the Church's teaching about the 'last things' is to characterize human life as merely temporary and confined to this earth, and therefore as insignificant. Life here on earth is life subject to recall – man's true home is, after all, not earth, but heaven.

Paul provided a classical formulation of the nature of the eschatological vision, which has acted like opium on the minds of men, in his letter to the Romans (viii, 18): 'I consider that the sufferings of this present time are not worth comparing with the glory that is to be revealed to us.' Imaginary treasures in the life after death are offered to men as a consolation for real suffering and deprivation here and now. The continued presence of unhappiness and injustice on earth is justified by encouraging men to think that their longing for happiness and justice will be satisfied in heaven.

WHAT IS CHRISTIAN?

The threat to bring the eschatological stick out of the bag and use it has, however, proved even more effective as a social psychological weapon. In the course of the history of theology, the Church's projections of men's wishes have remained remarkably pale and lifeless. They have, moreover, always been subject to conditions that are too difficult to fulfil – 'many are called, but few are chosen'. Who could, under such conditions, ever hope to realize his wishes? The horrors of ultimate eternal punishment in hell, on the other hand, have played a much more important part in the conscious and subconscious minds of men. The essential reason for this is quite clear – the idea of hell was not just something existing in the imagination, but was the result of man's experience of real happenings, such as the barbaric actions that took place within the legal system in the Christian world.

What, then, has this brief outline of the main themes in Christian theology proved? It has shown that every form of human suffering, every deprivation and every injustice can be substantiated, glorified or made harmless by Christian teaching, which deadens man's sense of humanity and takes a fundamentally cynical view of human dignity.

THE PERSECUTION OF THE PAGANS[8]

The whole of the New Testament resounds with extreme aggressiveness towards everything which deviates only very slightly from the Christian norm. The Sermon on the Mount provides us with a perfect example of this urge to destroy – the well-known statement, 'Whoever says [to his brother], "You fool!" shall be liable to the hell of fire' (Matt. v, 22). The New Testament abounds with threats of punishments which, as soon as the idea of guilt and atonement is recognized, are placed in a completely false relationship with the 'offence' and can only be called 'terrorist' statements.

8. In the parts connected with the history of the Church, I owe a great deal not only to the full histories of Heussi, Loewenich and Schmidt, but also to Benz' *Ideen zu einer Theologie der Religionsgeschichte*, Beumann, Blanke, Deschner, Erdmann, Holl, Kühner (*Tabus der Kirchengeschichte*), and Las Casas.

THE MISERY OF CHRISTIANITY

This need to punish is violently expressed in the New Testament writers' idea of God, which serves, together with the expectation of the day of judgement, as the extended arm of the authors' own impotence. Nowhere in the New Testament is there any indication that the theme of vengeance is transcended. The very opposite is true – the almighty big brother is far more effective in taking care of the destruction of one's enemies. As Paul told the Christians of Rome, 'Beloved, never avenge yourselves, but leave it to the wrath of God; for it is written, "Vengeance is mine, I will repay, says the Lord"' (Rom. xii, 19).

All the statements attributed to Jesus presuppose a very primitive concept of justice which categorizes men as either good or evil. The most obvious example of this black and white division of mankind is the parable of the last judgement (Matt. xxv, 31–46), in which all men are separated like sheep and goats. The blessed sheep on the king's right hand enter the eternal glory of the Father. The goats on his left, however, are told, snappily enough: 'Depart from me, you cursed, into the eternal fire prepared for the devil and his angels'.

What this tradition in the sayings of Jesus of dividing mankind into two groups is based on is the relationship with Christ. 'For whoever is ashamed of me and of my words in this adulterous and sinful generation, of him will the Son of man also be ashamed, when he comes in the glory of his Father with the holy angels' (Mark viii, 38). A definite ethical demand is derived from this religious norm – love of one's neighbour. Since only those who believe in Christ are thought to be theologically justified as human beings, all non-Christians are immediately regarded as inhuman. In the parable of the last judgement, the goats on the left hand of the judge were, as a matter of course, hard-hearted and did not visit the sick and those in prison, while the sheep on the right gave their neighbours food and drink.

The out-and-out sadism of this entire mythology is all too clearly revealed in the small but not unimportant detail in the gospel that no one knows when the judgement will take place (see, for example, Matt. xxiv, 50 f.; xxv, 13) – the victims are to be taken by surprise in the most cunning way.

The apostle Paul's view was no different. He quoted, for example, a sentence taken from an ancient liturgy at the end of his first letter to the Corinthians: 'If anyone has no love for the Lord, let him be accursed. Maran atha! (that is, Our Lord, come)' (xvi, 22). Ernst Käsemann, professor in New Testament studies at Tübingen, has elaborated this eschatological *ius talionis* or right of retaliation as something that was fundamental to the theology of Paul in his 'Sätze heiligen Rechts im Neuen Testament'.

All sins and vices could conveniently be projected on to the pagans. In addition to this stereotyped enemy theme, which underlies the crude division of mankind into good and evil, there is also the similar idea, which is especially popular in the New Testament, that the godless are quite simply sexually unchaste. What is more, 'they are filled with all manner of wickedness, evil, covetousness, malice. Full of envy, murder, strife, deceit, malignity, they are gossips, slanderers, haters of God, insolent, haughty, boastful, inventors of evil, disobedient to parents, foolish, faithless, heartless, ruthless' (Rom. i, 29–31). These subhuman beings have, of course, no right to live – they are already (in their sins) dead and God will not be slow to punish them as they deserve with eternal damnation.

It is, of course, not difficult to realize that this attitude is one that thirsts for destruction. When the prevailing power structures are favourable, those who think in this way do not hesitate to exterminate the enemies of God. God himself wields the sword in the hands of his believers. The political situation was favourable in this way in the fourth century, when Christianity ceased to be a conviction held by an ostracized minority and began to play the privileged part of the state religion. Before Christianity came to occupy this privileged position, theologians such as Tertullian had argued in favour of unrestricted religious freedom in the Roman Empire. The fourth century, however, marked the end of religious toleration and the freedom and rights both of non-Christians and of non-Catholic Christian minorities were systematically curtailed. Constantine had tolerated all religious cults and had only recommended, in his imperial decrees, that the Christian faith should be accepted. His sons, however, began to persecute the pagans and, in 380, the Catholic Church was given exclusive rights as the official state church by the emperors Theodosius and Gratian. From that time onwards, every Roman citizen had to be an orthodox Christian. Practising a pagan religion or heresy was regarded as committing a crime against the state (*crimen maiestatis*) and visiting a pagan temple or offering a pagan sacrifice was punished by banishment or death. Christian mobile detachments, monks, bishops and laymen, stormed and plundered pagan places of worship. Huge numbers of art treasures of immeasurable value were destroyed and most of the pagan literature was burnt. This process of christianization within the Roman Empire was ultimately concluded in the sixth century during the reign of Justinian I (527–565), who imposed compulsory baptism, renewed the death penalty and outlawed all pagans and non-Catholic Christians. This marked the completion of the setting-up of a totalitarian system which was to have a deep impact on the Christian centuries which followed – some traces of this system can still be detected even today.

Although Christianity did not become exactly a 'state' religion in Franconia, a similar situation soon developed there after the death of Clovis in 511. Christian noblemen were given preferential treatment at court. This was the first step, and it was quickly followed by a ban imposed first on non-Christian worship in public and later even on private pagan worship. From 626 onwards, Dagobert I forced the non-Christian remnant of the population to be baptized. This development, which was fostered by the Germanic tradition of a sacral monarchy, came to a peak during the Carlovingian period in the eighth century. Since the papacy had allied itself, in the figure of Stephen II, with the Frankish ruling house under Pepin the Short, the king assumed direct responsibility for defending and championing the Church. From this time onwards, it was the task of the rulers of God's grace to protect the Church against enemies from within (heretics) and enemies from without (pagans). The wars of expansion waged against the Franks' non-Christian neighbours were accordingly more often than not indirectly missionary wars – indirectly, because the direct aim of these wars was, of course, to subdue the enemy and to annex his territory. This immediate aim, however, was fully justified by the missionary activity that followed in the wake of the victorious armies. Charlemagne, for example, compelled the vanquished Saxons, by threatening death as an alternative, to be baptized.

This alternative of baptism or death was, of course, what especially characterized the ideology of the crusades. It should, however, be noted right away in this context that the sword was not always used immediately in the attempt to missionize the pagan world. Missionaries without swords were also sent by the Church into pagan territory that had not yet been subdued by force. But even when this happened, pressure was used, since those sent in the name of Christ only entered foreign lands under military protection and on behalf of their sovereign ruler – even Boniface was in the service of the Franks. Thus the Christian missionaries to the pagans were rightly regarded as heralds or helpers of ultimate subjection. To say no to their message and to refuse their offer of baptism could provoke a war. To say yes, on the other hand, could also be the prelude to a loss of political and economic freedom.

The most decisive form that the debate between the Church and the non-Christian world took was that of the crusades. The ideology of the crusades, as defined by Pope Gregory the Great round about the year 600, was, very briefly, an either/or. Either the pagans surrendered unconditionally and submitted to the political and economic domination of their Christian conquerors, with, as a consequence, baptism and indoctrination by the Church to follow, or they were, also in the name of God, exterminated.

I cannot, of course, examine in detail here either the historical and social causes of this imperialism or the concrete forms in which it appeared. All that I can do is to sketch out the progress of this imperialist expansion during the Middle Ages in the two principal directions in which it moved – very briefly in the Near East and even more briefly in Eastern Europe.

THE MISERY OF CHRISTIANITY

The seven great crusades in the Near East, which together covered more than two centuries (1095–1270 or 1291), were wars of conquest embellished with religion. They were undertaken in order to satisfy the economic greed of the northern Italian cities of Venice, Pisa and Genoa and the lust for political power of kings and popes, knights and princes. Objectively, these wars resulted in the colonial subjection and exploitation of the Saracens, who had, until that time, been relatively peaceful. The Christian arms manufacturers and dealers – who, of course, also sold weapons to the Mohammedans – made rapid and substantial profits. Those who kept the crusaders supplied and equipped had the most prosperous businesses of the period. The pedlars of holy relics also did a very good trade. (The tiny fragments of the true cross, which still abound today, would, if put together, have made a small forest.) The flourishing slave trade was entirely concentrated in Christian hands – the cardinal legate Pelagius was particularly active in this field.

The unsuspecting masses of the people were stirred up by such ecclesiastical demagogues as Pope Urban II, Peter the Hermit of Amiens, and Bernard of Clairvaux, the *doctor mellifluus*. They were persuaded to join the crusades by the promise that all their sins would be remitted – a step which rendered the planned crime morally neutral in advance – and by the clarion call 'It is God's will' – which acted as an additional justification – and they became the *militia Christi* and *militia sancti Petri*, the soldiers of Christ and St Peter, with the holy task of wresting the sepulchre of the Lord out of the hands of the enemies of God.

How did these pious pilgrims behave in the Holy Land – those, at least, who were fortunate enough to survive the long journey there without dying of disease or hunger? An eyewitness has described, in the *Gesta Francorum*, the blood-lust of the crusaders who entered Jerusalem after its capture in 1099:

Soon ... all the defenders were leaving the walls and running through the city, pursued by our men, who drove them along, cutting them down and killing them and following them as far as the Temple of Solomon, where there was such a blood-bath that our men were

WHAT IS CHRISTIAN?

wading ankle-deep in blood. ... Soon the crusaders were rushing through the whole city, seizing gold, silver, horses and mules and looting the houses that were full of costly things. Then, happy and indeed weeping for joy, our men went to venerate and pray at the sepulchre of our Redeemer.[9]

Richard Lionheart had two to three thousand Muslim captives massacred during the Third Crusade, when negotiations with Saladin had broken down. The entrails of the victims were examined for swallowed gold and then their corpses were burnt and the ashes also inspected for gold.

I cannot go into the complex and chequered history of the conquest and forcible Christianization of Eastern Europe in any detail. I will simply mention the well-known crusade against the Wends in 1147 and the activity of the Order of Teutonic Knights, about which the Catholic historian Hans Kühner has said that it 'was nominally a spiritual order with the task of missionizing the pagan eastern province, but was in fact a large-scale and barbaric military dictatorship organized on capitalistic lines, a "state within a state", the main activity of which was to exterminate pagan nations. It is very difficult for us to visualize this clearly enough'.[10]

Contrary to what many people, in their unsuspecting innocence, imagine, the crusades did not end with the close of the Middle Ages – colonialism and imperialism, the characteristic activities of the modern age, also flourished under the banner of the Christian faith.

After the troops led by the Portuguese Prince Henry the Navigator had conquered the north-west coast of Africa in 1450, Pope Nicholas V confirmed, in his bull *Romanus Pontifex* of 1454, that the subjugated territories belonged to Alphonsus of Portugal and authorized him to subdue and exploit other islands and countries in Africa and 'India' in the future. By virtue of his total supremacy as pope over the whole world, including the pagan world, he was able to give the Portuguese king provinces, principalities, duchies, kingdoms and all kinds of lands already

9. Quoted from Deschner, *Abermals krähte der Hahn*, p. 512.
10. Kühner, *Tabus der Kirchengeschichte*, p. 42.

conquered and still waiting to be conquered and, what is more, to give them to him for all eternity. In return for this enormous gift, which had never belonged to the pope and which he had never even seen, the bull demanded that the occupied colonial territories should be christianized. This 'patronage of the missions' or *ius patronatus* meant that the Catholic missionaries had to be sent out, paid, equipped, supplied and protected by the Portuguese crown.

When Columbus discovered America or, as he believed, India, in 1492 in the name of the Spanish throne, the problem arose as to how the spheres of influence should be divided between Portugal and Spain. The pope came promptly to the rescue with a clear-cut solution in the bull *Inter caeterae divinae*, of 1493. He simply divided the world into two halves by drawing a line on the map through the Atlantic from the North Pole to the South Pole – the famous demarcation line of Pope Alexander VI – and said that the eastern part should belong to Portugal and the western half to Spain. This bull, which enjoyed binding force in the international law of the period, also gave the whole of the New World, most of which had still to be discovered, to the rulers of Spain, Ferdinand and Isabella, and entrusted them with the task of missionizing the natives. The Catholic mission in America was in fact financed by the Spanish crown.

The method used to spread the Good News is strikingly evident in the so-called 'proclamation of the conquistadores', which was read out to the 'Indians' in order to persuade them to capitulate without a struggle:

God the Lord has delegated to Peter and his successors all power over all people of the earth, so that all people must obey the successors of Peter. Now one of these popes has made a gift of the newly discovered islands and countries [in America] and everything that they contain to the kings of Spain, so that, by virtue of this gift, their majesties are now kings and lords of these islands and of the continent. You are therefore required to recognize holy Church as mistress and ruler of the whole world and to pay homage to the Spanish king as your new lord. Otherwise, we shall, with God's help, proceed against you with violence and force you under the yoke of the Church and the

WHAT IS CHRISTIAN?

king, treating you as rebellious vassals deserve to be treated. We shall take your property away from you and make your women and children slaves. At the same time, we solemnly declare that only you will be to blame for the bloodshed and the disaster that will overtake you.[11]

Anyone who has read the unforgettable account of the devastation of the 'West Indian' countries published by the Dominican, Bartholomé de las Casas, will know what was done in those countries during the Golden Age of Spain and Portugal – in a word, the mass murder of twenty thousand Indians. Those who were not massacred at once died later in the gold mines, the pearl fisheries and the plantations. There was an endless succession of the most horrifying crimes. Indians were impaled, hanged or slowly burnt alive, or had their hands, feet, ears and other parts of their bodies cut off.

What did the Catholic priests who came with the colonists do while this was going on? They gave them absolution and the body of the Lord and assured them that He would bestow His grace and favour on them.

The predominantly Protestant Christians – mostly Congregationalists – who brought the faith to North America were no less cruel. The conquest of New England and the extermination of its Indian inhabitants was accomplished according to the pattern of the occupation of idolatrous Canaan by the Israelites. At that time, Yahweh spoke, through Samuel, to King Saul, telling him: 'Now go and smite Amalek, and utterly destroy all that they have; do not spare them, but kill both man and woman, infant and suckling, ox and sheep, camel and ass' (1 Sam. xv, 3). This was the will of the Father of Jesus Christ and those who clung stubbornly to the worship of the false Indian god, Manito, had to experience it. The English colonists were, in this, the instruments of the Father's will and, true to the tireless preaching of their Anglican and later Puritan theologians, they behaved in North America as though they were the chosen people, the successors of Israel.

Even more recently, in the nineteenth century, colonial ex-

11. This is how the content of the proclamation is formulated by Blanke, *Missionsprobleme des Mittelalters und der Neuzeit*, p. 92.

ploitation and the preaching of the gospel went hand in hand. A good example of this is the opium war in China (1840–1842). Opium was forbidden in England as a narcotic and it was also a punishable offence to take opium in China. Imperialist Britain therefore unleashed the opium war – her motives were purely and blatantly economic – and forced China to allow the drug to be imported. The Peace of Nanking, concluded in 1842, opened the Chinese ports to opium and, at the same time, to Christian missionaries. Just as no representative of the Church had raised his voice in protest against the unscrupulous sale of alcohol, hitherto unknown to the Indians, by Christian merchants in North America, so too no Christian objected publicly to the open crime of the Opium War. On the contrary, the missionaries rejoiced – their God, who was not averse to using crooked ways, was clearly opening a door to admit the gospel into pagan China. As the Protestant pastor Karl Gützlaff wrote, 'Now that the way to China lies open, my heart has begun to beat with joy'.[12]

The missionaries, then, often followed trade. But it often happened the other way about, the exploiters following the Christian missionaries and fleecing the newly-won converts mercilessly. The order of escalation, greatly simplified, was, in this case, 'gospel – financial exploitation – political subjection' and, in this, the apostles who preached the love of one's fellowmen were guilty of a double crime. In the first place, they preached humility and obedience and directed the minds of the people they were converting towards an imaginary hereafter. Every murmur on the part of the converts that might have sounded like a desire for emancipation was stigmatized as a 'worldly preoccupation'. This has been touchingly expressed by a Maori: 'While we [under the influence of the mission] were looking up to heaven, your [that is, the missionaries'] brothers came and took our land away from us.'[13]

In the second place, the missionaries were directly involved in the horror of colonialism and did not utter one word of protest, but held their tongues and took advantage of the military

12. Quoted from Blanke, p. 111, note 46.
13. ibid., p. 126.

WHAT IS CHRISTIAN?

protection offered by the European powers and trading companies. They were not interested in humanity, but in making the greatest possible number of baptisms.

Is this only something that took place in the past? I know it is not. Colonization by Christian nations is still going on, but is now more cunningly camouflaged (as 'help for the underdeveloped countries') and brutality and violence are less clearly visible. The German Confessing Church and the Catholic Church both supported the Second World War as a crusade against the godless Bolsheviks and, quite recently, the American Cardinal Spellman, who died in 1967, defended the war in Vietnam as a war for the Christian faith.

It is possible to glorify any war with the equipment provided by theology.

THE PERSECUTION OF THE JEWS[14]

The New Testament is permeated with the spirit of anti-semitism. This has already been made clear in my brief survey in the previous section of the attitude taken by the early Christian writers towards the pagans. Anti-semitism, it must be remembered, seldom appears as an isolated phenomenon – it is secretly present everywhere whenever the world is divided, as it was in the New Testament, into sheep – the good, to whom one, of course, belongs oneself ('You are the light of the world', Matt. v, 14) – and goats – the evil rest of mankind. It is present wherever the idea of a heavenly reward for some is indissolubly linked to that of a punishment in hell for others and wherever the hope exists that everyone who thinks differently, believes differently and acts differently from oneself will be destroyed.

The fact that the New Testament authors were incapable of ordinary human experience and of thinking for themselves is clearly revealed in the stereotyped patterns of which the gospels,

---

14. In this section, I have depended to a great extent on Bienert, Deschner, Eckert, Heer, Gamm, Grässer, Huss, Kühner (*Tabus der Kirchengeschichte*, and *Neues Papstlexikon*), Kraus ('Kirche und Synagoge'), and Schultz (*Juden Christen Deutsche*).

both as a whole and as separate documents, are made up. For example, the part of Jesus' opponents is almost always played by the scribes and pharisees, who are treated, from the very beginning, as his stubborn and bloodthirsty enemies (see, for example, Mark ii, 6, 16; iii, 6). The inability of the evangelists to distinguish between fantasy and reality reaches its peak in the gospel of John, in which the Jews – quite simply and without any inner distinction, the Jews as such – are presented as Jesus' opponents.

Another clear example of the evangelists' latent anti-semitism is their anxiety to transfer the guilt for Jesus' death from the shoulders of the Roman authorities – in this case, Pilate – and place it entirely on the shoulders of the Jews. Even in the earliest of the gospel accounts, that of Mark, Pilate refuses to condemn Jesus – 'For he perceived that it was out of envy that the chief priests had delivered him up' (Mark xv, 10). Luke made Pilate affirm Jesus' innocence even more emphatically – 'Pilate said to the chief priests and the multitudes, "I find no crime in this man"' (Luke xxiii, 4; see also xxiii, 14, 20, 22, 25). Matthew also added to Pilate's affirmation of his innocence the well-known washing of the Roman governor's hands – 'He took water and washed his hands before the crowd, saying, "I am innocent of this man's blood; see to it yourselves"' (Matt. xxvii, 24). This is followed, in Matthew's account, by the notorious verse which was to be fulfilled in the most horrible way in later centuries – 'And all the people answered, "His blood be on us and on our children!"' It has, of course, been known for a long time now, as a result of historical research, that Matthew fabricated this infamous curse pronounced on the Jewish people, which saddles them with the entire blame for the death of the Son of God.

Paul was also anti-semitic in his attitude and blamed the Jews entirely for the death of Christ. In his first letter to the Thessalonians, for example, he wrote: 'You killed both the Lord Jesus and the prophets, and drove us out, and displease God and oppose all men by hindering us from speaking to the gentiles that they may be saved – so as always to fill up the measure of their sins. But God's wrath has come upon them at last' (1 Thess. ii, 15-16). Paul's attribution of collective guilt to the Jews and his condemnation of the whole people is in keeping with the rest of his theology, in which he called Christians, on the other hand, 'blameless and innocent, children of God, without blemish, in the midst of a crooked and perverse generation, among whom you shine as lights in the world' (Phil. ii, 15).

John's gospel, however, represents the summit of anti-semitism in the New Testament. It is especially clear from the fourth gospel that the Jews were absolutely necessary to Christian theology as the mythical projection of the arch-enemy. Although a dualism is present in all the New Testament writings, it is nowhere more evident than in this gospel, with its contrasting concepts of light and darkness, truth and falsehood, above and below, heaven and earth, God and devil, freedom and servility and life and death. A man belongs to the light if he believes in the one who has revealed the light and who said: 'I am the way, and the truth, and the life: no one comes to the Father, but by me' (John xiv, 6). The man who rejects the one who was sent from heaven and indeed who simply questions whether he has been legitimately sent becomes the property of darkness and falsehood. The decisive concept which is attributed to those who do not believe is that of the 'world' – or that of the 'Jews'. Both these terms are generally used without distinction in John's gospel. The Jews were descended neither from God (like Jesus and the Christians), nor from Abraham, but from the devil (John viii, 44), and, as children of the devil, the father of lies and a murderer from the beginning, they were bound to seek Jesus' life.

Erich Grässer, New Testament professor at the University of Bochum, has made a detailed analysis of the anti-Jewish polemics in the gospel according to John.[15] He has come to the conclusion that the passages in which the Jews are referred to contain 'no anti-semitism of any origin whatever'.[16] The 'Jews' are not a

---

15. An article, which I have not listed in the bibliography, but which is included in Eckert's symposium.

16. Grässer, 'Die antijüdische Polemik . . .', p. 90.

historical people in the fourth gospel, Grässer claims, but 'stylized types' exemplifying and embodying the world's lack of faith. John's intention was not to vilify real Jews – his polemics were 'purely the result of theological reflection', 'the product of a compellingly logical way of thinking' and 'one of the earliest attempts to give a firm theological basis to the absolute claims of Christianity'.[17]

Objectively speaking, this is quite right, but, as apologetics, it is astonishingly naïve. After all, has any form of anti-semitism ever had anything essentially to do with the Jews as a historical people? Whether they are defamed as the children of the devil or whether they are branded as an inferior race of people is really beside the point. Both these attitudes are mythological and both are the result of the same need to have an enemy.

Even in the New Testament, then, the Jews formed an essential part of Christian theology, making satanology and demonology concrete.

This tradition was continued in the early Church. Many of the treatises written at this time clearly betray this tendency, some simply in their titles – *Adversus Iudaeos* or *Contra Iudaeos* ('Against the Jews') – and others in their united aim to present the Jews as the people who had been rejected and disinherited by God. Examples of the latter are the letter of Barnabas (*c.* 130), Justin the Martyr's 'Dialogue with the Jew Trypho' (*c.* 160), Tertullian's polemical treatise against the Jews (*c.* 200) and Origen's work against Celsus (*c.* 250). What, then, did these Fathers of the Church claim? They insisted that all the privileges of the chosen people of God had been transferred to the true Israel, the Church. They regarded the Old Testament purely as a prophecy of Christ and they blamed the Jews for what Christians have always done and still do – for falsifying Scripture. It goes without saying, too, that all these claims were made in the most violently abusive language.

The eight sermons written by John Chrysostom ('Gold Mouth') in 387 were epoch-making. 'The whole arsenal of all the weapons that have ever been used against the Jews is to be

17. Grässer's article in Eckert, pp. 164, 168, 170.

found in these documents. The Jew is a sensual Jew, an obscene, lascivious Jew, a demonic Jew, a money-making Jew, an accursed Jew. He is a murderer of the prophets, a murderer of Christ, a murderer of God. He worships the devil. All Jews are drunkards, whoremongers and criminals.' The frequently quoted judgement of the synagogue also occurs in these sermons: 'Whatever name is given to the synagogue – whorehouse, den of iniquity, pandemonium, house of Satan, soul-destroying habitation or yawning abyss of perdition – it cannot be described as it deserves to be described.'[18]

From the beginning of the Constantinian period in the fourth century, there was no longer any need for the anger that Christians felt towards the Jews to be expressed simply in words. They continued to defame the Jews, but their verbal attacks were from now on accompanied by repressive acts on the part of society and the state. Constantine imposed heavy penalties not only on anyone who went over to Judaism (as the pagan Trajan had done before him), but also on the Jewish community that received him. Constantine's sons confiscated a Christian's entire property if he became a Jewish convert. Mixed marriages between Jews and Christians were punished by death. In the *Codex Theodosianus* of the Emperor Theodosius II (408–450), the Jews were forbidden to hold any public office or function or to build new synagogues. Justinian completed this process of discrimination against the Jews in the sixth century by outlawing them together with all pagans and 'heretics'. Their synagogues were confiscated by the state and converted into churches. Justinian was also the first to make the crime of burning down and pillaging Jewish synagogues by Christian bishops and monks – often canonized later – legal. Finally, it was he who gave the order, after his commander Belisar had conquered the North African city of Borion, for the compulsory mass baptism of all Jews. This was a pleasant Christian custom which was to be repeated often enough throughout the history of the Church.

I can do no more than mention a few especially striking cases of the countless sufferings endured by the Jews in every Chris-

18. Quoted from Heer, *Gottes erste Liebe*, p. 67.

tian country during the Middle Ages. In 638, the Sixth Council of Toledo ordered all Jews living in Spain to be baptized and, in 694, the Seventeenth Council of Toledo declared all Jews to be slaves, ordering all that they possessed to be confiscated and their children to be taken away from them when they were seven years old and later to be married to Christians. In 1179, the Third Lateran Council threatened with excommunication all Christians who lived with Jews, and thus encouraged the growth of special Jewish quarters or ghettos. In 1205, Pope Innocent III called the Jews 'damned slaves'. This idea was given a firm theological foundation and a practical conclusion by Thomas Aquinas in his treatise *De regimine Iudaeorum ad Ducissam Brabantae* – popes, kings and princes were henceforth allowed to dispose of property belonging to Jews as though it belonged to them. The Fourth Lateran Council of 1215, which set up the Inquisition and declared transubstantiation – the changing of bread and wine into the body and blood of Christ – to be a dogma of faith, also laid down that Jews should wear distinctive dress.

A yellow spot on their outer garments and a horned cap or *pileum cornutum* became the striking distinguishing marks of the stubborn murderers of Christ and reminded those from whom they were thus separated of their descent from the devil. The Jews were also forbidden to visit Christian inns and baths and even to appear on the streets during Christian feasts. They were, of course, excluded from all public offices.

The shameful ill-treatment of a minority group was in this way elevated to the level of a good work. This feeling of hatred was further intensified by certain aspects of the Church's liturgy, the Good Friday and Easter services especially having a marked anti-Jewish emphasis. The defamatory intercession, *Pro perfidis Iudaeis* ('For the perfidious Jews'), in which the word 'perfidious', literally 'unbelieving', also had the undertone of 'cunning', and the fact that this prayer, unlike the intercessions for other groups of people made at this point during the Good Friday liturgy, was not accompanied by a genuflection often helped to incite Christians to the bloody massacre of Jews.

WHAT IS CHRISTIAN?

This practice was retained in the Catholic liturgy until only a few years ago, the genuflection being introduced in 1955 and the intercession itself being made *pro Iudaeis*, and not for the 'perfidious' Jews, in 1959.

Countless treatises and legends of the saints and all kinds of mystery plays, passion plays and other semi-religious entertainments mocked and vilified the Jews. The devil is frequently represented in medieval pictures with a typically Jewish nose.

Jews were again and again accused of ritual murder and desecration of the host. A projection of inner guilt on to others is, of course, always present in such accusations. Accusing others of practising ritual murder is a phenomenon which occurs in widely different societies and at different periods of history. Almost always, a minority group is accused of killing members of the majority – usually their children – and of eating them in a ritual meal. In this way, the repression practised by the majority is conveniently projected on to the minority.

The myth of the desecration of the host, on the other hand, could only occur in a specifically Christian environment. In this case, the Jews were accused of stealing consecrated hosts and of trampling on them or pricking holes in them so as to make Christ suffer and die again. This accusation was first made, as far as we know, in the thirteenth century and, of course, presupposes the dogma of transubstantiation. Christians secretly doubted the absurd dogma that they were expected to believe and projected their own revolt against it on to the Jews who were, of course, not expected to believe the myth of the consecration of the host and who were consequently punished for the repressed doubts of the Christians. It was, of course, no coincidence that the Fourth Lateran Council of 1215, which raised the doctrine of transubstantiation to the level of dogma, in which all Christians were bound to believe, should at the same time institute the Inquisition in order to persecute the Albigensians, a group of 'heretical' Christians who refused to believe in 'Roman fraudulence'.

Two events of great importance in the Middle Ages led to widespread and horrifying mass persecutions of the Jews. In the first case, the fanaticism aroused by the crusades unleashed a furious hatred of the 'enemies of Christ' in Europe. The second event was the Black Death, which was the point of departure for a second series of bloody pogroms. This great plague, which ravaged Europe between 1347 and 1349 and carried off millions of people, was, of course, regarded as a punishment sent by God and a scapegoat had to be found at once. Only one group of people could have caused this terrible disaster – the Jews. They had poisoned the wells and springs. Their extermination in the fourteenth century is comparable to the pogroms that took place more recently under Hitler.

The proceedings taken by the Spanish Inquisition against the compulsorily baptized Jews, the *marranos*, are also reminiscent of the madness of the Nazi era in Germany. These recent 'converts' in Spain were suspected of continued secret adherence to their Jewish faith and were consequently forbidden to hold any office at all in the Church or the state. Every candidate for the priesthood had to produce a certificate proving that he had 'purity of blood' (*limpieza de sangre*) going back to the fourth generation. Clearly, this was usually impossible to establish and, as a result, cases of perjury were frequently heard by the Inquisition because many *marranos* had forged their genealogies and because Jewish descent had been imputed to old Christian families by their enemies. It was not until 1865 that this article of the Spanish law, which was so similar to the Nazi *Arierparagraph* – those laws relating to the Aryanization of the German people – ceased to apply to appointments to official positions in the state in Spain.

From the very beginning, Protestantism was no less antisemitic than Catholicism. Martin Luther, who, as a young man, had hoped that the Jews would be converted to Christianity, persecuted the Jews rabidly in his later life. He might well have used the German slogan: 'If you won't be my brother, I'll knock your brains out'. In 1543, in his treatise 'On the Jews and their Lies', he demanded:

In the first place, that their synagogues or schools should be set on fire and what does not burn be sprinkled and covered with earth, so that no man may see a stone or a cinder of the places ever again. . . . In the second place, that their houses may also be broken down and destroyed . . . . In the third place, that their prayer books and their talmudists may be taken away from them. . . . In the fourth place, that their rabbis may at all cost be prevented from teaching in the future. . . that they may be prevented from praising and thanking God and from praying and teaching publicly here among us and among our Christian people, on punishment of loss of life. . . . And once again, that they may be prevented from uttering the name of God in our presence. . . . We Christians can hardly believe that a Jew's foul mouth is worthy to speak the name of God in our presence and if any one of us should hear a Jew speak that name, he should at once inform the authorities or else throw pig shit at him. . . . In the fifth place, that the Jews should be refused safe conduct and permission to use the streets. . . . In the sixth place, that they may be forbidden to practise usury and that all their cash and all their jewels be taken from them, all their gold and silver, and that this be set aside. . . . In the seventh place, that all strong young Jews and Jewesses may be given flails, axes and spades . . . and made to earn their living by the sweat of their brows . . .[19]

It was clearly not without good reason that Julius Streicher, the editor of the Nazi paper *Der Stürmer*, used the example of Martin Luther in an attempt to justify his own conduct in the military court at Nuremberg in 1946.

The pattern of Christian anti-semitism that I have already outlined continued in the modern age. Again and again, the Jews have been accused of ritual murder and desecration of the host. Again and again, Christian sermons have, consciously or unconsciously, stirred up hatred of the Jews. Let me mention one or two cases at random. In 1819, there were numerous and widespread pogroms in Germany, accompanied by Christian slogans. 'Aliens' could not be permitted in the German Christian empire. Pope Leo XII (1823–1829) once more confined the Jews living in the Papal States to the ghetto and once more subjected them to the Inquisition. In 1892, Adolf Stöcker, the Protestant court chaplain at Berlin, once again revived the legend of ritual murder at the Reichstag. In 1923, the Federation of German Catholic

19. Quoted from Kraus, 'Kirche und Synagoge', p. 45 f.

THE MISERY OF CHRISTIANITY

Student Societies required all its members to produce a certificate proving that they had Aryan grandparents.

The most appalling single case of anti-semitism that has up till now occurred in human history and for which Christianity was also partly responsible resulted in the extermination of some six million Jews. Adolf Hitler, the leading exponent of German fascism, was a Catholic Christian who never left the Church and was never excommunicated. His book, *Mein Kampf*, was never placed on the Index of prohibited books which, until recently, included all books and articles that were contradictory to Catholic teaching in matters of faith and morals. Apparently Hitler's political aims did not contradict Catholic moral teaching in any way.

On 26 April 1933, he had a conversation with Bishop Berning and Monsignor Steinmann. 'Theme – common struggle against liberalism, socialism, bolshevism. Conversation had very friendly tone. Hitler also says he will take no steps against the Jews that the Church has not taken in 1,500 years. Not opposed by prelates of the Church! Hitler says he is a Catholic and states discussions with Poles imminent, we need obedient soldiers – hence religious schools!'[20]

From the very beginning of the Nazi period until its end in 1945, the churches gave ideological support to Hitler in all essential questions. Their protests in the so-called 'struggle of the churches', which we now regard as heroic, referred, with the single exception of the churches' opposition to the Nazi programme of euthanasia, exclusively to Hitler's religious policy, which aimed at the curtailment of the churches' privileges – for example, the removal of crucifixes from Bavarian schools. The churches did *not* protest against the suppression of constitutional democracy or of freedom of the press and of speech and the freedom to hold public meetings. They did *not* protest against the countless judicial murders committed against liberals and communists. They did *not* protest against the concentration camps, which were set up as early as 1933. They did *not* protest against the invasions of Austria, Czechoslovakia,

20. Heer, *Gottes erste Liebe*, p. 406.

WHAT IS CHRISTIAN?

Poland, Denmark, Norway, Belgium, Holland, France, Yugoslavia and the Soviet Union. Not at all – the churches offered prayers to the divine 'Lord of battles' in all religious services for the victory of the Führer and his human cannon fodder.

What is more, unless a few, isolated charitable actions, such as the work of Pastor Grüber, are blown up to the size of nation-wide movements, the churches did not oppose the Jewish policy of the Nazis. On the contrary, the new laws relating to the Aryanization of the German nation were simply accepted by the churches and often administered by functionaries in the churches. Thousands of servile parish priests performed a useful service by producing evidence from their church records that some parishioners were Aryan and non-Jewish. The clergy thus served the state machinery very well by handing over those who did not belong to the master race to be murdered. A Protestant minority, the Confessing Church, did champion the cause of Jews who had been baptized and who had married Christians, although this group did not take up the cudgels for practising or secularized Jews. The majority of German Christians, however, excluded even baptized Jews from their ranks. On the 17 December 1941, the Church Presidents and Bishops of Saxony, Mecklenburg, Schleswig-Holstein, the Anhalt of Saxony, Thüringen and Lübeck published the following declaration:

> The National Socialist leaders of Germany have provided indisputable documentary evidence that the Jews are responsible for this war in its world-wide magnitude. They have therefore made the necessary decisions and taken the necessary steps, both internal and external, to ensure that the life of the German nation is protected against Judaism.
>
> As members of that same German nation, the undersigned leaders of the German Evangelical Church stand in the forefront of this historical struggle to defend our country, because of which it has been necessary for the national police to issue a statement to the effect that the Jews are the enemies of the German nation and of the world, just as it was also necessary for Dr Martin Luther to demand, on the basis of his own bitter experience, that the severest measures should be taken against the Jews and that they should be expelled from all German countries.
>
> ... Christian baptism does not change in any way the Jew's racial

character, his membership of the Jewish people and his biological nature. It is the duty of a German Evangelical Church to foster and to promote the religious life of the German people. Christians who are Jews by race have no place in that Church and no right to a place.

The undersigned leaders of the German Evangelical Church have therefore decided not to accept Jewish Christians as members of the Church community.[21]

After the Second World War, some Christians had a guilty conscience with regard to the Jews. Nonetheless, as is all too clearly revealed by a careful study of the stages in the development of the short section dealing with Judaism in the totally inadequate Declaration, *Nostra aetate*, on the Church's attitude towards the non-Christian religion,[22] made by the Second Vatican Council, a narrow-minded anti-semitism is still prevalent among Christian leaders and theologians. But how could it ever be otherwise, in view of the fact that Christianity has an inherent need of an enemy?

THE PERSECUTION OF CHRISTIAN 'HERETICS'[23]

Even in the earliest Christian community in Palestine, with its centre in Jerusalem, Christians were divided into different groups which strenuously opposed one another. The earliest literary records of this inner division in Christianity are to be found in the letters of the apostle Paul, almost all of which contain some polemics directed against one or other group of 'heretics', in other words, Christians with different theological views. Paul's most violent battle of words was conducted against the right wing of the community at Jerusalem, the members of which had begun a counter-mission in Galatia, in opposition to the work the apostle to the gentiles himself was doing. What was Paul's attitude towards his fellow-Christians? He accused them of having impure motives (Gal. iv, 17; vi. 13), called them

21. Quoted from Deschner, *Abermals krähte der Hahn*, p. 461 f.
22. See Hirschauer, *Der Katholizismus vor dem Risiko der Freiheit*, p. 60 ff.
23. In this section, I have consulted especially Deschner, Grundmann (*Ketzergeschichte des Mittelalters*), Heussi, Kühner (*Tabus der Kirchengeschichte*), Nigg (*Das Buch der Ketzer*), Pfister and Schmidt.

'false brothers' (ii, 4) who were preaching a gospel that was different from the gospel that Paul had preached to them (i, 8) and even pronounced them to be anathema, calling them accursed (i, 8) and handing them over to the eschatological anger of God at the last judgement.

In his second letter to the Corinthians, Paul dealt just as harshly with those Christians who opposed him, calling them 'false apostles, deceitful workmen, disguising themselves as apostles of Christ' and going on to say 'And no wonder, for even Satan disguises himself as an angel of light. So it is not strange if his servants also disguise themselves as servants of righteousness. Their end will correspond to their deeds' (2 Cor. xi, 13–15).

Defamation of the enemy within began, therefore, in the New Testament. But during the first four centuries of Christianity, Christians sent one another to hell purely with words. This was really only because there was no existing power structure to reinforce these words with actions. As soon as the emperors Theodosius and Gratian, however, raised the numerically strongest community of Christians, the Catholics, to the status of a state church, by the edict of the 28 February 380, 'heresy' at once became a crime against the state. The law stated:

> We order those who follow this law to assume the name of 'Catholic Christians'. The rest, on the other hand, whom we declare to be mad and insane, have to bear the shame of being called heretics. Their meeting places may not be known by the name of churches. They must first be struck by the vengeance of God and then also by the punishment of our anger, for which we derive our power from the heavenly judgement.[24]

Appealing to a parable in the gospel (Luke xiv, 23) – *cogito intrare*, 'compel them to come in' – Augustine supplied a theological justification for compulsory measures taken by the state against Christian minorities which was covered against all risks. In his struggle against the Donatists, a North African group of Christians, round about the year 400, he developed the doctrine

24. Quoted from Deschner, *Abermals krähte der Hahn*, p. 474 f.

that Christians persecuted because of love, whereas unbelievers persecuted because of cruelty, and that a war conducted to preserve or to restore unity in the Church was a *bellum Deo auctore*, a war waged by God himself.

The first Christian to be executed by other Christians because of theological differences was the Spaniard Priscillian. He was decapitated in 385 in Treves on the initiative of Catholic bishops because he denied the doctrine of the Trinity and the resurrection.

Until the High Middle Ages, it was mostly only individual Christians who were hanged or burnt because their religious views differed from those put forward by the Church. The systematic persecution of dissident Christians only began in earnest when the individuals began to form groups – groups which, in many places, were numerically far greater than the Catholics. The Roman Church could not permit any inner opposition without endangering its very existence as a feudal structure. Any criticism of the scandalous practices of the hierarchy and any deviation from the official teaching of the Church had to be eradicated at once. This need led, by a very complicated historical process, the details of which do not really concern us here, to the Inquisition, one of the most horrifying instruments of terror that the world has ever known. The Protestant church historian, Walter Nigg, has said of it: 'The only answer that I can make to the statement that the Inquisition was surely not as bad as that must be that it *was* bad, very bad – so bad that it could not have been worse!'[25]

The Inquisition, which was set up by the Church, not by the state, made it the duty of bishops and their synods to seek out 'heretics' by appointing a few laymen in every parish to carry out this task. This was the original plan worked out at the Fourth Lateran Council in 1215, but when it was discovered that the Church could not be 'purified' in this way, Pope Gregory IX changed the Inquisition into an institution that was controlled centrally by the Curia and, in 1232, handed it over to the Dominicans – the *Domini canes* or 'hounds of the Lord',

25. Nigg, *Das Buch der Ketzer*, p. 199.

as the name of the order was interpreted according to folk etymology. The Dominican, Thomas Aquinas, who is known in the Catholic Church as the *doctor angelicus* or 'angelic teacher', not only justified slavery and anti-semitism but also made the death penalty for 'heretics' theologically legitimate. Just as forgers were put to death by the princes of this world for circulating false money, so too were 'heretics' executed for disseminating false doctrines like a contagious and soul-destroying disease.

The Inquisition usually announced beforehand that it was going to visit a town so that the people could assemble at the time stated. Anyone who did not put in an appearance at that time was viewed with grave suspicion from the very beginning. It was forbidden to leave the place where the Inquisition was meeting – a kind of state of emergency was proclaimed. Every Catholic was bound to denounce 'heretical' Christians. (Even at the time of the earlier episcopal Inquisition, every Catholic had to swear to track down 'heretics' and was obliged to renew this oath every two years.) Parents had the duty, if necessary, to betray their children, children were obliged to betray their parents and husbands and wives each other. Anyone who did not do this made himself an accessory to the crime. Anonymous letters were preferred.

The trial of a 'heretic' began with his arrest and imprisonment. The accused was regarded from the very beginning as guilty. He was kept in chains in a prison cell and refused the sacraments. He had, at the beginning of his trial, to swear to the Inquisitor, who was his prosecutor, judge and father confessor all in the same person, that he would obey all the commandments of holy Church, answer all questions truthfully, betray all his fellow 'heretics' and willingly accept any penance imposed on him. He was not granted any defending counsel in the proceedings. Hardly anyone could have been found to carry out this task – any such person would automatically have been suspected of 'heresy' himself.

If the victim voluntarily admitted his criminally 'heretical' ideas and practices, then he was spared a great deal of suffering. If, on the other hand, he made no confession, he was tortured.

Pope Innocent IV had ordered 'heretics' to be tortured in his bull *Ad Extirpanda* of 1252 and had regulated the use of torture in canon law.

The heretic was dragged into the torture chamber and shown all the terrible instruments of torture. If this dreadful display did not make him confess his errors, then the instruments were applied to his body, one by one, in a process of slowly increasing pain.... Tortures lasting three or four hours were not unusual. While the victim was being tortured, the rack or other instrument was frequently sprinkled with holy water. Countless frightful means were used in the procedure, all with the sole purpose of crushing the victim's resistance and making him confess.... A cloth was usually pushed into the victim's mouth to prevent the torturers from being distracted or irritated by his wild screams. A heretic might be tortured in this way for hours, until his body had become a flayed, bruised, broken and bleeding mass of flesh. From time to time he would be asked whether he was at last ready to confess. Overwhelmed by pain and half out of his mind with anguish, he would usually, after a few hours of this torment, give all the information that the Inquisitors wanted to hear...[26]

'Heretics' who had confessed and were repentant were treated very mercifully by the Church, which was quite content that the penitent should be punished only in this world. This punishment often took the form of a public scourging. Every Sunday, the penitent had to appear during the celebration of Mass with a stick and the priest would beat him before the altar in the presence of the people. Fines were also imposed, in which case everything that the penitent possessed was usually confiscated and found its way into the pockets of the members of the court, who used it to support themselves. As the Catholic church historian, Hans Kühner, has said, the Inquisition was set in motion 'in at least fifty per cent of cases purely for the purpose of self-enrichment'.[27] The Spanish Inquisition especially was an instrument of clerical exploitation and preferred to try prosperous Jewish Christians – the *marranos*.

A long pilgrimage, often as far as Palestine, undertaken

26. ibid., p. 210.
27. Kühner, *Tabus der Kirchengeschichte*, p. 59.

entirely on foot, was regarded as a very lenient punishment for repentant 'heretics'. Others were consigned to what was called a living grave – they were chained for the rest of their lives in a tiny dungeon without windows.

The true Church of Christ had only one punishment for those who stubbornly persisted in or reverted to 'heresy' – burning alive. (From 1231 onwards, this was carried out on the instructions of the pope himself.) What is more, even dead 'heretics' were sometimes burnt – when their false doctrines became known after they had died. Amalrich of Bena, for example, who died in 1206 or 1207, was exhumed in 1210 and burnt. It was believed that, if a man's body was burnt and the ashes were scattered, it would be impossible for him to rise again at the end of time. A 'heretic' could thus be effectively punished for all eternity in this way. ('I will give you the keys of the kingdom of heaven, and whatever you bind on earth shall be bound in heaven, and whatever you loose on earth shall be loosed in heaven', Matt. xvi, 19.)

It is, of course, true that the Church herself did not carry out the sentence, in accordance with the principle of canon law, *Ecclesia non sitit sanguinem* – 'the Church does not thirst for blood' – but this principle is undoubtedly cruelly cynical, because the civil authorities would quite simply have been excommunicated had they refused to burn an unrepentant 'heretic'. Furthermore, the burning of a 'heretic' was regarded as a meritorious act and anyone who brought wood to the stake was given a full remission of all his sins.

Autos da fé were usually held on Sundays and feast days, so that the biggest possible audience could be attracted. Horsemen went around the district inviting people to attend the spectacle. High prices were paid for places at windows with a good view of the stake. Whereas the Nazis at least gassed their victims before burning them, the Inquisitors simply burnt them alive. Very few were granted the special grace of being throttled before being burnt – most were bound, while still alive, to the stake, which was raised high enough on the pile of wood for most of the Christian audience to follow every stage of the victim's death

THE MISERY OF CHRISTIANITY

agony. Depending on the direction of the wind, he either quickly choked to death or experienced a slower death by burning. If he screamed with pain, the assembled Christians joined in with a hymn of praise to God.

In Auschwitz, prisoners were sent to the gas chambers to the accompaniment of operetta music. Was this a more cynical practice than that of the Church's executions of 'heretics'? In his study of the death penalty over a period of three thousand years, Kurt Rossa makes the remarkable statement: 'Anyone who wants to know everything about us Christians should read the Sermon on the Mount. Anyone who wants to know more about us, should read a history of the death penalty.'[28]

The Inquisition, which continued to exist in the Papal States until they were dissolved in 1870, caused countless people to suffer unspeakable torments for centuries. Figures signify very little and they are, in any case, very difficult to get hold of, because no one is granted access to the Vatican archives of the Inquisition. Despite this, it is known that four thousand people were burnt and thirty thousand were condemned to other severe punishments in the space of forty years in the Spanish town of Seville in the fifteenth century. In Guadalupe, a town of three thousand inhabitants at the time, fifty-three people were burnt alive and forty-six exhumed corpses were also burnt in one year (1485); sixteen people were condemned to everlasting imprisonment and others were sent to the galleys. The Grand Inquisitor of Spain, Thomas de Torquemada, who died in 1498, sent 10,220 people to the stake and 97,371 to the galleys.

The Inquisition was not, however, the only instrument used by Christians to punish other Christians with death. When individual action proved inadequate, wars were waged. For example, when all prohibitions and all attempts at conversion, mostly by Cistercian monks, had come to nothing, Pope Innocent III called upon true Christians, in 1209, to undertake a crusade against the Cathari (or Albigensians) in Southern France. All Catholics who took part in this campaign were promised eternal happiness and the French king and nobles were also

28. Rossa, *Todesstrafen*, p. 9.

WHAT IS CHRISTIAN?

promised the Albigensian lands – the earldom of Toulouse and Provence. On the strength of these promises, the land was laid waste in a terrible war of extermination which lasted for some hundred and twenty years. After the first peace treaty of 1229, the pope offered a reward of two silver marks for every 'heretic' brought in, alive or dead.

A further example of a bloody struggle fought between Christians is that of the Hussite wars in the first half of the fifteenth century. When John Hus was burnt as a 'heretic' at the Council of Constance in 1415, his Czech supporters rose against the Roman Church. In retaliation, Pope Martin V and Pope Eugene IV preached a crusade against the Hussites and the result was one blood-bath after another. Each side gave visible evidence of its orthodoxy to the other by having crosses cut into the foreheads of the Catholics and chalices into the foreheads of the Hussites. Whole towns and villages were butchered, and the scorched-earth policy practised, during these cruel wars.

Christians of both the main streams of the Reformation – the Lutherans on the one hand and the Calvinists and Zwinglians on the other – showed themselves from the very beginning to be no more and no less intolerant than their Catholic enemies and fellow-believers. In fact, all that the Reformers usually did was to give a fresh theological justification to traditional practices. Luther's struggle against the Catholic Church was certainly not conducted under the banner of individual freedom of conscience. The famous confession which he made on 18 April 1521 at the Diet of Worms and which has been immortalized in the words: 'Here I stand. I can do nothing else. God help me. Amen' is very far from being a proclamation of man's inalienable right to religious freedom and freedom of conscience. Luther was simply fighting against the authority of the pope in the name of an authority which was even higher than that of the pope – the word of God. Submission to this objectively present authority was freedom of conscience as he understood it.

Luther was convinced that the government of the Church ought to be in the hands of the reigning princes of each country. It therefore became the duty of the civil authorities to prevent unrest and rebellion and to ensure peace and order in the sphere of religion. This inevitably led to only *one* religion being tolerated in each country. What is more, each state authority was responsible for saving the souls of its own subjects and therefore had the task of enforcing by the sword the right religion and the form of worship demanded by the first tablet of the ten commandments.

In 1527, all non-Protestants were compelled by the Saxon Visitation, for which Luther was to a great extent responsible, to emigrate from Protestant lands. In 1531, Luther gave his consent to Melanchthon's suggestion that the Anabaptists should be punished by death. Then, in 1536, he persuaded Philip, the Landgrave of Hesse, to accept the principle of the death penalty for all 'heretics'. As blasphemers who went against Christian teaching and who disturbed public order, they could not be tolerated.

Huldreich Zwingli also used the death penalty as a weapon against 'heretics'. The Anabaptist Felix Manz, for example, was condemned to death on 5 January 1527 by the city council of Zürich, which was supported by Zwingli, and drowned in the Limmat.

It is, of course, well known that Calvin exercised a stranglehold over dogmatic questions in Geneva in the sixteenth century. The Spanish physician, Michael Servet, was burnt alive there on 27 October 1553 because he disputed the doctrine of the Trinity. Between 1545 and 1546, Calvin had been in correspondence with Servet about various matters of Christian dogma, but had terminated the correspondence as soon as it became clear to him that the Spaniard was inflexible in his insistence that the doctrine of the Trinity was unbiblical. Calvin threatened even then that, if Servet ever visited Geneva, he would never leave the city alive. At the beginning of 1553, he informed the Catholic Inquisition at Vienne, where Servet lived. Servet was captured when he passed through Geneva in an attempt to escape to Italy and was put to death at the instigation of Calvin.

In the centuries that followed, Protestants fought one another with a brutality which was in no sense inferior to that of the Catholics. Melanchthon's son-in-law, for example, Kaspar Peucer, who was physician to Augustus, the Elector of Saxony, was imprisoned for twelve years for 'crypto-Calvinism' and was tortured with red hot pincers by the Lutheran inquisitors to force him to recant. Chancellor Cracov, who held similar views to Peucer, died under torture in prison. The Dutch Calvinists led the lawyer John of Oldenbarneveldt to the scaffold in 1619 because, together with the Arminians, he rejected the doctrine of predestination and taught that Christ had died to redeem all men.

These three cases make it quite clear that the Protestant countries were completely totalitarian as far as religion was concerned. It was often compulsory for people in those countries to go to church on Sundays and failure to do so was punished by the civil authorities. The sextons often had to go up and down the aisles during services on Sundays with long sticks in their hands prodding people who fell asleep during the sermon.

Confronted with the emergence and consolidation of the new Protestant 'heresies', the Catholic Church could hardly remain inactive. The Inquisition was completely remodelled on the Spanish pattern and became the favourite organ of Pope Paul IV (1555–1559), who made the famous assertion: 'Even if my own father were a heretic, I would gladly gather wood to have him burnt'.[29]

In this way, Spain and Italy were quickly 'purged' of Protestants. This was also a time of bitter religious wars fought between Catholics and Protestants. The Huguenot wars raged in France and several thousand Protestants were massacred on the single night of St Bartholomew, 24 August 1572. Pope Pius V was so happy that he commemorated the event by having a medal struck with his own image on one side and a picture of an angel killing a Huguenot on the other.

The climax was reached with the Thirty Years' War, which ravaged almost the whole of Europe. Most Lutheran theologians protested indignantly when peace was planned in 1648 because

29. Quoted from Kühner, *Neues Papstlexikon*, p. 119.

the proposed treaty granted equal rights to the Calvinists, and they almost succeeded in having the treaty rejected. Even Pope Innocent X had harsh things to say about it in a special bull, *Zelo domus Dei*.

Do religious wars between Christians belong entirely to the past? Unfortunately not. The Catholic fascist movement in Croatia, which flourished between 1941 and 1944, proves this. The Ustaša, as this terrorist organization was called, was responsible for the forcible conversion of some 240,000 Orthodox Serbs to Roman Catholicism and for putting about 750,000 of these people to death. There was, from the very beginning, close collaboration between the Catholic clergy and the Ustaša. Archbishop Stepinać, whom the Vatican appointed in 1942 to be the spiritual leader of the Ustaša, had a place, together with ten of his clergy, in the Ustaša parliament. Priests were also employed as police chiefs and as officers in the personal bodyguard of the fanatical Croatian head of state, Pavelić. Nuns marched in military parades immediately behind the soldiers, their arms raised in the fascist salute. Abbesses were decorated with the Ustaša order. The most cruel part in this movement was played, however, by the Franciscans, whose monasteries had for some time been used as arsenals. Several monks and priests agreed to work as executioners in the hastily set up concentration camps to which the Orthodox Serbs were sent for mass execution by decapitation. These massacres were so brutal that even the Croatians' allies, the German Nazis, protested against them and petitions were sent to the Vatican. Pope Pius XII, however, said nothing, just as he also said nothing about Auschwitz. It was not until some ten years later, in 1953, that he broke his silence by promoting Archbishop Stepinać, who, as one of those bearing the greatest guilt, had been sentenced by the Supreme People's Court of Yugoslavia to sixteen years' forced labour, to the rank of cardinal for his 'great services' to the Church.

WHAT IS CHRISTIAN?

THE DEFAMATION OF SEXUALITY AND OF WOMEN[30]

The ideological basis of the hostility of Christian ethics towards the sexual impulse, which has been and still is so disastrous in its consequences, is to be found in the New Testament. Jesus' teaching in the gospel was quite clear: 'For when they rise from the dead, they neither marry nor are given in marriage, but are like angels in heaven' (Mark xii, 25). Sexuality, in other words, belongs to a sinful world which is passing away. It is something that is overcome and left behind. In the kingdom of God, where human life is ultimately fulfilled, sexual pleasures have no place, with the result that there are some believers who castrate themselves here on earth for the sake of the kingdom of heaven (Matt. xix, 12). Existing marriages have either to be given up for the sake of Christ (Matt. xix, 29) or, according to the categorical evangelical prohibition against divorce (Mark x, 11 f.), they must be endured like lifelong imprisonment, with the result that even a desirous glance makes a person fit for hell (Matt. v, 28 f.).

Paul was also convinced that sexuality was a bar to ultimate human fulfilment. His statement, 'flesh and blood cannot inherit the kingdom of God' (1 Cor. xv, 50), is one of the most misanthropical statements in the whole of the New Testament. Our 'lowly' bodies (Phil. iii, 21) will perish and God will destroy our stomachs (1 Cor. vi, 13). In eternity, 'there is neither male nor female' (Gal. iii, 28). At the resurrection, Christians will be clothed with an asexual body made of ethereal, heavenly substance (1 Cor. xv, 42 ff.; 2 Cor. v, 1 ff.). A man who despised and ridiculed everything to do with the body as much as Paul was, of course, bound to say that 'it is well for a man not to touch a woman' (1 Cor. vii, 1) and that it was best if all people remained unmarried (1 Cor. vii, 7, 26).

---

30. In this section, the following have been consulted: Althaus (*Die Ethik Martin Luthers*), Baschwitz, Deschner, Glaser, Gottschick, Hansen, Heer (*Mittelalter*), Heussi, Knoll (*Katholische Kirche ...*), König, Marsch, Morus, Nigg (*Das Buch der Ketzer*), Pfister, Schmidt, Seeberg, Taylor, Zscharnack, and Zurhellen.

Some Christians, however, are unfortunately unable to do without it and they are allowed to marry – marriage is here permitted for the limited period of life on earth. Every act of sexual intercourse which has not been made legal, as the lesser evil, by a marriage contract is regarded as a sin of unchastity, incurring eternal punishment by God. Paul outlawed extra-marital sexual intercourse, but characteristically not because of the danger that the couple might treat each other as objects that could be exchanged or as instruments of purely physical satisfaction – any idea of this kind was very far from the apostle's mind – but because 'the immoral man sins against his own body' (1 Cor. vi, 18). In giving this as his reason for condemning sexual relationships outside marriage, Paul reveals his deep egocentricity. He goes on, in the same passage, to show that he does not believe that marriage is based on personal love, but that, in his view, it has only one purpose – that of satisfying, in a legalized manner, the sexual urge that so many Christians unfortunately cannot deny. As a result of this, the partners in marriage are bound to give each other the 'conjugal rights' that each owes to the other (1 Cor. vii, 3).

Paul also demanded that 'those who have wives' should live 'as though they had none' (1 Cor. vii, 29). Marriage for the Christian, then, was to be a joyless brothel in his own home, a situation which Tertullian, faithful to Christian tradition, attempted to correct by insisting on the renunciation of marriage since it was based on the same act as harlotry.

The defamation of sex inevitably leads to the defamation of women, who tend to be regarded as inferior beings. The New Testament provides plenty of evidence of this attitude. What is common to all its authors is a traditionally Jewish patriarchal view which was unable to concede equality to women. The gospels, for example, depicted Jesus as a man who treated women as second-class people, someone who certainly allowed himself to be served, looked after and supplied with money by them (see Mark xiv, 3–9; Luke vii, 36–50; viii, 1–2; x, 38–42), but who did not accept any into the intimate circle of the twelve, not even, as might well happen nowadays, as an alibi. There are other indications too in the gospels that he was in no sense concerned with the emancipation of women – for example, his use of the word 'marry' for men and the phrase 'being given in marriage' for women (Mark xii, 25; Luke xvii, 27).

Paul similarly justified the specially privileged position of men by pointing out that it was not the man, Adam, who was tempted, but Eve, the woman (2 Cor. xi, 3), and that man was not created for the sake of woman, but woman for the sake of man (1 Cor. xi, 9). The hierarchy of creation, then, according to Paul, was, from the highest to the lowest level – God, Christ, man, woman (1 Cor. xi, 3). Only man, not woman, is the image and glory of God – woman is only the glory of man (1 Cor. xi, 7). Even in communal worship, woman's subordination to man had to be made quite clear by her wearing a veil (1 Cor. xi, 5 ff.) and by her keeping silent (1 Cor. xiv, 34). If she wanted to know anything, she was to wait till she got home and then ask her husband (1 Cor. xiv, 35).

The later letters especially – the Deuteropauline and the Catholic epistles – stress that the woman's place is in the home. 'Let a woman learn in silence with all submissiveness. I permit no woman to teach or to have authority over men; she is to keep silent. For Adam was formed first, then Eve; and Adam was not deceived, but the woman was deceived and became a transgressor. Yet woman will be saved through bearing children ...'(1 Tim. ii, 11 ff.). In the letter to Titus, women are required 'to love their husbands and children, to be sensible, chaste, domestic, kind, and submissive to their husbands, that the word of God may not be discredited' (Tit. ii, 4f.).

The New Testament is the work of neurotic philistines, who regarded human sexuality not as a source of joy, but as a source of anxiety; not as a means of expressing love, but as a means of expressing sin. Sometimes overtly, but sometimes in a more concealed manner, the New Testament writers outlawed everything to do with man's body.

Suppression of man's natural instincts inevitably leads to psychological repression and aggressive fixation on a scapegoat. Apart from non-Christians – the lascivious pagans and Jews –

the obvious objects on to which impulses which were contrary to the norm could be projected were women. It was, after all, not Adam, but Eve who brought sin into the world. The fact that woman humbly accepts an inferior position, is submissive to man as her lord and master and confines her sexual activity to the task of bearing children is quite in accordance with an ideology which justifies male domination by appealing to mythological arguments.

The earliest Christian theologians were almost unanimous in regarding sexual abstinence as superior to marriage. Anyone who was able to do so had to lead the more perfect life of strict continence. The second century Marcionites and Montanists totally rejected marriage, but even those theologians who did not go as far as this only permitted marriage in the case of Christians who were too weak to live without it. The ideal form of marriage which was recommended by theologians was the 'spiritual marriage' in which husband and wife lived in continence, as Joseph and Mary were supposed to have lived.

Until the beginning of the third century, extra-marital sexual intercourse was regarded, like murder or apostasy, as an unforgivable mortal sin and the believer who committed it was excluded from the Christian community. The Roman bishop, Callistus, was the first, in 217 or 218, to make it possible for the penitent sinner to be readmitted, although, in so doing, he lost the Novatians, who left the Church because they insisted on the more severe sexual ethics.

The practice of bishops, priests and deacons remaining celibate after consecration or ordination became gradually more and more widespread throughout the course of the third century. The ideological justification for this practice was, of course, that the sexual act made a man unfit to preside at an act of public worship. The Synod of Elvira, which took place round about the year 310, required married altar servers to refrain from all sexual intercourse. A similar fear of everything to do with sex – an anxiety which was, of course, based on a magical understanding of man and the world – was the reason why women were forbidden to attend religious services during menstruation. In

Syria, a penance of seven years was imposed on any woman who defied this ban.

Many of the Church Fathers are characterized by an attitude of deep hostility to women which is quite obscene. Tertullian's defamatory view of woman is clearly revealed by his calling her the 'gate through which the devil enters', giving as his reason, of course, the fact that it was she who made man – the image of God – fall and that she was therefore ultimately to blame for the death of the Son of God. Jerome, who was responsible for the Latin translation of the Bible, the Vulgate, wrote: 'Woman is the gate of the devil, the way of evil, the sting of the scorpion, in a word, a dangerous thing'.[31] It is therefore hardly surprising that Jerome, who would have liked most of all to have shaved off the hair of all women, was later made the patron saint of misogynists! He was convinced that married people lived 'like cattle' with each other and were in no way different from 'pigs and irrational animals'. He was one of the earliest protagonists of that 'metaphysical eroticism'[32] which allowed the repressed sexual urge to be transferred to Christ as the bridegroom, who became, in this way, 'spiritually' united with the pure soul. This religious substitute for sexual satisfaction has played an important part at different times throughout the history of the Church, especially in the various mystical and pietistic movements.

The cult of Mary occupies a similar position in the domestic life of the soul. It commenced very early in the history of Christianity – there are indications of it in the New Testament (see Luke i, 28, 48; xi, 27) – and began to flourish after the proclamation, at the Council of Ephesus in 431, of the dogma of Mary's motherhood of God. Despite all the claims made by Christian apologists that womankind is ennobled by the example of Mary as the antitype of the sinful Eve, the cult of Mary undeniably dishonours women. Mary has, after all, been venerated since the second century as *semper Virgo* – always a virgin – in other words, as a woman who never experienced sexual intercourse either before or after the birth of Jesus, since

---

31. Quoted from Heer, *Mittelalter*, p. 527.
32. Marsch, 'Frau', p. 1071.

this, as Pope Siricius (384–399) stated, would have defiled her. The cult of the blessed Virgin is the product and the expression of an infantile and a mutilated sexuality, of a mother fixation or psychological virginity.

Augustine (354–430) summed up all the most important views in the Church about sex and, in so doing, determined the whole attitude of fundamental hostility towards sexuality taken by theologians in the later history of the Church. This may be summarized very briefly as follows. Sin – *concupiscentia* – reaches its peak in sexual desire, that is, in the *'libido . . . qua obscenae partes corporis excitantur'* ('the desire in which the indecent parts of the body are excited').[33] Sin is inherited physically, by way of the sexual act. This is why Jesus had to be born of a virgin. If he had not, he would not have been sinless. There is no essential difference between sexual intercourse between married people (*copula carnalis*) and sexual intercourse with a harlot (*copula carnalis fornicatoria*). Both are equally sinful. Any teaching about the *triplex bonum coniugii*, the three virtues of marriage, has therefore to justify in some way the sexual act within marriage. The first *bonum* of marriage is the *bonum sacramenti* – marriage is indissoluble and the type of Christ's union with mankind. The second is the *bonum fidei* – the mutual faith and trust of the partners on which marriage is based. The third virtue is the *bonum prolis*, according to which the only meaning and purpose of the sexual act within marriage is to beget children.

The whole history of the Middle Ages is characterized by an increasing attempt on the part of theologians to repress man's sexual urge or at least to regulate it. Private or auricular confession proved to be an excellent weapon for achieving this domination of sex life by the Church, with the result that it was imposed on all Christians as a duty by the Fourth Lateran Council in 1215.

The Church's rules concerning sex were, on the one hand, recognized as God's will. On the other hand, however, it was almost impossible to keep them, with the result that people

33. Quoted from Loofs, *Leitfaden zum Studium der Dogmengeschichte*, p. 306.

experienced oppressive feelings of guilt and fear. But to whom could they turn for relief, except to their priests, who alone possessed the 'power of the keys', that is, the power to forgive sins and to protect men from purgatory and hell? In this way, men's actions and even their thoughts were directed by the clergy.

Sexual intercourse was forbidden on Sundays, Wednesdays and Fridays, which amounted to almost half the year. In addition to this, it was prohibited during the forty days of Lent and forty days before Christmas. In case this was not enough, it was also forbidden for three days before receiving communion. What is more, even the position of love-making was prescribed and the Church laid down punishments for anyone who wished to vary this official position. The sexual act had to be performed as quickly and as uninterestingly as possible. Long, heavy night clothes with an opening at the requisite place were worn, so that the husband could fertilize his wife without it being necessary or even possible to touch her too closely.

If a man had an involuntary nocturnal emission, he knew that he had committed a sin and had to get up at once and recite seven penitential psalms. The next morning he had to recite another thirty. The Church's penitential books prescribed the most severe punishments for masturbation, which Thomas Aquinas described as a greater sin than harlotry.

It will be obvious that this was very favourable soil for priestly celibacy to flourish in and it was, of course, energetically fostered, especially by the Cluniac reformers of the eleventh century, who firmly opposed the marriage of priests. Finally, at a lenten synod in 1074, Pope Gregory VII made celibacy obligatory. Monks who were faithful to the pope incited the people to mob those priests who refused to leave their wives.

But, although priests could be compelled to live as celibates, it was not possible to ensure that every priest was completely continent. Concubinage with the cook was, of course, the most harmless way of leading a double moral life. In many dioceses, however, bishops permitted their priests to live in sin so long as

THE MISERY OF CHRISTIANITY

they paid a tidy sum of money for the privilege. There was no end to the succession of scandals in monasteries and nunneries. In his *De contemptu mundi* – 'Contempt of the World' – Pope Innocent III complained about members of the clergy who embraced Venus at night and worshipped the Virgin Mary in the morning. It is true to say that even the higher clergy were hardly concerned at all with the practice of the Church's rules of celibacy and sexual conduct, either in the tenth century, at the time of papal pornocracy, or later, during the heyday of the Renaissance popes.

When Pope Innocent IV (1243–1254) left Lyons, where he had been because of a Council of the Church, after ten years, Cardinal Hugo said, in a farewell speech to the citizens: 'We have made great improvements since we have been here. When we arrived, we found three or four brothels. We are leaving only one behind us. We must add, however, that this one brothel stretches from the east to the west gate.'[34]

Prostitution also flourished during the period the popes spent in exile at Avignon (1309–1377). The whores had to keep strictly to certain hours of prayer and were not allowed to miss Mass. Their clients were also subject to the Christian rule – in other words, the brothels were closed to pagans and Jews.

Friendly relationships continued to exist between the clergy and the prostitutes in later centuries. During the Council of Basle (1431–1449), for example, about fifteen hundred whores provided for the physical well-being of the Fathers of the Council and the Basilica of St Peter in Rome was to a very great extent financed by papal courtesan taxes.

These outlawed sexual urges, however, could not always be shed in such a relatively harmless way. It should not be forgotten, in this context, that the libertinism of privileged members of the clergy was contrary to the commandments of God and that this resulted in feelings of guilt and anxiety which were inevitably transferred to the temptress woman.

Medieval theology was characterized by a brutal hostility towards woman. As early as the sixth century, the bishops atten-

34. Quoted from Taylor, p. 40 f.

WHAT IS CHRISTIAN?

ding a synod in Macon (Gaul) had earnestly debated whether woman was really a human being at all and later, in the Middle Ages, the 'angelic' teacher, Thomas Aquinas, defamed her by calling her a 'failed man' (*mas occasionatus*) and by insisting inflexibly that she should not be permitted any equality in the Church or in civil society. He did not hesitate to speak about the 'use of necessary things, of woman, who is necessary for the continuation of the human race, or of food and drink'. 'Woman was created to help man, but only in procreation ... since, in any other work, man can be helped better by another man than by a woman.'[35] In expressing this opinion, of course, the angelic teacher failed to observe that agriculture in the High Middle Ages, for example, would have been totally impossible without the serf labour of women, quite apart from the domestic function they performed.

This deep hostility towards woman reached a horrifying climax in the Christian witch-hunt, which resulted in several million women being tortured and burnt at the stake from the thirteenth until the eighteenth century.

Although they were very closely interwoven in this persistent illusion that witches existed, two essential elements can be distinguished. The first is, of course, the unbridled and aggressive hostility towards women to which I have already referred several times and the second is a widespread belief that devils and demons really existed.

The real existence of devils and demons is presupposed in all the gospels. Diseases are attributed to their presence and Jesus is represented as an exorcist who cures people by driving out devils – although even ancient scientists would have called this pure superstition. Paul also believed firmly in spirits. At baptism, evil spirits are said to be driven out at the name of Christ.

The early Church must have been swarming with demons, because there was a special office, that of exorcist, to deal with them. There were devils at work everywhere and holy water, prayers and exorcisms were helpful in warding them off. The

35. Quoted from Heer, *Mittelalter*, p. 526 f.

longer Christianity existed, the deeper became men's fear of occult powers.

Thomas Aquinas taught that the rain, hail and wind were caused by demons. He also believed that the Huns were descended from demons. He thought too that the devil could and did have sexual relationships with human beings and reflected about the origin of the seed used in this process. The devil could either change into a man – *incubus*, 'lying on' – and make a human woman pregnant or he could change into a woman – *succubus*, 'lying underneath' – and be made pregnant by a human man. The monsters that were presumably begotten in this way – creatures with wolves' heads or fishes' tails – had to be fed with ordinary human children.

Luther also believed quite firmly in the existence of changelings. In a sermon given on 13 June 1529, he gave an emphatic warning against bathing in lakes and rivers because the devil lived in them and laid traps for human beings – which was why so many people had drowned in the Elbe.

Witches were women who had taken an oath renouncing Christ and had assigned their souls to the devil. They were, of course, also 'heretics' because they had fallen away from God and gone over to the devil. As a reward for concluding this blasphemous pact with him, Satan had given them the power to practise magic. What, then, did they do? They made men impotent and women infertile. They caused miscarriages, bad harvests, and made cattle die. They were also responsible for plagues and other inexplicable illnesses.

Their most important characteristic, however, was their lechery – and this, of course, provides the key to the whole phenomenon of witchcraft, at least from the psychological point of view. They were the devil's whores who, at night-time, flew up to the top of the Brocken and, after celebrating a black mass there with their lascivious partners, the demons, plunged into a wild orgy.

Gregory IX (1227–1241) was the first pope to instruct the Inquisition to take legal action against witches and the first trial was held in his pontificate near Treves. The second call to hunt witches was made by Pope John XXII in his bull, *Super illius specula*, of 1326, and other official documents were published by the Church in 1374, 1409, 1418, 1437, 1445 and 1451. Innocent VIII finally promulgated his notorious 'Witches' Bull', *Summis desiderantes affectibus*, on 5 December 1484, and thus extended the whole criminal process of legitimate persecution. Three years later, the infamous 'Witches' Hammer' (*Malleus maleficarum*) appeared. This disgraceful concoction was the work of two Dominicans, Heinrich Institoris and Jakob Sprenger, and had been reprinted twenty-nine times by 1669. Later popes, such as Alexander VI, Julius II, Leo X, Hadrian VI and Clement VII, also called upon Christians, in various bulls, to murder innocent women and the leaders of the Reformation did exactly the same. In the sermons that he delivered in Wittenberg, Luther again and again urged his followers to hunt and torture witches, and Calvin, without doubt one of the greatest sadists who ever lived, constantly advocated mass executions in order to exterminate witches (*extirper telle race*). He was convinced that the court of Geneva, despite its barbarity, was far too lenient.

What happened at a witch trial? It was quite enough for a woman's nose to be too long, for her to have red hair or a humped back or for her to be exceptionally beautiful or intelligent – in such cases, she might easily be suspected of being a witch. A person thus suspected would at once be thrown into prison and put in chains. The first question that the Inquisitor would ask her was whether or not she believed in witchcraft. The answer 'no' was regarded as immediate proof of the alleged offence, since, as Innocent VIII's 'Witches' Bull' and the famous 'Witches' Hammer' put it so clearly, the slightest doubt that witchcraft really existed was regarded as the greatest heresy of all. There was, then, no escape. If the accused woman answered 'yes' to the Inquisitor's question, she would immediately be subjected to cross-examination and asked, for example, what she had been doing in the field before the storm broke, why she had gone into her neighbour's stable and so on.

If the suspect did not, in the course of the trial, accuse herself, she would be examined for physical signs that might show beyond any doubt that she was a witch. She would be stripped naked and all the hair on her body would be shaved off so that it might be possible to find, in some hidden place, the mark that Satan had imprinted on the body of his mistress. Moles and warts were regarded as infallible signs of a lewd association with the devil.

If no mark was found on her body, the victim would be tortured, to force a confession from her and to make her reveal the names of other witches. In order to terminate the terrible pain, a so-called witch might even betray her own mother, sister or daughter as an accomplice and, even if she withdrew her confession or the names she had given at a later stage, this would not be accepted.

Tortured almost to the point of death – as one phrase expressed it, 'You are to be tortured so thin that the sun will shine through you' – the unhappy woman would then either be tied to a wooden cross in a damp, underground, rat-infested dungeon or be chained and hung up in a witches' tower, where she would have to endure cold and hunger until she was ultimately roasted over a slow fire.

If she confessed to the crime of complicity with the devil, she had to be burnt alive. It was impossible for her to be pardoned, because, as the Bible clearly stated, 'You shall not permit a sorceress to live' (Exod. xxii, 18). Anyone who dared to criticize this procedure was regarded as someone who despised the word of God, and was therefore at once suspected of heresy.

Witches were burnt all over Europe. 'The flames were rising everywhere and it seemed as though they would never be put out. Everyone was being burnt – men and women, Catholics and Protestants, idiots and scholars, four-year-old children and eighty-year-old women. Everyone was being sent indiscriminately to the stake and burnt to ashes.'[36]

In 1678, the Archbishop of Salzburg sent ninety-seven women to the stake because so many cattle were dying of disease. Bishop Fuchs von Dornheim of Bamberg had some nine hundred

36. Nigg, *Das Buch der Ketzer*, p. 280.

witches and sorcerers put to death round about the year 1630 and his victims included the five burgomasters of the town. Bishop Adolf von Ehrenberg of Würzburg also sent about twelve hundred witches and sorcerers to the stake at about this time, but had the kindness to endow masses to be said for the repose of their souls. Archbishop John of Treves had so many witches burnt in 1585 that there were only two women left in each of two villages.

Witch-hunting reached its peak during the Thirty Years' War. Altogether, there were more Protestant than Catholic victims. In Protestant Sweden, many witches were burnt after having been denounced by their children – since, in the words of the Bible, 'Out of the mouth of babes and sucklings thou hast brought perfect praise' (Matt. xxi, 16). The last witches were burnt in Switzerland in 1782 and drowned at the witches' ordeal near Danzig in 1836.

Only the Enlightenment, of course, could bring this mad witch-hunt to an end, although it has not yet completely disappeared even now. I should like, however, to leave this unpleasant subject, and consider Luther's hostility towards sex and women.

The fact that Luther married the ex-nun Catharine von Bora and that he also became extremely critical of priestly celibacy tends erroneously to make us believe that he ceased to practise or to preach the traditional Christian asceticism. Nothing could be further from the truth. Like the other reformers, Luther regarded marriage above all as a cure for sin (*remedium peccati*), as a dyke against the unbridled sexual urge or as a 'hospital for the sick'. Even within marriage, he believed, sexual intercourse was sinful, since it was always mixed with 'carnal lust' – 'no marital duty takes place without sin'.[37]

He insisted crudely on the husband's rights with regard to his wife, including his right, as her lord and master, to beat her. 'The woman's place is in the home' – the saying was coined by Luther. Motherhood is woman's greatest glory and she should give birth to as many children as possible, so that all

37. Quoted from Seeberg, 'Luthers Anschauung . . .', p. 114.

the more people may be led to the gospel. Even if she should die, worn out and exhausted, from bearing too many children, motherhood is still her true task and her true health. 'If they become tired or even die, that does not matter. Let them die in childbirth – that is why they are there.'[38] Luther saw women, in other words, as child-bearing machines. Finally, it should be noted that, despite his teaching about the universal priesthood of all believers, he did not think that women were fit to be ordained. When, at Wittenberg in 1591, the Lutheran theologians once again discussed the old question of whether women were really human beings at all, they were, of course, being quite consistent with Christian tradition.

The hostile attitude towards sexuality that has characterized Christianity throughout history is basically unchanged today. Let me give one example to prove my point, that of the Vatican *castrati*. Until as late as 1920 or thereabouts, many members of the choir of the Sistine Chapel were men who had been castrated simply for the sake of church music. Two hundred and thirty popes, beginning with Sixtus V, who died in 1590, had men mutilated because God could be praised more sweetly by eunuchs. The Viennese psychoanalyst, Wilfried Daim, had this to say about the use of *castrati* in church choirs: 'It is the last, the most open and the clearest expression of a clerical castration-wish directed against a laity which is viewed with sexual envy'.[39]

Finally, there is another and far more recent example of the fact that the history of the Christian attitude towards sexuality continues to be a history of aversion to normal human desire, of fear, repression, guilt complexes and envy, and of Christians being constrained to lead a double moral life. This is clearly borne out by the latest papal encyclical of July 1968, *Humanae Vitae*, and the debate which followed its publication.

In this encyclical letter – which, it should be noted, claims to have binding force not only for Catholics, but for the whole of mankind – Paul VI has endorsed the traditional repressive sexual morality of the Church. Cynically, he evokes the ideas of

38. Quoted from Althaus, *Die Ethik Martin Luthers*, p. 100, note 82.
39. Quoted from Knoll, *Katholische Kirche* . . ., p. 78.

'nobility' and human freedom in order to subject people to crushing anxiety by condemning all forms of contraception except that of periodic continence.

What about the very many Catholic theologians critical of this encyclical? They are regarded here in northern Europe as very progressive, yet they are really only adapting themselves to an existing and powerful tendency in society today and are, at the same time, worried about a loss of papal authority among the sheep of their flock. Their attitude is not fundamentally different from that expressed by the pope in the encyclical – it is only different in degree. Whereas they might have argued in favour of the total liberation of man's erotic and sexual life, they have talked a great deal of cant and hypocrisy about 'the personal choice of married people based on their private consciences', 'responsible parenthood' and 'world population'. These advanced Catholic theologians are convinced of their own philanthropic spirit, but, for them, extra-marital sexual relationships are still taboo.

The false morality of the churches is objectively reflected in the existing criminal law of Western Germany, for example, with the result that anyone found guilty of unregulated desires can be prosecuted for indecency, especially under those sections of the law relating to divorce and adultery and to procuring and homosexuality.

But has this rigid juridical framework of Christian ethics not been at least very strongly influenced by recent developments in social attitudes? Have the Christian taboos not been swept away at last in the increasingly promiscuous tendencies in modern society? Anyone who believes this is, I am afraid, merely dazzled by appearances, because the Church's fundamental hostility to normal human desire is still able to control forms of sexuality which are quite different from those approved of by the clergy.

To what extent does this happen? Christianity has never accepted man's sexual urges as valid human impulses in the good sense. Every physical act of love has always been shrouded in darkness and has only been permitted by the churches as a means of begetting children. Sexual relationships have thus always been experienced as something alien to and separated from the human personality as such. Even nowadays, in our modern age of libertinism and pseudo-emancipation, they are still experienced in this way.

Certainly sexuality is no longer regarded by all people simply as a means of producing children, but it is used as a means of making money. The capitalist machinery of advertising shamelessly exploits human sexual instincts and stimuli to promote higher rates of profit and defames woman even more totally, but so subtly that she is usually not even aware of it.

Sexual intercourse itself has been reduced to the level of a thing, an object. The idea of marital faithfulness was debased in the Christian ethos of marriage to the level of property and woman herself was degraded to the level of a possession – '*my* wife'. In the same way, sex has today come to assume the character of 'goods' and, under the cover of freedom, the capitalist laws of exchange have penetrated into the most intimate sphere of human relationships. With the constantly increasing production and consumption of goods, consumers are not simply content to 'own' a woman – they also want to be able to replace a used woman by a new one as often as they like.

The attempt to grant full equality to women has so far been as unsuccessful as the movement towards full sexual emancipation. Woman is not recognized as man's equal either in the professional sphere or in social life. It is also clearly quite untrue to say that woman enjoys equal rights in the Church as long as there are still no women as priests, bishops, cardinals and popes.

POSSIBLE OBJECTIONS ARE REFUTED

It is possible for Christian apologists to react in several different ways to the facts of Christian history that I have given in the preceding sections. In this section I shall discuss some of the more common of these attitudes.

The simplest and by far the most widespread method of dealing with the events of Christian history is either to deny

WHAT IS CHRISTIAN?

them or simply to pass over them in silence. Hans Conzelmann, who is Professor in New Testament Studies at Göttingen, said rather bitterly some time ago that Christians were nourished by their radical ignorance of the results of historical and scientific research into the Bible. How much more appropriately could the same be said of that 'hotchpotch of error and violence', as Goethe once described the history of the Church!

Christians are ignorant of the history of their religion very largely because they are so imperfectly informed by theologians and Church historians, who succeed in denying the scandalous facts either by twisting them into their complete opposite or by drawing a veil over them. Let me give an example of each of these cunning devices.

In his popular pamphlet questioning whether atheism was not really self-deception, the Protestant theologian, Gunther Backhaus, said: 'Even the most determined atheist cannot go on denying the fact that woman could never have become ultimately emancipated in Western society – however incomplete this process may still be – without the biblical teaching about woman.'[40] What this biblical teaching about woman in fact is, I have already shown, at least as far as the so-called 'New' Testament is concerned.

In his *Kleine Konziliengeschichte*, the Catholic Professor in Church History at Bonn, Hubert Jedin, had this to say about the Fourth Lateran Council of 1215: 'The Church's defensive action against the false doctrines of the Cathari, the Waldensians and other sects is reflected in the regulations concerning the Inquisition'. But, instead of going on to illustrate the nature of these regulations, in other words, instead of showing that they prescribed barbarous measures and justified them by divine authority, Jedin continues in a philistine tone: 'The famous section, chapter 21, which makes it the duty of every Christian who has reached the age of reason to confess his sins and receive communion at least once a year, is still in force.' Then, after discussing further details of conciliar decisions about the organization of the Church – which proves that he was not

40. Backhaus, *Atheismus* . . ., p. 21.

writing a mere summary of the Council – Jedin says: 'The legislation forbidding the Jews to go out during Easter and making it obligatory for them to wear special clothes was not the result of racial prejudice, nor was it thought of as a disparaging insult, because it was also applied to Mohammedans living among Christians. It was introduced simply in order to protect the Christian faith. It was nonetheless an expression of the spirit of the age.'[41]

Here, too, important information is hushed up and an attempt made to soften the harsh facts by appealing to the spirit of the times. Why should discriminating regulations be any less disparaging and insulting because they applied to two minority groups? The distinctive dress which Jews were expected to wear was, after all, a horned cap, which showed clearly enough to people of those times that they were descended from the devil.

These two examples of the falsification of history by Christians are not by any means exceptional. 'Falsifications have, from the very beginning, always played a truly historical part in Christianity.'[42] Letters, books, documents, decrees, reports on the martyrs and the saints, minutes and monastic records – they have all been forged, invented or rewritten to mean the exact opposite and this has been done unscrupulously in order to satisfy the honour of God. (Clear examples of this are the Constantinian donation and the false decretals of Pseudo-Isidore.) Even since the recent Second Vatican Council, there has been quite audacious falsification of the facts – an example of this is the encyclical *Pacem in Terris*, a product of the reactionary, triumphalistic elements in the Roman Curia.

A second way of reacting to summarily reported events in the history of the Church is to admit in the abstract that they may to a greater or lesser extent be true and then at once to minimize them. For example, Heinrich Fries, Catholic Professor in Fundamental Theology at the University of Münster, has this to say about the pact between the Catholic Church and the dominant powers in state and society: 'It is true that many of

41. Jedin, *Kleine Konziliengeschichte . . .*, p. 48 f.
42. Heer, *Gottes erste Liebe*, p. 197.

these decisions have been and still are open to question. Compromises have been and still are being made. A great deal might, no doubt, have been done very differently or better. There has been weakness, guilt and failure on the part of the Church – this cannot be denied, nor can it be justified. But it would be asking too much of the pastors of the Church, who so often have to make concrete decisions, to expect them to take all the possibly evil consequences and all possible abuses into account in their plans and to be able to foresee these, as it were divinely.'[43]

What is so often done in this kind of apologetics is to appeal to the 'spirit of the age' – 'Luther was also a child of his time' or 'the whole problem must be viewed in its historical context' are typical remarks. I have, of course, already given a good example of this technique above. This type of argument is, I believe, both dishonest and impossible to believe because it presupposes that there is some element in the history of the Church that is not entirely determined by history. The supposedly positive aspects of Christianity are in this way regarded as transcending time and as directly brought about by God himself. The negative aspects – I would prefer to call them the notoriously corrupt elements – are, on the other hand, purely the result of historical circumstances and the Church is thus completely exonerated. I would simply ask this: What was the factor that determined the spirit of the age for centuries? And I would reply – the Church, in its alliance with the worldly powers.

A favourite variation of the theme of the spirit of the age is the criticism that a completely one-sided selection has been made of unrepresentative examples from the history of Christianity. The reality of Christianity is certainly not as uniform as the critics of the Church would have us believe.

The Catholic Professor of Church History at the University of Innsbruck, Hugo Rahner – the brother of Karl Rahner – has made use of this type of objection to adverse criticism of the Church.

43. Fries, *Ärgernis und Widerspruch*, p. 146 f.

It has to be freely admitted that ideological and physical force was used, for example, to convert the Saxons or to missionize many pagans. But, when we speak in such broad terms of fateful and wrong developments of this kind, we should at the same time not forget to mention the truly Christian principles which Ambrose, for example, advocated in connection with the pagan missions, or the purely biblical policy which Gregory the Great proclaimed with regard to the mission to the Anglo-Saxon people, or the heroism shown by the Cistercian communities or by the Franciscans in Morocco and China, or the exemplary missionary work of Francis Xavier which was so free of any alliance with the state. The Church of 'established power' played no part in this work. Of course, it is true that this heroism was often covered over by the patronage of the Spanish or Portuguese state Church.... But it is grossly simplifying history to speak of an epoch of the Church of established power lasting some one thousand five hundred years until its ultimate dissolution in our own age.[44]

Whatever force the events and personalities mentioned by Hugo Rahner in the above passage may have as examples to convince us of the positive aspects of Christianity, I cannot and will not overlook a single human Christian or group of Christians or try to hush up their actions or their intentions. Quite the reverse – the existence of a few Christian nonconformists or minority groups who have refused and still refuse to follow the practices of the churches of established power only serves to make criticism of the established churches more cogent. Although they can, of course, never succeed in undoing the recorded crimes that have been committed by established Christianity or in minimizing their importance, they do show quite clearly that Christianity cannot be defined without ambiguity. The following facts may help to prove both that the history of the Church cannot be treated, as it were, in bulk and that Christianity is a mass of inner contradictions.

The Carpocratians, a Christian gnostic group centred in Alexandria, abolished slavery in their community and gave equal rights to women in the name of the equality of all mankind. At the time of the Reformation, the Protestant pastor Thomas Münzer fought on the side of the exploited peasants and miners

44. Rahner, *Abendland*, p. 192 f.

WHAT IS CHRISTIAN?

for an early form of democracy which also included social equality. In the nineteenth century, the journeyman-tailor Wilhelm Weitling was the first to create the image of a socialist Jesus, the revolutionary carpenter, and to demand, in the name of the gospel, a revolution which would bring about a classless Christian society.

Even the ideology that led to the crusades did not go unchallenged in the Christian world. From time to time, theologians, Individuals and groups of Christians who believed in peace have emerged – Francis of Assisi, Brigid of Sweden and the theologians Anselm of Canterbury and Peter Damian all rejected the crusades and the two theologians were even strongly opposed to any kind of war, like the Waldenses, who further rejected all forms of jurisdiction by blood, including, of course, the Inquisition. Other Christian pacifists are the Anabaptists, the Mennonites and the Quakers.

What is more, anti-semitism, as practised by Christians, has not always been given unqualified approval by all the clergy and laity of the Church. A number of medieval popes and bishops tried repeatedly to protect the Jews from pogroms.

Before going on to consider in greater detail the real meaning of the demand, made again and again by Christians throughout the history of the Church in the name of their God, that mutually exclusive norms of conduct be imposed, I shall first discuss the third way in which Christians believe that it is possible to lessen the oppressive weight of Christian crimes.

The most cunning form of apologetics used by Christians is to admit openly and without reservation that the atrocities of the Inquisition and witch-hunting certainly took place, but then to argue that the men who committed it were not Christians. Characteristic of this method is the very detailed and basically sympathetic discussion of Karlheinz Deschner's book *Abermals krähte der Hahn* by Fritz Blanke, who was, until his recent death, Professor of Church History at Zürich University.

He says that, although Deschner's book is incomplete, it contains enough to bear out what the English historian, William E. H. Lecky, has said, namely that it is in no sense an exaggera-

THE MISERY OF CHRISTIANITY

tion to say that the Christian Church has caused a greater measure of undeserved human suffering than any other religion. Then, however, Blanke makes the theological manoeuvre which he is bound to make at this point and states that these crimes were, of course, an 'embezzlement' of the true gospel and that it should really be a question of making people 'enthusiastic about genuine Christianity'.[45]

The Church historian Walter Nigg used a similar device to try to slip through the mesh when he was writing about witch hunting in the Church:

> In this chapter of the history of heresy in the Church, gloom increased until it became the impenetrable darkness of night, inspiring men with fear and trembling. Even in trying to portray these stepchildren of Christianity, one has the feeling that one will never again be able to emerge from one's sadness and be normally happy again. Even today, a fearful nightmare presses down on one's mind as soon as one attempts to describe what this burning of witches was like.... Understandably enough, no one likes to be reminded of this nocturnal aspect of Christianity. It is such an oppressive burden to bear that it calls both the Catholic and the Protestant churches fundamentally into question.[46]

What is Nigg's solution to this problem? Quite simply, that it was not the witches themselves, but the mad delusion of those who persecuted them that came from the devil:

> The devil was at the centre of the problem of witchcraft like a cosmic monster. His servants were involved in the game, but they were not on the side of the poor women who were tortured and burnt to ashes. Quite the reverse is true – the devil's servants were the Inquisitors and jurists whose minds he had turned.[47]

Let us pause to take stock. On the basis of pure experience, we can say that Christians – appealing to God, to Jesus Christ and to the Bible – have committed and justified the most widely divergent and indeed mutually exclusive actions. Norms of

---

45. Blanke's review is printed in Deschner, *Mit Gott und den Faschisten*, p. 270 ff.; the quotations will be found on pp. 273-4.
46. Nigg, *Das Buch der Ketzer*, p. 271.
47. ibid., p. 287.

WHAT IS CHRISTIAN?

human conduct which were regarded as the glorious and most sacred will of God by earlier followers of Jesus are condemned by present-day believers as diabolical delusions. It is clearly possible – in the name of the God of the Bible – either to exalt or to reject the burning of witches, either to curse or to bless the Jews, either to force pagans to be baptized or to leave them full freedom of conscience, and to find crusades either glorious or abominable.

The name of God, the name of Jesus Christ, the Bible and the *testimonium Spiritus Sancti internum* – the 'inner testimony of the Holy Spirit' – hold good, in all fundamental and really decisive questions, for mutually exclusive norms of human behaviour.

To apply the idea of the 'historicity of God's word', which is so much favoured by theologians nowadays, would, in this context, be simply cynical and bound to fail miserably, because the fantastic fact of being able at the same time to commit and to abhor murder in the name of Jesus Christ cannot be explained away by an appeal to the difference between one period of history and another. It has always been so.

There is even now no question of any importance to which contradictory answers are not given by Christian theologians and Church functionaries. Even within the same Christian confession, there are enormous differences of opinion as to what in fact constitutes obedience to God's will. The death penalty, the distribution of property, war and peace, birth control, homosexuality, educational policy, divorce – in these and so many other questions, God's word is rather like an oracle whispering cryptically in the ears of Christians, instead of being a clear unequivocal message, as the theologians would have us believe. In the name of Christ, Protestant pastors belong to fascist groups. In the name of Christ, Catholic bishops sympathize with the aims of neo-Nazis. As a Christian, it is possible to be either a loyal communist or a fanatical anti-communist. As a Christian, it is possible to preach pacifism or to give one's blessing to the production and the use of the atomic bomb.

The word 'God' and the name 'Jesus Christ' are exposed in

this moral anarchy – to which there seems to be no end – as blank formulae that can be filled up and manipulated at will, as figures of speech which do no more than simulate facts and realities. Their only function is to remove changing moral standpoints, which are not in any way essentially different from those of non-Christians, from the sphere of man's intellect and to invest them with the appearance of absolute validity. They can then be used as ideological icing-sugar to decorate and superficially sweeten the still very sour cake. 'God' turns out, at every level of man's existence, to be a spirit that can be used by man, and there is nothing that cannot be made to look beautiful by this religious therapy – that cannot, in other words, be doctored. This is, of course, why Franz Overbeck called theologians the 'quacks of Christianity'.[48]

Christians find themselves in a fix which is very difficult indeed to get out of. To reduce the problem to its simplest terms, there seem to be two possible solutions.

Firstly, one group of Christians can call another within the same Church heretical – or both groups can call each other heretics – and each group can call the appeal made by the other group unchristian and blasphemous. In an extreme case of mutual defamation, this can come to a division within the Church and the formation of a new Christian group, sect, confession or church – call it what you will. The result of this is that there will now be two separated groups, each with its own organization and each calling itself Christian, but both in competition with each other and both appealing to the same authorities when their interests are opposed, yet denying each other any right to these authorities.

Christians hardly ever choose to solve their problems in this way nowadays, because experience has taught them that it is extremely difficult to heal breaches in the Church once they have been made. (Towards the end of the nineteen-fifties, West

---

48. Overbeck, *Christentum und Kultur*, p. 274. (Overbeck's phrase is the 'Figaros of Christianity', in other words, the barbers (or surgeons); *frisieren*, to dress the hair, has the same pejorative sense as the English 'to doctor' – *Translator*.)

German Protestantism was threatened by division because of irreconcilable differences of opinion about atomic warfare. Now, at the end of the nineteen-sixties, a schism occasioned by violently opposed views in the debate about demythologization cannot be ruled out.) As a rule, then, quarrels are settled within one's own particular Christian group. This brings us to the second possible solution to the problem.

Christians can, if they follow this second course, 'remain together under the authority of the gospel', as it is sometimes expressed in theological jargon. They accept the painful fact that fundamental differences do exist between them, but they do not draw any conclusions from this fact. They prefer, in other words, to delude themselves and others into thinking that unity exists. But what does this unity 'under the authority of the gospel' consist of, if it is not made clearly manifest, at least in fundamental questions?

There is one very obvious objection to this. Do not all Christians recognize the commandment to love their fellow-men? In theory, this commandment does indeed unite all Christians at all times. But only in theory. Quite apart from the fact that the commandment to love one's neighbour is not simply confined to Christians, but is widely recognized outside Christianity, it has, in practice, proved to be the perfect example of an empty formula. In the concrete, all the insurmountable differences that exist between Christians continue to divide them. It is clearly necessary to be aware of the beneficent function carried out by the empty formulae of Christianity – that of hushing up fundamental differences within a given group by means of a suitable linguistic device – before it can be discovered at work in theology. Christianity would be even more radically divided if Christians were not protected by a theological vocabulary which deludes them into believing that they are still united.

So, whether Christians remain united 'under the authority of the gospel' or whether they continue to defame one another, one thing is certain – nothing can put an end to the anarchy that reigns in their ethics. But what use is a message containing nothing, a message that is, in fact, completely elastic, a message which can be interpreted in so many mutually incompatible ways? What is a 'Lord' who protects everything his 'servants' do? Both the Christians' message and their 'Lord' are not only superfluous; they are also harmful.

They are superfluous because non-Christians have also come to very much the same conclusions – with regard to both good and evil – without the theological claptrap of Christian teaching. They are harmful because certain actions are proclaimed by Christianity to be unconditionally obligatory. Something that is unconditionally binding is removed from the sphere of rational debate. This criticism also applies to those Christians with whom I am in partial agreement on many questions – for example, Christians who are opposed to nuclear armament, and left-wing Catholics and Protestants in general. Let us now consider their contradictory manoeuvring in the field of apologetics.

Their basic tactics are to play off the perfect concept of the true Christian faith against the imperfect realization and falsification of that faith in practice. They usually succeed in reading a religion of perfect love into the New Testament, where they discover the norms of authentic faith, love of one's enemies and concern for peace and justice in human society, embodied, of course, in the figure of Jesus Christ.

The history of the Church has, however, been marked by a massive decline from the original gospel. The beginning of this movement away from the true Christian message has been set variously at the time of the death of the first apostles, the ascendancy of Paul or, more usually, the Constantinian era, when Christianity became a state religion. This concept of an ideal form of primitive Christianity and a later falling away from this ideal has a long history and is widely accepted among non-Christian thinkers such as Nietzsche, Overbeck and, more recently, Karlheinz Deschner. All the same, it is wrong. All the crimes that have been committed by Christians throughout the history of their religion are to be found in embryo in the New Testament, so that it would be more correct to speak of an escalation than of a decline.

WHAT IS CHRISTIAN?

Let me give two examples. In the first place, slavery is accepted without question as an institution in the parables of Jesus. Paul called on slaves to remain in a state of slavery. The later Church not only opposed all attempts by slaves to become emancipated, but even enslaved countless people – an instance of this being the slave-hunting expeditions of the papal galleys in Africa.

In the second place, Jesus, in his Sermon on the Mount, and Paul both threatened terrifying punishments in hell, using words alone. Later, to make up for this absence of the real punishment of hell on earth, the Church instituted severe disciplinary measures and harsh penances which culminated in the horrors of the Inquisition.

The New Testament commandment to love one's neighbour and one's enemies, which Christians so cheerfully peddle from door to door – although it is not unknown in other religions[49] – has also to be considered in this context. It cannot be treated ahistorically, like a purely philanthropic ethical commandment, and used outside the context of the Bible, as some apologists fondly imagine in their ignorance.

Paul says, for example, 'Repay no one evil for evil, but take thought for what is noble in the sight of all' (Rom. xii, 17). Then he goes on, 'Beloved, never avenge yourselves, but leave it to the wrath of God; for it is written, "Vengeance is mine, I will repay, says the Lord"' (Rom. xii, 19). Vengeance is not renounced – on the contrary, it is increased. God does not love his enemies and the enemies of those who believe in him, but condemns them to everlasting punishment.

It is quite clear, too, from Paul's famous hymn to love in 1 Cor. xiii that he did not base his teaching about the Christian commandment to love objectively and disinterestedly on his neighbour's well-being. In 1 Cor. xiii, 3, he says distinctly: 'If I give away all I have, and if I deliver my body to be burned, but have not love, *I gain nothing*'. His own gain and his own salvation are absolutely central. Only the man who 'loves' has any chance of survival before God's judgement seat, which is

49. See Deschner, *Abermals krähte der Hahn*, p. 136 f.

THE MISERY OF CHRISTIANITY

why Paul refers again and again to the imminent judgement according to one's works.

The same state of affairs is also clearly apparent in the gospels. The well-known parable of the good Samaritan (Luke x, 25-37), which allegedly depicts boundless love, is introduced by a question put to Jesus by a lawyer: 'Teacher, what shall I do to inherit eternal life?'

The basis of the Christian commandment to love, then, is a selfish aspiration towards heavenly joys. This is clearly confirmed in what is said about the love of one's enemies in the Sermon on the Mount: 'For if you [only] love those who love you, what reward have you?' (Matt. v, 46). Even the commandment not to judge others is made more pointed by the threat of being judged (Matt. vii, 1). This is surely the theme of reward and punishment again. The Sermon on the Mount lays down the conditions for admission into the kingdom of heaven and what is stressed is always the selfish interests of the individual – '... shall be called great in the kingdom of heaven' (v, 20), '... shall be liable to judgement' (v, 21), '... shall be liable to the hell of fire' (v, 22), '... you will have no reward from your Father who is in heaven' (vi, 1), '... they have their reward' (vi, 2) and so on and so on.

The fourth gospel has nothing whatever to say about love of one's enemies and restricts love purely to the Christian community: 'By this all men will know that you are my disciples, if you have love for one another' (John xiii, 35). It is clear from the so-called high priestly prayer that this gospel was not concerned with love of one's enemies, because Jesus explicitly excludes the world, which hates him and his disciples (vii, 7; xv, 18; xvi, 20; xvii, 14), from his intercession to God: 'I am praying for them; I am not praying for the world but for those whom thou hast given me, for they are thine' (xvii, 9).

Theological criticism is a useless weapon against these biblical texts, because they are the inevitable consequence of the Christian consciousness of being chosen, which is, in turn, what sociologists would call a form of ethnocentrism or group egoism.

WHAT IS CHRISTIAN?

When left-wing Catholics and Protestants reject authoritarian behaviour as unchristian, I cannot challenge or dispute this. It is, after all, up to them what they wish to regard as Christian or unchristian. They should, however, realize that they cannot base their arguments on the New Testament and they ought to ask themselves more radically than they have in the past why it is that the overwhelming majority of Christians have always allied themselves, and even identified themselves, with every possible form of nationalism, anti-semitism, fascism and anti-communism. This has not happened purely by chance. There is a logical process at work here from which not even people like Helmut Gollwitzer, Martin Niemöller, Friedrich Heer and Gerd Hirschauer have been able to escape.

They also base their arguments on authorities, although they do this under different auspices. Nevertheless, anyone who relies on authorities of any kind is acting inhumanly and is certainly thinking irrationally, and we can never be sure that an irrational thinker will not manipulate the facts and arguments. Although it cannot be denied that Christianity as presented by Gollwitzer, Niemöller, Heer and Hirschauer has, under certain circumstances, a progressive social function which is worth supporting even though it can act like a two-edged sword, their form of Christianity is really no more exemplary than any other.

The Impossibility of Knowing the Historical Jesus

The quest for the historical Jesus, which has been central in theological debate, especially among Protestants, for at least fifteen years now, has always been of use in the field of apologetics. Ernst Käsemann has expressed the meaning of this quest in the following way: 'It is a question of separating the true Christian message from the false and this can only be done with the help of him who was and had to be the historical Jesus. The norm that is chosen should therefore not be a bad one. This has become not only obligatory for Christianity, but, in my opinion, also indispensable.'[50]

50. Käsemann, *Exegetische Versuche und Besinnungen* II, p. 55.

Theologians, then, have been looking for a continuous thread which will lead them out of the maze of contradictory forms of Christianity and conflicting theological systems into the open. They would like to be able to say with binding force what Christianity really is.

Innumerable difficulties which are proverbially connected with the nature of historical knowledge in general and with this source in particular present themselves, however, and they appear to be insuperable. As Ernst Troeltsch once pointed out in an important essay on the historical and dogmatic method, the value of historical knowledge is always purely that of probability. The historian can never make statements which have an undoubted guarantee of fundamental certainty without first defining the limits of more probable solutions and marking these off from the more improbable. Historical knowledge is here too seen to possess, in its own special way, the same very important structural characteristic of all human knowledge. It is, in other words, open to error and this makes it impossible for any infallible dogmatic pronouncements to be made and necessary to reconsider all views.

Applied to the fundamental question: 'Did a man called Jesus of Nazareth ever exist?', this means, formulated as precisely as possible: which hypothesis does greater justice to the available source material – the assumption that a historical figure was deified and raised to the level of a celestial being by his followers after his incomprehensible death, or the opposite assumption that what was in the first place a myth was subsequently made into a historical figure?

The second view, which has a representative today in Hermann Raschke, a Protestant pastor in Bremen,[51] gives rise to more problems than it solves and cannot be made to harmonize with the guaranteed results of form criticism.

For the time being at least, I shall – together with the overwhelming majority of biblical scholars – assume, in the paragraphs that follow, that the Jew, Jesus of Nazareth, did in fact exist as a historical figure. All the same, I must at the very

51. 'The unhistorical Jesus'; see Deschner, *Jesusbilder* . . ., p. 343 ff.

outset dissociate myself here from Bultmann, who reduced the problems to an absurd level when he observed: 'It is hardly worth while refuting doubts, which are in any case unfounded, about whether Jesus really existed or not. It is beyond dispute that he was the originator of the historical movement, the first tangible stage of which was represented in the earliest Palestinian community.'[52]

The certainty of this statement is, I am afraid, unfounded and it is all the more surprising because the man who wrote it is otherwise so careful to stress the purely probable aspect of all the results of historical research. It can only be explained in the light of Bultmann's theological standpoint, which is unshakably based on the pure fact of Jesus – the '*that* of his having come'.

All theologians who – however vaguely – regard the existence of the historical Jesus as a fundamental fact seem to revel in all kinds of fiction, and this must be because the unconditional certainty of faith cannot be made to agree with the constantly relative results of historical research.

Is it, however, possible to go beyond the historical fact that a man called Jesus existed at a date and place which can be established approximately and learn something about the peculiarities, the life, the teaching and the fate of this person? If we cannot find out this kind of information, the name of Jesus is bound to remain cryptic and meaningless, indistinguishable from a myth. I will now try to show, by discussing the sources, that this is so, and that it confirms my conclusion that the name of Jesus is empty.

The point of departure for every quest for the historical Jesus must be the fundamental fact that Jesus himself did not leave behind any written records. Everything that we know about him can only be derived from the reports made about him by his followers, the evangelists. When we reach the farthest point in history, we come only to the Christian community, never to Jesus himself.

The fourth gospel, according to John, can be excluded at once as a possible source – I cannot go into my reasons for this

52. Bultmann, *Jesus*, p. 15.

here, but the reader can take it that critical and historical research into the New Testament has shown conclusively why this is so. There remain, then, only the three other gospels – those according to Matthew, Mark and Luke and known as the synoptic gospels because they provide a fairly consistent view of Jesus.

The earliest gospel is that of Mark. It was written round about the year 70, perhaps in Rome or more probably in Syria, by an unknown author. The other two gospels were also the work of unknown authors who were no more personally acquainted with Jesus than the author known as Mark. The so-called Matthaean text probably also originated in Syria and is usually dated between the years 70 and 90. Although the date of Luke's gospel can be placed between A.D. 70 and 90, the place of its origin is quite uncertain.

Leaving aside all the individual, more detailed, problems, the mere existence of these Greek texts, which I have described so cursorily above, poses two fundamental questions. First of all, there is the linguistic problem – Jesus spoke a Hebrew dialect, Aramaic, and the gospels were written in Greek. Secondly, there is the problem of time – Jesus died round about the year 30 and the earliest gospel was not written until at least forty years later.

According to the most competent authorities, then, we have to assume that Jesus spoke an unimportant provincial dialect with hardly any literature. What he said and did was therefore reported, to begin with, only in this dialect. The message was eventually taken by bilingual Jewish Christians into the hellenistic zone, to Syria, where Greek, which was a world language at that time, was spoken. There were people there who only understood Greek and these spread the Christian message further afield. The original texts of all the gospels are in Greek and there is nothing whatever to prove that these were translations of even earlier Aramaic texts. So according to this tradition, men speaking a different language passed on the Christian message and it was clearly impossible for that message to be verified. In view of this, it is almost impossible to suppress the suspicion

WHAT IS CHRISTIAN?

that misunderstandings and distortions crept into the original message.

This suspicion is increased when one recalls that some forty years elapsed between Jesus' death and the appearance of the earliest gospel – forty years during which Jesus' words and actions were handed down *by word of mouth*. It frankly baffles me how anyone can really hope to learn anything reliable about the historical Jesus when the tradition was not only oral, but also so long and so completely anonymous. But, before going into this question more fully, I must attempt briefly to answer the question: why were the gospels not written until so late?

The most decisive reason for this very late written record is to be found in the social structure of the earliest Christian groups. The first Christians were overwhelmingly members of the lower and even lowest social classes – vassal peasants, fishermen and artisans – who naturally had neither the inclination nor the ability to write books. What is usually regarded as the principal reason for the late emergence of the gospels in fact goes back to this real, underlying reason – the prevalence of social and spiritual misery. The earliest Christians did not think in terms of a history of the Church lasting for at least two thousand years. They expected that the great miracle, the mythical revolution, the cosmic catastrophe by means of which God and Christ, coming for the second time, would put an end to this evil world might happen any day.

This final establishment of the tradition of Jesus in writing presupposes that Christians realized that their hope that the world would soon come to an end was illusory and that they had ultimately decided to accommodate themselves to the existing world. They prepared themselves for longer periods of history. The earliest generation of Christians, who had had personal experience of Jesus and could speak of having seen him and witnessed his actions themselves, were dying and their memories – or what passed as their memories – had to be recorded.

As the leading representatives of the school of form criticism – Karl Ludwig Schmidt (*Der Rahmen der Geschichte Jesu*), Martin

Dibelius (*Die Formgeschichte des Evangeliums*) and Rudolf Bultmann (*Die Geschichte der synoptischen Tradition*) – have shown in some detail, only separate sayings and actions of Jesus – parables, memorable phrases and reports of miracles – were at first handed down. The earliest Christian missionaries used these as examples and evidence in their preaching, which aimed, of course, to convert people within their environment to faith in Jesus the Messiah. The central statement in this preaching was that Jesus had died for the sins of all men, had been resurrected by God from the dead for the salvation of mankind, and would descend from heaven in the near future and appear again as judge.

Since interest was centred in Jesus' crucifixion and resurrection, the story of the Passion and the Easter story had, of necessity, soon to be joined together to form a single narrative and then extended backwards to cover the life of Jesus before his suffering, death and resurrection. So the various separate traditions which were going the rounds were connected together to form a single whole, a complete story.

In this sense, the gospels are what Bultmann has called 'extended cultic legends',[53] which brought the figure of Jesus vividly to life in the minds of Christians when they were assembled for worship, reminded them of his teaching and the events in his life and, what was even more important, represented the mysteries of salvation – baptism and the eucharist – as firmly rooted in the fate of the cultic deity.

The method of form criticism seeks to discover how literary works, such as the gospels, were formed. It shows, for instance, that the framework of the history of Jesus – both the temporal and causal combination of events and places indicated – is the editorial fabric used by the evangelists. It was they who composed the discourses of Jesus, for example, the Sermon on the Mount, even putting them together from separate sayings. In the same way, they also invented the times, the places and the circumstances – a house or a road, for example, a mountain, a boat, a meal, a crowd of people, opponents or followers. Above

53. Bultmann, *Die Geschichte der synoptischen Tradition*, p. 396.

all, they placed all the traditions that they used in the right theological light. They wrote as the representatives of the community of Christ and therefore, in accordance with the theology of that group, they presented Jesus in various ways – as the son of man, as the son of God or as the suffering servant of God. The consequence of this is that 'it is no longer possible to establish the sequence of events in the life of Jesus, to write a biography of Jesus and to provide a picture of the figure of Jesus'.[54]

Looked at purely from the literary point of view, the gospels cannot be regarded as great literature. They are essentially minor literary works. Their closest parallels are certainly not the hellenistic biographies or the memoirs of great men in the ancient world. These early Christian writings are hardly concerned at all with Jesus as a human personality, with his early life and education, with his character or with the way in which he developed as a person. To some extent they resemble the popular books and collections of stories of the late Middle Ages which provided accounts, in the style of the people, of the sayings and doings of such well-known and perhaps semi-legendary figures as, for example, Doctor Faustus. In these books, as in the gospels, actions and statements are loosely assembled in the form of anecdotes without any concern for chronological sequence or psychological motivation. What is certainly true is that the primary aim of the gospels was not to keep alive the memory of the Jesus who worked miracles, but to stimulate faith in Jesus the *Kyrios* or Lord, who was present in Christian worship.

Let us now consider in greater detail whether it is possible to know with certainty anything about the historical Jesus from the sources which we possess. Since Jesus, the first source, did not himself leave anything written behind, the gospels are, of course, all secondary sources.

A fundamental rule of all work in the humanities, which every first-year student knows, is to verify in the first sources all quotations in secondary sources. Experience has shown that even practised scholars seated at their desks in their studies cannot always copy correctly from other books, that they distort the

54. Conzelmann, 'Jesus Christus', p. 620.

views of other authors either out of negligence or out of malice, and that they sometimes even twist them round to mean the precise opposite.

If this can truthfully be said of professional scholars who are concerned with accuracy and reliability, then how much more truthfully can it be said of men who lived in an environment of primitive superstition, who were for the most part illiterate and who certainly did not care at all for the actual historical content of Jesus' message! And, what is more, all this applies to an oral tradition going back several decades to its first source.

Everyone knows from personal experience that the spoken word can be falsified from one day to the next; scientific research into legends, fairy tales and sagas, and form criticism of the Bible, have shown that all oral tradition is subject to certain laws – exaggeration and idealization play an important part, a human figure tending to become first a miracle worker and then a god.

Although theologians active in the field of form criticism are prepared to admit openly to their more conservative colleagues that the tradition of Jesus was greatly influenced and even changed by the interests of the primitive Christian community – its dogmatics and polemics, its discipline and its ethos – they are not equally prepared to accept the ultimate conclusions of this admission. Let me give three examples which will show quite clearly the extent to which the present position of New Testament studies carried out according to the principles of form criticism demonstrates the truth of Franz Overbeck's contention, that form criticism of the Bible as practised by theologians today is really no more than 'pseudo-criticism'.[55]

1. Form criticism presupposes that the tradition of Jesus was originally based, at least partly, on the testimony of witnesses who could testify from what they had seen and heard[56] and that the reliability of the tradition was thereby to some extent guaranteed. This, however, is very naïve, because, even assum-

---

55. See Nigg, *Franz Overbeck*, pp. 119, 120.
56. See, for example, Kümmel, *Einleitung in das Neue Testament*, p. 23; Dibelius, *Die Formgeschichte des Evangeliums*, pp. 9, 11 f.

ing that these witnesses observed the events correctly and grasped their true meaning, there is absolutely no guarantee that their accounts of these events were passed on correctly by those who narrated them subsequently.

The very concept of eye and ear witnesses is questionable, however, because even direct witnesses are not tape recorders or documentary films – and it is a notorious fact that these too can be forged. On the contrary, the witnesses were only fallible men who were capable of lapses of memory, misunderstanding and even deliberate distortion. What is more, man's experience of any event is always selective. Anyone who thinks for a moment about the cultural revolution in China or the anti-Shah demonstration in Berlin on 2 June 1967, for example, will know that there are as many different kinds of eyewitness reports as there are political and philosophical views. As long as we are obliged to rely on the real or alleged eyewitness accounts of Jesus' own followers, we shall, I feel sure, never be able to know for certain what Jesus of Nazareth really said and did.

2. A second trick employed in form criticism is to ignore all biographies of Jesus and descriptions of his personality and to base all arguments on the words which are regarded as authentically those he used in proclaiming his message. This is also directly opposed to one of the most elementary rules of all work in the humanities – that of observing the context in which words are spoken or written. How can a man's words be understood if it is not known when, where, how, to whom, on what occasion and with what kind of undertone they were uttered?

3. The period of time which elapsed between Jesus' death and the first written record of the tradition was so fatally long that theologians have naturally enough looked for texts which could be dated back to previous periods.

The hypothetically reconstructed source known as 'Q' has a part to play in apologetics here. This collection of Jesus' words, composed in Greek, must have been available to Matthew and Luke as a second source in addition to Mark's text. If this source 'Q' did perhaps originally go back, at least partially, to the primitive Christian community in Palestine, then the collection as a whole could not have been written down until a few decades after Jesus' death, that is, not until round about A.D. 50 to 70. In any case, it could not have been available to Mark, so that a period of at least forty years separating the oral and the first written tradition must be assumed in the case of the earliest gospel.

The New Testament does, however, contain earlier texts – the Pauline letters, all of which originated between about A.D. 50 and 60. If Paul did not know Jesus personally, and if, as his letters show, he knew almost nothing at all about him, there is nonetheless a short passage in the first letter to the Corinthians which has aroused a lively interest among theologians.

In the fifteenth chapter of this letter, the famous chapter on resurrection, Paul says, in verse 3 ff.: 'For I delivered to you as of first importance what I also received, that Christ died for our sins in accordance with the scriptures, that he was buried, that he was raised on the third day in accordance with the scriptures, and that he appeared to Cephas, then to the twelve . . .'

Hans Grass, Professor in Systematic Theology at the University of Marburg, said this about the historical value of these words of Paul:

> 33 A.D. or shortly afterwards is the generally accepted date of the conversion of Paul and the year 30 that of the death of Jesus. If Paul received the kerygmatic formula soon after his conversion, then this formula must already have been extant during the first five years after Jesus' death. . . . Paul's testimony of the resurrection of Jesus therefore brings us very close indeed to the original events. This is the *best possible guarantee* of the authenticity of the historical data contained in the kerygma.[57]

What an extraordinarily naïve statement this is! So many things can happen in a few years. Think, for example, of the death of the American president, John Kennedy, in the autumn of 1963. Only a few months after his assassination, myths and legends which threatened to cast a veil over the true facts and background of the event were flourishing. Another example in recent history – a few days after the press report that Ernesto

57. Grass, *Ostergeschehen und Osterberichte*, p. 95 f.; my italics.

'Che' Guevara, the friend of Fidel Castro and the leading theorist of the South American socialist partisans, had been killed in Bolivia, left-wing supporters in Europe were spreading the message (which clearly expressed their own wish) 'Che lives'.

The impossibility of ever getting a glimpse of the historical Jesus is clearly revealed in the evidence I give in the following brief survey of some of the most valiant attempts to penetrate the problem in the light of the gospels as a whole.

The Protestant theologian, Martin Kähler, who died in 1912, said once – and the statement became famous in theological circles – that the gospels were 'stories of the Passion with a detailed introduction'. He was, among other things, referring here to the selective quality of the reports – the fact that they represented only the final and shortest part of Jesus' life. In fact, if the dual traditions are left out, the words of Jesus that the gospels provide can be contained in no more than a few pages. If it was ever given, the Sermon on the Mount would have lasted for about three minutes.

The consequence of this is that we cannot know that the primitive Christian community did not misrepresent Jesus or that its members did not suppress some of the facts about him because they might have placed him in a compromising position. Gerhard Ebeling, the Protestant Professor in Systematic Theology at Tübingen, has in fact admitted: 'There was undeniably a tendency to omit. From the very beginning we cannot rule out the suspicion that a distortion of the facts, in the manner of idealizing simplification, might have been practised.'[58]

A shrewd comment – but I would go even further. Not only can this suspicion not be ruled out – it simply cannot be refuted. Ebeling has therefore to back, rather miserably, out of the difficulty. At first, however, he continues quite perspicaciously: 'This therefore brings us in contact with a particularly critical aspect of the quest for the historical Jesus. Should our knowledge of Jesus be called into question because of this difficult point, about which we can learn nothing, even indirectly, from tradition? Should we, then, take into account the possibility

58. Ebeling, *Wort und Glaube*, p. 309.

that we are completely misunderstanding Jesus, or at least understanding him insufficiently, when we say that faith is expressed and discussed in him?' (This is, of course, the quintessence of the historical Jesus according to Ebeling.) 'Certainly, in the matter of history, there is basically nothing that cannot be called into question.'

So far, so good. After saying this, however, Ebeling seeks refuge in the world of pious aspirations. He 'solves' the difficulty by appealing – in a manner which is typically that of a theologian – to his fundamental conviction and asserting: 'But, quite apart from all the arguments that are uppermost in this question, what is really convincing in this case is that all the various lines of tradition in the expression and discussion of faith came together here, not in man's imagination, but in his existence'.

But why is this so convincing? How can it be convincing? Since when have convictions replaced arguments? What cannot be disputed is that Jesus only comes to us through the filter of the dogmatics of the evangelists. The fact that whole nations can be completely tricked is clear evidence of the strength of such a barrier to real information and knowledge.

Let me give one example. Both Mark and Matthew state that Jesus died with the words 'My God, my God, why hast thou forsaken me?' (Mark xv, 34 and Matt. xxvii, 46) on his lips. One might perhaps think that here a text was handed down which placed Jesus in a compromising position by showing him in despair. But what Christian would ever have dared to assume that Jesus in fact broke down under the strain, especially since God raised him up again from the dead three days later and thus acknowledged his life? No – those words which Jesus uttered, according to the evangelists, before he died on the cross are the opening words of Psalm 22, and anyone who dies with the words of a psalm on his lips is not dying in despair, but at peace with God. Moreover, these words were also subordinate to the purpose of the reports of Jesus' passion and death in the gospels, which was 'to show the defeat of the crucified Jesus as his victory'.[59]

59. Harenberg, *Jesus und die Kirchen*, p. 94.

WHAT IS CHRISTIAN?

So, since the gospels only contain selective fragments of what Jesus must have said (this is obvious because they are so short) and, what is more, since historical and critical research into the New Testament has reduced the number of possibly reliable traditions to a strict minimum, those theologians who practise form criticism are faced with a very difficult problem. (This problem may, incidentally, be made worse by the attitude of theologians who, although they are to some extent prepared to approach the New Testament critically, are still dominated by a pious reverence for it.)

The Heidelberg professor, Günther Bornkamm, has put it in this way: 'If we were to reduce the tradition of Jesus to what can no longer be doubted for any historical reason whatever, we should be left with no more than a *torso* that would have hardly anything at all in common with the history to which the gospels bear witness'.[60] Since what may not be cannot be, exegetes tend to use all kinds of jugglers' tricks. They say, for example, that even if a saying may not be authentic in the 'formal' sense – if, in other words, it is something which was fashioned by the primitive Christian community and subsequently attributed to Jesus – it may still be authentic in a 'more profound' sense, in other words, it may accurately represent Jesus' view. If it is not authentic, then it is at least authentically invented.

It should in this way be quite easy to claim, as was done in the past, that almost the whole of each gospel text went back to the historical Jesus, and thus to render the destructive effect of form criticism completely harmless.

This process is, of course, scientifically unjustifiable. A novelist can work in this way, but not a historian. It is quite easy to imagine theologians of the German fundamentalist movement known as 'No Other Gospel' devising Bultmann sayings, on the basis of what they believe Bultmann would in fact certainly say, instead of keeping to his published statements. According to the practices of form criticism, it would be quite correct for Gerhard Bergmann, Bultmann's adversary, to say that his supposition that Jesus rose again, according to

60. Bornkamm, *Jesus von Nazareth*, p. 13; my italics.

Bultmann, 'like Goethe', was a literal quotation from Bultmann.

In its own special way, the pseudo-criticism of form criticism is simply repeating what was done by the primitive Christian community nineteen hundred years ago. The early Christians not only omitted many of Jesus' sayings – they also invented new sayings and showed no inhibitions at all in adding these to the rest of Jesus' words whenever the need arose for an authoritative directive or affirmation. Such 'communal formations' can usually be recognized by the fact that they presuppose situations, practices, problems, interests or doctrines that were current in the primitive community. Thus, even many years ago, the so-called prophecies of Jesus' passion were recognized as communal formations; the three passages in Mark's gospel in which Jesus is alleged to say: 'The Son of man must suffer many things, and be rejected by the elders and the chief priests and the scribes, and be killed, and after three days rise again' (Mark viii, 31; ix, 31; x, 33 f.) – these words presuppose a detailed knowledge of the history of the suffering and death of Jesus and faith in his resurrection after three days.

Other statements fashioned by the primitive community are rather shamefacedly called 'words of the exalted Lord' by theologians of the school of form criticism. These are sayings devised by primitive Christian prophets who played an important part in the very early Church. These prophets

clothed their crystallized thoughts, as we see clearly enough in the Apocalypse of John, in the form of words spoken by Jesus himself and spoke as men inspired in the name and the authority of the exalted Christ. If these words were handed down, the distinction between the exalted Lord and Christ here on earth soon became blurred, all the more so because the early Church was not really interested in the latter. In this way, countless [!] words attributed to Christ revealing himself through the prophets entered the synoptic tradition as Jesus' sayings.[61]

This form of prophecy, which is the prototype of all later

61. Käsemann, *Versuche I*, p. 234; my exclamation mark.

WHAT IS CHRISTIAN?

Christian theology, produced, for example, the commandment to baptize and missionize all people at the end of the gospel of Matthew. This commandment runs: 'All authority in heaven and on earth has been given to me. Go therefore and make disciples of all nations, baptizing them in the name of the Father and of the Son and of the Holy Spirit ...' (Matt. xxviii, 18 ff.). These words were a very late Hellenistic addition, because they presuppose a practice of baptizing and missionizing the known world and this was something which the primitive Jewish community of Christians in Jerusalem did not recognize.

The inevitable consequence of this confusion in connection with the sources of the New Testament has been strikingly expressed in the following way by Ernst Käsemann:

> On the basis of form criticism, our quest has become so extended and at the same time so concentrated that we no longer have to test and make credible the possible unauthenticity but rather the authenticity of each individual datum. Nowadays we do not have to prove our right to criticize, but have to establish the limits of criticism.[62]

Only very few New Testament scholars ever realize consciously what this methodical research really implies. It is this. It must be proved conclusively that these particular words could only have been said by Jesus and by no one else and that they could not have been, under any circumstances, put into his mouth, either in the course of the Jewish tradition or as something devised by the primitive Christian community. But, as Bultmann himself has admitted, it is completely impossible to prove this. He has stressed 'that definite proof of authenticity can never be provided for a single individual saying of Jesus'.[63]

He breaks off the fatal point of this perception at once, however, by going on to argue that, although it is true that no proof of authenticity can be established in the case of individual sayings, it is certainly possible 'to point to a whole series of sayings which go back to the earliest traditional level and which convey a picture of the historical preaching of Jesus ... either

62. ibid., p. 203.
63. Bultmann, *Glauben und Verstehen* IV, p. 30.

because they have to be understood as the direct radiation of Jesus' preaching or because they must be interpreted as the broken effect of that preaching in a different kind of historical material'.

Bultmann goes to work here like a judge who reasons thus: 'The charges brought by the three witnesses certainly cannot be proved beyond all doubt, but I still condemn the accused because, however fragmentarily, his actions are reflected in these charges.' But I maintain that, according to the rules of formal logic, if the authenticity of Jesus' individual sayings cannot be proved, then we cannot have any proof of the authenticity of Jesus' preaching as a whole.

Seen in the perspective of this fundamental insight, the material criterion of authenticity used by theologians of the school of form criticism is also very questionable. Tradition which 'for any reason whatever cannot be traced back to Judaism or attributed to the primitive Christian community, especially if the traditional material was too audaciously changed or subdued' is regarded by Käsemann as authentic. We can therefore never be certain 'what really bound Jesus to his Palestinian environment and his later community'. It would be impossible for us to know this today, but it is, Käsemann believes, 'more important to gain an insight into what separated him from his opponents and friends'.[64]

Käsemann can therefore write about a saying in the Sermon on the Mount that 'the unprecedented nature of the saying bears witness to its authenticity'.[65] Bultmann has said that such sayings 'lay a claim to the highest degree of authenticity' when they are filled 'by the feeling of eschatological power which Jesus' appearance must have contained'.[66] Finally, Conzelmann maintains that Jesus' words show themselves to be sayings 'which express an unrepeatable consciousness of situation' and reflect a 'sharply outlined consciousness of self'.[67]

64. Käsemann, *Versuche* I, p. 205 f.
65. ibid., p. 206.
66. Bultmann, *Die Geschichte der synoptischen Tradition*, p. 174.
67. Conzelmann, 'Jesus Christus', p. 623.

WHAT IS CHRISTIAN?

Can these formal and extremely flexible criteria ever put an end to the misery? Of course they cannot, because the proof of authenticity based on the distinction that those sayings of Jesus which were derived neither from Judaism nor from the primitive Christian community are the authentic words of Jesus presupposes that what has first of all to be proved is that Jesus himself was distinct both from Judaism and from primitive Christianity.

In Bultmann's opinion, Jesus' preaching was 'not new in its content of ideas, because, as far as this content is concerned, his preaching was nothing but pure Judaism and pure prophetism'.[68] As for Käsemann's 'unprecedented sovereignty' and Conzelmann's 'sharply outlined consciousness of self' which presumably typified Jesus' appearance, these characteristics, we are bound to admit, also applied equally well to the prophets of the primitive Christian community. The enormous self-confidence that inspired them is reflected, for example, in the well-known words about the unforgivable sin against the Holy Spirit in Matt xii, 32: 'Whoever says a word against the Son of man will be forgiven; but whoever speaks against the Holy Spirit will not be forgiven, either in this age or in the age to come'.

As Käsemann has said:

It is perfectly clear what these much disputed words mean. The primitive Christian missionaries encountered resistance which, because they were convinced that their mission was the work of the Holy Spirit, they at once regarded as directed against the Spirit and could only interpret as a sign of malevolence and hardness of heart ... God's epiphany was carried out on earth in prophecy, and, what is more, with an eschatological glory which outshone the glory of Jesus on earth. His life was still, insofar as can be judged from the experience of Easter, overshadowed by a concealed quality which made doubt, ignorance and lack of faith understandable and forgivable. But to oppose the unconcealed epiphany of God in the prophetic spirit was the one simply unforgivable sin.[69]

To conclude, then, let us consider very briefly what can in fact be known about the actions and the fate of Jesus of Nazareth.

68. Bultmann, *Glauben und Verstehen* I, p. 265.
69. Käsemann, *Versuche* II, p. 100 f.

At the very outset, we are bound to recognize that two basic truths apply fully to the case of the historical Jesus. Firstly, all our knowledge of Jesus' activity comes to us through his followers, whose aim was to glorify him and who were most anxious to avoid reporting anything that might do him harm. Secondly, all historical knowledge, including that of Jesus, has the value of pure probability, never of certainty.

Critical research into the gospels has also proved conclusively that all the stories of miracles, such as the virgin birth, Jesus' walking on the water, his resurrection after three days and his ascension, are in fact myths or legends. The historical and critical method does not, in this connection, dogmatically take the fact that a man cannot walk on the water of the lake of Gennesareth or emerge from his grave three days after having died as its point of departure. It does not seek to find out what is possible – everything may be possible so long as the opposite is not proved to be true – but rather seeks to establish what did in fact happen.

As soon as the accounts of miracles in the synoptic gospels are, however, examined in the light of their inner harmony, then the only possible criticism of them is destructive. The question has to be asked, for example, who can have observed and then reported this or that incident?

A further argument against the historical authenticity of the miracles, and one which should never be underestimated, is the overabundance of parallels in the immediate environment of Israel which have been revealed by the scholars of comparative religion. In the later ancient world, both in Judaism and in Hellenism, there were innumerable miracles, sons of God and saviours. Virgin births, resurrections from the dead and ascensions into heaven were the order of the day. It was commonplace for storms over lakes to be miraculously calmed and for great multitudes to be fed by miraculous means. Even those who were violently opposed to the religions which taught these miracles believed in them.

Every New Testament scholar holds a different opinion here, of course, but let me quote one. Bultmann claims that it is possible to say this, 'with some caution', in respect of 'Jesus' works':

> Exorcisms, the breach of the commandment to observe the sabbath, the violation of the laws of cleanliness, polemics against the Jewish emphasis on the law, keeping company with classless people such as publicans and prostitutes and a strong sympathy for women and children – these are characteristic of him. It is also obvious that Jesus was not ascetic like John the Baptist, but a man who liked to eat and drink a glass of wine. We may perhaps also add that he called on people to follow him and gathered a small band of supporters, both men and women, around him.[70]

Let us assume that this may in fact be evident from the works of Jesus. But what would be achieved by it? In my view, nothing, since Jesus' actions are also either shrouded in silence or completely equivocal simply because we are unable to know anything more about his words and his expressed intentions. Exorcisms were also carried out by other rabbis. The laws of cleanliness and the commandment to observe the sabbath were also broken, or partially broken, in the primitive Christian community as well, so that a back-dating of this type of action from the early community to the life of Jesus himself cannot be entirely ruled out. (This has in fact been demonstrated in the analysis of the controversial passages in the synoptic gospels provided by theologians of the school of form criticism.) Jesus' association with publicans, his 'keeping company' with prostitutes and his 'sympathy for women and children' might also have had quite a different background from the one that theologians are inclined to accept. All that we can really say with some certainty is that Jesus was not an ascetic. As bare facts, his call to people to follow him and his gathering of supporters around him really mean nothing at all. What is important is precisely what Jesus called on men to do and this is something that cannot be known.

All the necessary information about Jesus' crucifixion as a probable historical fact can be found in Bultmann, who has stressed 'the fact that we cannot know *the way in which Jesus*

70. Bultmann, *Urchristlichen Christusbotschaft* . . ., p. 11.

himself understood his end, his death'. He continues, 'We cannot know whether Jesus found any meaning in his death and, if so, what kind of meaning he found. We should not conceal the possibility from ourselves that he broke down under the strain.'[71]

The historical reasons which led to the crucifixion of Jesus are almost impossible to understand. As far as I know, three basic attempts have been made in recent years to provide a solution to this problem.

1. Bultmann's disciples regard Jesus' death as the necessary and organic conclusion to his preaching, which was so profoundly opposed to Judaism that the Jewish religious leaders had to get rid of this unwanted preacher. This theory is, however, purely hypothetical and cannot be proved, because it is impossible to reconstruct the preaching of Jesus.

2. According to Bultmann himself, Jesus was executed by the Romans 'like other rebels as a messianic prophet', because, as 'outsiders', they did not recognize the 'peculiarly unpolitical character' of his appearance.[72] 'From the historical point of view', his crucifixion was 'a meaningless fate',[73] the 'tragic end of a noble man'.[74]

3. For some outsiders – the philosopher Walter Bröcker,[75] the Protestant theologian Heinrich Buhr[76] and the non-Christian historian Joel Carmichael,[77] for example – Jesus was not only a religious prophet, but also a political revolutionary. This supposition, which was made as long ago as the eighteenth century by Hermann Samuel Reimarus, is based on such statements by Jesus as 'Let him who has no sword sell his mantle and buy one' (Luke xxii, 36) or on such incidents in the life of Jesus as the cleansing of the temple in Mark xi, 15 ff. The authors whom

---

71. ibid., pp. 11, 12; author's italics.
72. Bultmann, *Jesus*, p. 26.
73. Bultmann, *Urchristlichen Christusbotschaft* . . ., p. 12.
74. Bultmann, *Kerygma und Mythos* I, p. 46.
75. Bröcker, *Zur Theologie des Geistes*, p. 61 ff.
76. Buhr, *Der Glaube - was ist das?*, p. 87 ff.
77. Carmichael, *Leben und Tod* . . ., (*passim*, especially p. 142 ff.); see also the reference to him and Eisler in Deschner, *Jesusbilder* . . . p. 181 ff. (Friedrich Pzillas).

I have mentioned above regard texts such as these as the last traces of a failed messianic *Putsch*, which the primitive Christian community tried later to hush up. According to this view, the crucifixion of Jesus was not a misunderstanding on the part of the Romans, but something carried out in accordance with the usual way of dealing with real messianic rebels.

Can anyone decide between these three possible explanations? Is it at all possible to distinguish here between what is authentically historical and what is not? The third theory has much to recommend it, of course. The saying about the sword is certainly striking and it is understandable that attempts should have been made on the part of the primitive Christians to conceal the possible political character of Jesus' activity. On the other hand, however, such texts are so scattered and so few in the gospels, their historical authenticity is so disputed and their meaning is so ambiguous that they can hardly be used to refute Bultmann's thesis of a misunderstanding on the part of the Romans.

So, instead of continuing to struggle in the bog of suppositions, we may as well admit freely – we just do not know.

The Balance-Sheet of the History of Theology: Chaos in Dogma

The problem that I want to discuss in this section of my book is that of the unity or the identity of Christianity. This identity cannot, as the indelible events that have taken place during the history of the Church have proved, be discovered in the sphere of Christian ethics. Nor can it be found in the quest for the historical Jesus, since the latter is totally buried under the rubbish of primitive Christian myths and legends.

The chaos is not so immediately apparent in the dogmatic field, because both Catholic and Protestant Christians make every effort to conceal it from themselves and from others and try to demonstrate the constancy of faith throughout the centuries. The well-known principle of tradition in Catholic teaching was formulated by Vincent of Lerins, a monk who died before the year 450: 'Curandum est, ut id teneamus, quod ubique, quod semper, quod ab omnibus creditum est' – 'We must keep to *what has been believed everywhere, always and by everybody*'. This idea has, of course, been made concrete in the principle of episcopal succession – by the imposition of hands, the *charisma veritatis*, the gift of the true doctrine going back directly to the twelve apostles, is passed on to the bishops of the Church.

Protestant teaching also contains the idea of an unbroken chain of historical succession, although this is not necessarily thought of as a specifically episcopal succession. Luther taught that the authentic apostolic faith would always be preserved by a little band of true Christian believers.

This affirmation that the Church is one has, of course, always been accompanied by the liturgical practice of reciting stereotyped formulae which are intended to evoke the unchangeable nature and the inviolable constancy of the Church's treasury of faith – not only creeds, but also such formulae as 'As it was in the beginning, is now and ever shall be; world without end, amen'; 'Jesus Christ, the same yesterday and today and forever' (Heb. xiii, 8); 'One Lord, one faith, one baptism' (Eph. iv, 5).

Anyone, then, who really wants to expose the totally contradictory nature of Christian teaching should not allow himself to be deceived by the similarity of so many formulae used by the Church, but must penetrate further than this and examine the content.

He must also keep in mind the mutual relationships between individual doctrines. According to the environment, the same idea and the same action may be given an entirely different value. For example, it is possible to say, rather naïvely, that Protestants and Catholics all believe in Jesus Christ and that this unites them at the deepest level. Certainly, both Protestants and Catholics do believe in Jesus Christ, but there is a considerable difference between saying 'faith in Christ alone' and faith as well in Mary as the 'mediatrix to the mediator' and a countless number of saints and mediators in heaven.

Even the Lord's Prayer has a very different meaning for Protestants and Catholics, despite a text which sounds very similar in both cases. The Roman Catholic says *an* Our Father, whereas the Lutheran says *the* Our Father. As a penance, the

WHAT IS CHRISTIAN?

Catholic may say several Our Fathers, one after the other. Prayer is thus a pious work. The basic attitude of the Protestant, on the other hand, has been expressed in this way by Gerhard Ebeling: 'Jesus did not want to teach a prayer. He wanted to teach people how to pray, and this also means freeing oneself from the anxious and superstitious use of formulae.'[78]

For a modern Protestant, baptism is nothing but an embarrassment. For a Catholic, on the other hand, baptism is an essential part of an all-embracing sacramental view of the world. In addition to this, the Christian's understanding of the sacrament varies according to whether only an ordained priest or any Christian may administrate the means of grace.

Not even the most rigorous protagonist of the Christian battle-cry 'One Lord, one faith, one baptism' can, however, ignore the fact that the most widely divergent views are in competition with each other and are fighting each other for recognition in Christian dogma. This is no new phenomenon – it has been so since the second century at least, when the Church's theologians devised a scheme to elucidate this painful datum. This scheme, which even nowadays still determines the mind of the Church to a very great extent, can, with the help of the late Walter Bauer, the New Testament scholar at Göttingen, be set out briefly as follows:

1. Jesus reveals the pure doctrine to his apostles, partly before his death and partly during the forty days before his ascension.
2. After his ultimate departure, the apostles divide the world between themselves and each one takes the pure gospel to the country which has been allotted to him.
3. Even after the death of the apostles, the gospel continues to be spread. But it encounters obstructions within Christianity itself. The devil cannot refrain from sowing tares among the wheat in God's field and he is very successful. Deceived by him, some Christians give up the true doctrine. The development takes place in the following way – no faith, sound faith, false faith . . .
4. The true faith is, of course, invincible. Despite all the efforts of

78. Ebeling, *Vom Gebet*, p. 20.

Satan and his instruments, true faith repels no faith and false faith and spreads victoriously further and further afield.[79]

This scheme – which presupposes an ideal age in the past when all Christians were, according to the phrase used in the Acts of the Apostles to glorify the primitive Christian community, 'of one heart and soul' (Acts iv, 32) – proved long ago to be no more than a pleasant sounding but empty illusion. From the very beginning, there was violent conflict within Christianity about central questions of dogma. This is clearly revealed, for example, in the important work published by the scholar from whom I have just quoted, Walter Bauer, on 'orthodoxy and heresy in the earliest Church' (*Rechtgläubigkeit und Ketzerei im ältesten Christentum*). Martin Werner, the Swiss systematic theologian and historian of dogma, also helped, some years ago, with the publication of his book on 'the emergence of Christian dogma' (*Die Entstehung des christlichen Dogmas*), to shake the foundations of the traditional idea of the course of the history of the Church.

Both of these authors have shown that the teaching which ultimately prevailed in the early Church as orthodox was that of the victorious party after a long and bitter struggle, at the end of which the doctrines of the defeated parties were branded as heretical.

In all truth, measured by the same yardstick, according to which other groups and movements were condemned by her as heretical, the new and expanding Church was herself nothing but a heresy. She was, however, the most successful heresy and was driving all the others from the field in victory.[80]

The most painful fact referred to in Walter Bauer's book is this – the early Jewish Christians of Jerusalem, whose faith formed the historical basis of every aspect of Christianity, were very soon outlawed as heretical by the non-Jewish, Hellenistic Christians, who later became completely victorious. Even Paul fulminated against the conservative party because they were

79. Bauer, *Rechtgläubigkeit* . . ., p. 3 f.
80. Werner, *Die Entstehung des christlichen Dogmas*, p. 35.

opposed to the mission to the gentiles. This fact was later hushed up. In the catalogue of heretics, these Jewish Christians were classified and defamed as Ebionites. They had fallen away from the true gospel – despite the fact that all they had done was to preserve the original teaching.

It goes without saying that the gentile Christians also split into different groups at the very beginning of the history of the Church. As Walter Bauer has said,

> The form of Christian faith and practice which was the most unified, the most powerfully organized and the most suitable for mass consumption was the form which ultimately prevailed. Despite this, the total number of consciously orthodox and anti-heretical Christians was, in my opinion, far less than the sum total of Christian 'heretics' for a long time after the final closing of the post-apostolic era.[81]

A very important instrument in creating orthodoxy in the Church was the New Testament canon. The various texts which had allegedly been written by apostles and eye-witnesses were collected in the second half of the second century, so that these could be used as norms for sound faith and sound teaching. It hardly needs to be said that a number of historical and systematic fictions found their way into this work of dogmatizing Scripture. Let us now consider one of these fictions a little more closely – the 'harmonizing' view that the same or very similar answers are given in all the New Testament texts to the main questions of dogma.

THE NEW TESTAMENT

In an essay which has since become famous in theological circles, Ernst Käsemann summarized the results of form criticism of the Bible in these words: 'The New Testament canon does not, as such, form the basis of the Church's unity. As such, that is, in the state in which it is available to the historian, it only forms the basis of the multiplicity of confessions.'[82]

81. Bauer, *Rechtgläubigkeit* . . ., p. 233.
82. Käsemann, *Versuche* I, p. 221.

THE MISERY OF CHRISTIANITY

From the abundance of contradictions contained in the New Testament and conveniently brought together by Käsemann[83] and Herbert Braun[84] in their articles on the New Testament canon, I will select three examples.

The gospels of Matthew and Luke state that Jesus was born of a virgin (Matt 1, 18 ff. and Luke i, 26 ff.). According to Paul (Phil. ii, 6 ff.) and John (i, 1 ff.), however, he was a pre-existent celestial being who came down to earth, assumed a human form, and, after performing his work of salvation, returned to God in the eternal world. Both views are mutually exclusive. In the case of the first, Jesus first became the son of God at his birth, after having been begotten in a miraculous fashion by the Holy Spirit. In the second case, he had already been living as the son of God with the Father since eternity. This, however, is not all – the gospel according to Mark presents us with a third view. Jesus was not born of a virgin and did not have any existence before entering his human body, according to Mark, but was initiated as the son of God during his life on earth, namely when he was baptized by John (i, 9 ff.). There are also glimpses of even a fourth form of Christology in the New Testament, although this is only apparent in a few ancient fragments. Thus Paul quotes a traditional formula (in Rom. i, 3 f.) which indicates that, in the earliest Christian community, Jesus' messianic state dated from his resurrection.

The eschatological teaching of the gospel and the Apocalypse of John cannot be reconciled in any way. In the gospel, the dramatic eschatology of the Jewish apocalyptic vision is, in accordance with the gnostic pattern, completely abandoned and judgement and salvation are presented as taking place in the present (John v, 24 f.). The soul of the believer is seen as rising up into the glory of heaven immediately after death (xii, 32; xiv, 2 f.; xvii, 24). The Apocalypse, on the other hand, indulges in phantasmagoria of a catastrophe at the end of time, imagined on a massive scale and accompanied by fearful punishments. Satanic locusts are to torment man, for example (Apoc. ix, 3 ff.).

83. ibid., p. 214 ff.
84. Braun, *Gesammelte Studien* . . ., p. 310 ff.; see also p. 325 ff.

There will be a battle between Michael the Archangel and the great dragon in heaven (xii, 7 ff.). Bloody massacres will take place in which Christ, seated on a white horse, will kill the unbelievers, whose bodies will be devoured by birds (xix, 11 ff.). This wholesale slaughter will be followed by a peace lasting for a thousand years (xx, 1 ff.), at the end of which Satan and his angels will be thrown for ever into a lake of fire (xx, 7 ff.). Finally, the Apocalypse presents us with a vision of the descent of the heavenly Jerusalem to earth (xxi, 1 ff.).

My third example of irreconcilability between the teaching in two similar New Testament documents was also noted a long time ago by Martin Luther. It is this. There is a gap between Paul's doctrine of justification and that of the letter of James that cannot be bridged. In Rom. iii, 28, Paul taught: 'For we hold that a man is justified by faith apart from works of law'. In the letter of James, we read: 'You see that a man is justified by works and not by faith alone' (James ii, 24). However ridiculous it may seem, both Paul (Rom. iv, 3) and the unknown author of the letter of James (James ii, 23) appeal, for their totally opposing statements, to the same passage in the Old Testament (Gen. xv, 6): 'Abraham believed God, and it was reckoned to him as righteousness'.

To conclude, then, we can say with Käsemann that the New Testament canon allows us 'to regard Christianity as a glowing apocalyptic vision, as a mystery religion or as a kind of popular philosophy, as a nomistic cult or as an early Catholic faith, if not simply, with relative justice, as a syncretic conglomeration of all these different parts. All these possibilities have been practised in the course of the history of the Church and – how could it have been otherwise? – have been repeated in Protestantism right up to the present time.'[85]

In this fatal situation, then, we are bound to raise the question of what has been called the 'canon within the canon'. Käsemann and Braun have certainly pointed to the inner contradictions and diversity contained in the New Testament, but it is obvious that, as scholars who are also members of the

85. Käsemann, *Versuche* I, p. 231.

Church, they cannot accept what is ultimately a purely destructive result. Both of these men have therefore taken up one of the positions that it is possible to assume with regard to the New Testament canon. In the case of my third example of irreconcilable teaching, that of Paul's doctrine of justification by faith alone as opposed to the contradictory doctrine found in the letter of James, they have followed Luther in asserting that the Pauline teaching is central to the Bible. Käsemann has called this 'the test of minds in Scripture' and has honestly admitted that it is a question of 'decision'.[86] Even a Catholic would call it an arbitrary question. What else is it but a desperate leap from the chaos of the Bible into the dogma of the Reformation?

Braun makes the rather extravagant claim that his criterion for the 'canon within the canon' is based on the New Testament itself, but adds that it is 'admittedly not based on the *whole* of the canon',[87] but only on the main parts, in other words, on Jesus, John and Paul. But to what extent are Jesus, John and Paul the main parts of the New Testament? We can know, as we have seen, nothing about Jesus. And numerically – insofar as numbers are really relevant in the question of truth – John and Paul are certainly not the main parts. But, whatever the case may be, all that we can say with certainty is that the New Testament is a hotchpotch of irreconcilable opposites.

THE EARLY CHURCH

The confusion that prevailed among the different groups in the early Church is clearly revealed in these two quotations alone. Clement of Alexandria complained, round about the year 200, that Jews and gentiles both rejected conversion with the comment 'that, in view of the confusing controversy over dogma among the Christian parties, it was impossible to know which of them really represented the truth'.[88] Origen, who died in 254, admitted that 'so many of those who confess to faith in Christ

---

86. ibid., p. 232.
87. Braun, *Gesammelte Studien . . .*, p. 323; author's italics.
88. Werner, op cit., p. 32.

disagree among themselves not only in the most insignificant questions of secondary importance, but also in the most significant matters of great consequence'.[89]

About the beginning of the third century, then, three great parties were, despite the rule of faith and the New Testament canon, in competition with each other within the early Church. Each of these groups propagated a different view of Christ. The first of these Christologies was the doctrine of the *logos*, which regarded Jesus as a divine being, but subordinated him to the Father. The second doctrine was that of adoptianism, which believed that Jesus was filled with an impersonal, divine power, by which he had been raised to the level of God (adopted by God). Finally, there was modalism, which taught that Christ was a mode of appearance of God and thus prepared the way for the later, and orthodox, doctrine of the Trinity.

When the Roman emperors bestowed such high privileges on the Catholic Church in the fourth century, the dogmatic struggles took on a new character in the light of the need for a unified religious ideology in the Empire, which was unable to tolerate the presence of an inwardly divided imperial Church. The emperors themselves intervened in theology, and presided over imperial synods at which important dogmas were formulated and made legally binding. These early councils were not always like the synods or councils of the modern Church, but often resembled indoor battles of the kind that took place in the Nazi period, with cudgels and agitated bands of monks replacing argument and debate. Faith in the dogmas thus defined was regarded as immediately necessary for salvation. Those who opposed the decisions of these synods were threatened with excommunication and, although they returned these threats, they were henceforth regarded as heretics and blasphemers.

The Council of Nicaea (325) rejected the teaching of Arius of Alexandria – and, at the same time, several passages in the New Testament – and declared that Christ was equal in essence to God. At the Council of Constantinople (381), the Holy Spirit achieved the same status. In 451, the dogma that Christ was

---

89. Quoted from Werner, op. cit., p. 34; author's italics.

both true God and true man at the same time, undivided and unalloyed, was laid down at the Council of Chalcedon. The existing religious disagreements, which were, of course, not purely religious but also social and political, were not always entirely resolved by the definition of these dogmas. On the contrary, the fundamental differences were often emphasized by these declarations and even more passionately disputed because of them. In extreme cases, new church organizations were formed and independent national churches founded.

THE MIDDLE AGES[90]

The Middle Ages are sometimes rather naïvely imagined to be a period of complete religious unity. It is, of course, true that Christians did not begin to dispute the Church's teaching in really great numbers until the High Middle Ages. Nonetheless, there were, throughout the whole period, individual theologians who raised their voices against the prevalent Catholic dogmas.

Let me give a few names and facts. There were, for example, the Arian East and West Goths, the Burgundians and Lombards. In his letters, Boniface mentioned a certain Bishop Clement and a preacher known as Aldebert who were spreading 'false doctrines' in Catholic Franconia. Under Charlemagne, the theological doctrines of Archbishop Elipandus of Toledo and Bishop Felix of Urgel were condemned. The monk Gottschalk, who died in 868, proposed, like Augustine, the doctrine of double predestination and was condemned by two synods because of this 'heresy'.

'Heretics' became more numerous in the first half of the eleventh century. Like the earlier Manichees, a great number of priests, noblemen and peasants rejected the veneration of the cross, honour of the saints, marriage, baptism and other sacraments and even the killing of animals and eating of meat. They were tried in Arras in 1025 and eventually confessed that they regarded not only marriage and baptism, but also communion,

[90]. In this section, I have relied to a great extent on the works of Grundmann.

confession and penance, as well as the Church and the clergy, as superfluous, and believed instead in individual inspiration.

In 1054, the great schism between the Latin and the Greek churches took place and both sides cursed and excommunicated each other. (The excommunications were not repealed until our own times.)

In Tours, Berengar, a canon who died in 1088, disputed the traditional teaching about the eucharist, denied transubstantiation and interpreted the act symbolically and spiritualistically. He was forced to recant at the Lenten Synod of 1079. Other heads of religious groups which were opposed to the established Church were Tanchelm of Antwerp and Zeeland, who lived around the year 1110, the priest Peter of Bruis, who died in 1132 or 1133, the monk Henry of Provence, who lived round about 1140, and Arnold of Brescia, who was active in Lombardy and Rome.

Tanchelm openly called the churches brothels and taught that the effect of the sacraments was dependent on the holiness of those who administered them. The monk Henry opposed the Church's practice of infant baptism, on the grounds that children were not able to believe. Arnold of Brescia was a forerunner of the 'heretics' of the centuries which followed, in that he scourged the magnificence of the hierarchy and preached a return to 'apostolic poverty'. In 1155, Arnold was hanged and burnt by the papal prefects in Rome and his ashes were scattered in the Tiber.

Of the many great theologians who were branded as 'heretics' either during their lifetime or after their death, I will mention only one, the fascinating and commanding figure of Joachim of Fiore, who died in 1201 or 1202 and whose doctrine of the three eras had considerable effects on the history of later German thought – on Lessing, for example, and on the philosophical movement of idealism. He taught that, when the era of the Holy Spirit dawned in 1260, all forms of Christianity that had been known up to that date would die out. The dawn of this third era would mark the end of the second period, that of Christ, and the beginning of a free fellowship of the Holy Spirit, without pope, clergy, sacraments, Bible or theology. God himself would then enlighten the minds of men directly, there would be no further need of any mediator and the commandment to love one's fellow-men would be fulfilled.

The two most widespread 'heretical' groups in Europe during the Middle Ages, whose existence formed a serious threat from time to time to the feudal Church, were the Cathari, or Albigensians, and the Waldenses. The Cathari, who were most numerous in the south of France and in Upper Italy, were in the Manichaean tradition. They rejected the sacraments of the Church, marriage, the cult of the saints and of holy relics and the consumption of all food derived from animals, with the exception of fish. The Waldenses, who took their name from their founder, Peter Waldo, a merchant of Lyons, rejected war and all jurisdiction by blood, opposed the doctrine of purgatory and disputed the effectiveness of sacraments administered by unworthy priests.

Other groups of Christians who rebelled against the Catholic Church in the Middle Ages were the Franciscan spirituals, who based their way of life on the teachings of Joachim of Fiore, the apostolic brotherhood, the Amalricans, the brothers and sisters of the free Spirit and the beguines and beghards.

At the end of the Middle Ages, there was a period of division within the western Church. For thirty-seven years, from 1378 until 1415, one pope resided in Rome and another in Avignon. Both representatives of Christ on earth fulminated dreadful excommunications against each other and each other's adherents and threw the mass of ignorant Christians into painful confusion. The Synod of Pisa, which was summoned in 1409 to put an end to the schism, deposed both popes and elected a new one. Since the other two chief shepherds of the Christian flock refused to give up their office, the children of God suddenly found themselves blessed with three popes.

WHAT IS CHRISTIAN?

THE REFORMATION

The body of Christ was divided once more by the Reformation, which added to it the Protestant members. These at once subdivided themselves into Lutherans, Zwinglians and Calvinists. Each of these three main groups of Protestant Christians, of course, attacked the others violently – for Luther, Zwingli was, for example, a 'fanatic' and 'unchristian' because his teaching about the eucharist deviated from his own. It goes without saying that other Protestant movements very soon arose alongside these three main tendencies; these other Protestant Christian movements can be, broadly speaking, grouped under the three headings of anabaptists, antitrinitarians and speculative mystics.

These three groups were in many respects very similar to one another, but they were also very different from one another, so much so that they cannot be discussed as a whole. The anabaptists rejected infant baptism and emphasized the voluntary nature of Christianity and the fact that the Christian has 'come of age'. For this reason, they distrusted any form of the idea of a state church. Unfortunately, they very soon embraced a fanatical ideology based on the ideal Christian community. (The pastor Thomas Münzer, to whom I have already referred in the section entitled 'Possible Objections are Refuted', was an anabaptist.) The antitrinitarians, as their name indicates, denied the classical doctrine of the Trinity. Their writings, which were a mixture of naïve faith in the Bible and a rational criticism of Christian teaching, undeniably did much to pave the way, in the history of philosophy, for the criticism of religion which was practised in the Enlightenment (especially by the Socinians in their alliance with the Arminians). The speculative mystics included lone wolves such as Sebastian Franck and Kaspar Schwenkfeld as well as groups like the Familists, who claimed to be the 'Family of Love'. Sebastian Franck taught a radical individualism divorced from any kind of cult and insisted that the 'inner light' was the only source of certainty of faith. His teaching was, of course, rejected by Catholics, Lutherans, Zwinglians and anabaptists alike.

THE MODERN AGE

As it is quite impossible to discuss, even cursorily, the richly varied pattern of Christianity in the modern age within the framework of this book, I will limit myself to the provision of a simple alphabetical list of some of the most important Christian groups which have been added during the modern period to those already existing in the past. Unlike the theologians of the great churches, I make no distinction in this list between sects and free churches. The list will, if it does nothing else, at least give an idea of the diversity of Christian faith and teaching nowadays:

Adventists, Anthroposophists, Apostles of Christ, Baptists, Catholic Apostolic Church, Christadelphians, Christian Scientists, Church of Jesus Christ of Latter-day Saints (Mormons), Congregationalists, Darbyites, Free Church of Scotland, Jehovah's Witnesses, Mennonites, Methodists, New Jerusalem Church (Swedenborgianism), 'No Other Gospel' Movement, Old Catholics, Oxford Group (Buchmanism), Pentecostal Church, Philadelphian Church, Presbyterian Church, Salvation Army, Society of Friends (Quakers), Theosophists, Unitarians.

TODAY

I fully recognize that Protestant Christians especially may object to what I have said in the foregoing sections on the grounds that I have failed to take into account the essentially historical nature of the gospel and thus its legitimately changeable character.

The proclamation of the gospel can change, the Protestant theologian Gerhard Ebeling claims, 'because the Church has been sent out into the world and owes the world the testimony of Jesus Christ and because the world is in constant movement, is confronted with constantly new situations, speaks in con-

WHAT IS CHRISTIAN?

stantly new languages and is always changing spiritually'.[91] That is why, 'so that the *same* may be said, it must always be said *differently* for the sake of the historical differences'.[92] This 'accompaniment of changelessness and change, identity and variability'[93] is the very stuff of the history of the Church and is 'the sign of the infinite riches of the word of God in its interpretation in the world during its progress through history'.[94]

A view such as this, applied to all Christian groups and all theologies throughout the whole history of the Church, fails to take into account the full extent of the phenomenon of change in Christian teaching. Very often, it is not a question of the same teaching being subject to change, but of completely opposing teaching being quite irreconcilable. Instead of talking enthusiastically about the infinite riches of the word of God, we should by now be beginning to understand the infinite variety of ways in which the word of God can be manipulated. There is not one Christ. There are dozens. The unity of the Church is a notorious fiction. I will prove this by discussing in some detail the theology that is practised today in the Protestant faculties of most German-speaking universities. To limit the discussion to the inner differences within the same Christian confession, at the same period of time, in the same social and cultural environment and among men of the same professional and intellectual status has the effect of enormously heightening and intensifying the problem itself and of eliminating all motives for extending the range of the inquiry.

What is the situation, then, according to these theologians? Hans Grass has spoken cautiously of 'theological pluralism'.[95] Walter Künneth thinks that 'the present theological situation is characterized by a high degree of confusion'.[96] Gerhard Ebeling calls a spade a spade. For him, there is simply 'chaos'[97] in

91. Ebeling, *Die Geschichtlichkeit der Kirche* ..., p. 82 f.
92. Ebeling, 'Tradition', p. 983; author's italics.
93. Ebeling, *Die Geschichtlichkeit der Kirche* ..., p. 81.
94. Ebeling, *Wort Gottes und Tradition*, p. 27.
95. Grass, 'Der theologische Pluralismus ...', p. 146 ff.
96. Künneth, *Glauben an Jesus?*, p. 7.
97. Ebeling, 'Hermeneutische Theologie?', p. 484.

Christian teaching and he calls for 'hermeneutics of the theological [!] dialogue ... not simply in view of the understandable difficulties within the inter-confessional, ecumenical dialogue or in the attempts made by theologians and so-called lay Christians to come to an agreement [!] with one another. What not infrequently [!] occurs in discussions between theologians [!] of the same [!] confession nowadays ... is most stubborn [!] mutual misunderstanding and complete failure to understand each other.'[98] According to Professor Hermann Diem of Tübingen University, there is 'hardly any basis left upon which an agreement can be reached'[99] between Protestant university theologians today.

I certainly do not intend to provide a complete picture of the position of Protestant theology in Germany today. In view of the space at my disposal, that is neither possible nor necessary. It is impossible because there are so many different positions and unnecessary because I can demonstrate my thesis with only a few examples.

Nowhere is the disunity in Christian teaching revealed more clearly than in the two central themes of the science of or teaching about God (theology in the narrower sense) and Christology. Anyone who succeeds in pointing out disparities here will in fact be pointing out disparities in all the questions of faith.

Let us first consider the Christology of Protestantism today. At the very outset, we are bound to say that theologians disagree radically even about the basic question, namely, what would it mean for the Christian faith if it became apparent that the historical Jesus probably never existed? The answer that the vast majority of theologians would give to this question is that it would be the end of the Christian faith. Gollwitzer, for example, has said:

The Christian faith stands or falls by Jesus having lived. We cannot say with *Albert Schweitzer* that Christian theology 'would lose a great deal but by no means everything in the personality of Jesus, and

98. ibid., p. 485; my exclamation marks.
99. Diem, *Dogmatik*, p. 5.

WHAT IS CHRISTIAN?

liberal Christianity would continue to live from the knowledge and energy of immediate religion independent of any historical basis'. A Christianity which had become mystical or idealistically gnostic might boast that it was independent of history, but the Christian faith as such could not because, for faith, Jesus is not simply a vehicle or the symbol of universal truths, but the object of faith and love itself.[100]

Similarly, the leading exponent of the Bultmann school in the field of systematic theology, Gerhard Ebeling, has said: 'If Jesus had never lived or if faith in him were proved to be a misunderstanding of what the historical Jesus was concerned with, the whole of the Christian faith would clearly be without foundation.'[101]

Walter Künneth, the conservative Lutheran theologian, who is otherwise worlds apart from Gollwitzer and Ebeling, has come to the same conclusion.[102]

Other eminent theologians, including, as we have seen, Albert Schweitzer, have expressed views which differ from those of Gollwitzer, Ebeling and Künneth.

Paul Tillich, for example, said 'that historical research can neither give *nor take away* the foundation of the Christian faith'.[103] Elsewhere, he has said: 'The documentary proof of this change of interest is a set of propositions which I presented to a group of theological friends in 1911. I asked how Christian doctrine might be understood if the non-existence of the historical Jesus were to become historically probable, and then attempted to answer my own question. Even now I insist on raising this question radically rather than falling back on the kind of compromises that I encountered then and that Emil Brunner is now offering. The foundation of Christian belief is the biblical picture of Christ, not the historical Jesus.'[104] As this last sentence shows, Tillich's solution looks very much as

---

100. Gollwitzer, 'Der Glaube an Jesus Christus ...', p. 111 f.; author's italics.
101. Ebeling, *Das Wesen des christlichen Glaubens*, p. 51.
102. Künneth, *Glauben an Jesus?*, p. 121 ff.
103. Tillich, *Systematic Theology* II, p. 130; my italics.
104. Tillich, *On the Boundary*, p. 50.

though he interpreted the mythology of the Bible as symbols which remain true and effective without reference to a historical figure, Jesus of Nazareth.

It is already clear, then, that in the sphere of Christology alone there are very many contradictory and opposing answers even to this first basic question. What Albert Schweitzer, in his famous work on the quest for the historical Jesus, *Geschichte der Leben-Jesu-Forschung*, demonstrated with regard to the past two centuries obviously still applies today – there are at least as many (supposedly scientific) views of Jesus as there are professors of theology.

Karl Barth taught a Christology 'from above', which took the classical doctrine of the Trinity as its point of departure and in which the idea of the incarnation was central. Friedrich Gogarten, on the other hand, has developed a Christology 'from below', which takes the man Jesus as its point of departure and presents us with a prototypal faith in this Jesus. The doctrine of the Trinity is completely cast aside in Gogarten's teaching. Otto Weber believes that it is possible to put forward a point of view that goes beyond these attempts to create a Christology 'from above' or 'from below'.

As far as Bultmann is concerned, the historical Jesus belongs, from the religious point of view, to Judaism and can only be counted among the presuppositions of New Testament theology. The only important aspect of the historical Jesus is the pure 'that' of his life. As far as Bultmann's disciples are concerned, the historical Jesus is, in word and action, the real basis and content of the Christian faith.

Herbert Braun regards Jesus as a 'cryptic' figure, pointing the way to a new understanding of self. Paul Tillich and Fritz Buri have both proclaimed 'the Christ' as a principle or a symbol of the 'new being'. Whereas Paul Althaus believes *in* Jesus, Ernst Fuchs believes *like* Jesus.

According to Karl Barth, 'consent to the doctrine of the virgin birth is also an essential part of real faith'.[105] Paul Althaus, on

---

105. Barth, *Die kirchliche Dogmatik*, I, p. 2, 198.

WHAT IS CHRISTIAN?

the other hand, does not regard the virgin birth of Jesus 'as a necessary, an inalienable, part of faith in Jesus Christ'.[106]

I could go on *ad infinitum* with these examples, but I should like to turn now to another Christological problem and consider it a little more closely – that of Jesus' resurrection. Three basic standpoints are in competition with each other here.

1. The radical denial of a resurrection as a historical fact. Bultmann is 'convinced that a corpse cannot come to life again and rise from the grave'.[107] 'The Easter event as the resurrection of Christ is not a historical event,' he states elsewhere, 'only *the Easter faith of the first disciples* is capable of being grasped as a historical event.'[108] In the same article, he says: '*Faith in the resurrection is nothing but faith in the crucifixion as a saving event.*'[109]

2. Wolfhart Pannenberg insists on the exact opposite, affirming the resurrection of Jesus as a historical fact which can be proved by the methods of secular historical research.[110] According to Pannenberg, 'the historian is expected' – to our astonishment – 'to prove that God has revealed himself in Jesus of Nazareth'.[111]

3. Between these two extremes, there are, of course, very many theologians who take up an intermediate position. They regard the resurrection of Jesus as a real event which took place in space and time, but which cannot be established historically, but only believed. In the words of Paul Althaus: 'The resurrection of Jesus is not a historical datum like the personal characteristics and the history of Jesus to which I have referred. Only faith knows that the dates which the historian can grasp, the reports of Jesus' "appearances" and even the empty grave (see

---

106. Althaus, 'Jungfrauengeburt', p. 1069.
107. Bultmann, 'Zur Frage der Entmythologisierung', p. 51.
108. Bultmann, 'Neues Testament und Mythologie', p. 46 f.; author's italics.
109. Bultmann, 'Neues Testament und Mythologie', p. 46; author's italics.
110. Pannenberg, *Grundzüge der Christologie*, p. 85 ff., especially also pp. 95 and 107.
111. Pannenberg, 'Heilsgeschehen . . .', p. 278.

von Campenhausen) are historical "signs" behind which lies the mystery of the resurrection.'[112]

The different points of view that I have indicated above are, of course, often found in combination with each other and in many variations. As a rule, however, each theologian puts forward his own Christology as the only possible one and condemns the teaching of his colleagues as heretical. Ernst Fuchs has dismissed Pannenberg's Christology, for example, as an 'ideology'.[113] For Pannenberg himself, on the other hand, nothing less than 'the foundation of the Christian faith' itself is at stake in his Christology.[114]

Walter Künneth has taken Rudolf Bultmann and his disciples strenuously to task in connection with their teaching about Christ: 'It is regrettable that the concept "Christology" is still used in this philosophical undertaking, although the material content has nothing whatever to do with it any more'.[115] He testifies to the arch-heretic Braun: 'Faith in Jesus has melted away into nothing. The humanitarian remnants have left the *specificum christianum* far behind and are becoming a miserable documentation of anthropocentric morality.'[116]

One of the Christologists accused by Künneth, Gerhard Ebeling, has retorted with equal vigour. The Christian faith, he claims, has been 'falsified into a philosophical principle and – what an astonishing change of front! – the whole basis of faith has melted away into enthusiasm' in Künneth's 'pamphlet' which, he insists, is brimful of 'pseudo-orthodox pathos'.[117]

Let us now turn to the second of the two themes which I have chosen to illustrate the disunity in theological teaching in Germany alone today – that of the 'science of God'. Here, too, the confusion that prevails is bewildering. In view of the limited space at my disposal, I shall confine myself simply to Herbert Braun's teaching about God and that of his opponents. The

112. Althaus, 'Christologie. *Dogmatisch*', p. 1780.
113. Fuchs, 'Theologie oder Ideologie'.
114. Pannenberg, *Grundzüge der Christologie*, p. 79.
115. Künneth, *Glauben an Jesus?*, p. 129.
116. ibid., p. 301, note.
117. Ebeling, *Theologie und Verkündigung*, pp. 128, 132, 139.

WHAT IS CHRISTIAN?

teaching of this New Testament scholar at Mainz University, which is, in one direction at least, the most consistent extension of Bultmann's programme of demythologization that has appeared to date, has had a very inflammatory effect on other theologians. As I am here only concerned with the question of Braun's being condemned as a heretic, I will not refer to those teachings about God which are opposed to each other, although these too are clear indications of the extent to which theology is divided today.

For Braun, the mythological statements that are contained in the Bible, including, for example, the 'existence of a deity', simply 'cannot be afforded in philosophy today'. After a radical 'hermeneutical' cure, in which the New Testament is put through an anthropological mincing machine, Braun's teaching about God amounts to this:

> God is the expression for the phenomenon of being able to act according to one's conscience and with conviction and confidence . . . God is there wherever the moment is seized and lived in its fullness . . . Man as man, man in his fellow-humanity, implies God . . . God is then a special kind of fellow-humanity. The atheist fails to grasp *man*. Indeed, we may ask whether there is really such a thing as an atheist.[118]

These statements of Braun have aroused a storm of indignation. Gerhard Petry has claimed that they mark the 'end of theology'.[119] Wilhelm Andersen has accused Braun of holding a 'complete clearance sale of theology'.[120] Johannes Schneider has attacked him for 'carrying out a thorough evacuation of the biblical statements about God' and for turning 'theology completely into anthropology'.[121] Ernst Wolf[122] and Helmut Gollwitzer[123] have expressed similar views.

---

118. Braun, *Gesammelte Studien* . . ., pp. 325, 331, 338, 339, 341; author's italics.
119. Petry, 'Das Ende der Theologie?', p. 17.
120. Andersen, 'Selbstpreisgabe der Theologie?', p. 58.
121. Schneider, 'Zur Entmythologisierung Gottes' in Augustin, p. 143.
122. Szczesny, *Die Antwort* . . ., p. 98.
123. Gollwitzer, *Die Existenz Gottes* . . ., p. 63 f.; *Post Bultmann Locutum* I and II.

This process of branding theologians as heretics does not always take place entirely on one side. Friedrich Gogarten, whose teaching about God is very closely related to Braun's, has, for example, accused his Lutheran colleagues and opponents of denying God and his word by objectivizing them.[124]

How grotesque it all is! What one theologian rejects as something that cannot be afforded in philosophy today, the other regards as the gospel itself. What one puts forward as the quintessence of faith, the other condemns as a complete clearance sale of theology. Yet both contestants are, it should be noted, professors in Protestant theology at German universities today. Both were called to occupy their chairs with the consent of their church leaders. Both are ordained pastors who are in charge of the training of young pastors and who have to examine them in the teachings of the Church.

This scandalous situation is completely contrary to the exalted claim of theology to be a scientific reflection on the supposedly unequivocal and supposedly crystal-clear word of God which is supposedly so necessary to life and salvation. Since no other university discipline has, or can have, this kind of understanding of itself, any euphemistic reference to fundamental differences within theology is bound to be out of place.

124. Gogarten, *Entmythologisierung und Kirche*, p. 112.

2

Irrationality in Theology

ALTHOUGH many theologians freely admit that 'affirmations about God and the divine reality cannot be regarded as scientific statements',[1] most of the scholars who specialize in theology at universities proudly claim the stamp of scientific quality for their goods. Of course, they usually add that theology is an 'ecclesiastical' science, because, in German universities, professors of theology are appointed by the Minister of Education only with the consent of the church leaders. The fact that these professors are bound to the Church, however, is not regarded as an infringement of academic freedom, but is extolled as an aspect of their studies which makes them fully consistent with their object.

At the risk of being accused of believing rather naïvely in the scientific method as applied to theology, I am bound to affirm here that, in my opinion, the only suitable criterion for any theological thinking which can claim to be scientific and can therefore justify its existence in university circles is whether or not it is pancritically rational.

Pancritical rationality is a way of thinking which is free of any external domination, always regards all assumptions and all results as in principle open to criticism and does not cling stubbornly and dogmatically to any thesis. In the case of criticism also being directed against the method of pancritical rationality itself, then, because this method can never be made absolute and it is especially, even triumphantly, valid in cases where it can itself be subject to criticism, it still continues to apply fully. Whereas, in the sphere of theology, doubt is acknowledged only as a challenge that has to be overcome and has in fact already been overcome in faith, doubt about the correctness

1. Loewenich, *Glaube Kirche Theologie*, p. 17 f.

of any assumptions and any affirmations forms an essential part of scientific, pancritically rational thought.

It cannot be denied, of course, that several other disciplines which are practised today in university circles also fail to come up to this standard, but they do not, as it were, fail in this way of necessity and by their very nature. A distinction must therefore be made between the essentially unscientific nature of theology and the character of other disciplines which may simply 'happen' to be unscientific. Theology is essentially dogmatic. Dogmatism in other university subjects, on the other hand, is always a sign of degeneration, and this is almost always traceable to inadequacy on the part of individual teachers or to the climate of thought prevailing within the particular university faculty or department.

The Two Structural Principles of Theology: Adherence to Authority and Maximum Content

I have no need to discuss Catholic theology in detail to prove that it is unscientific because it is immediately obvious that it is. The Catholic theologian, Joseph Ratzinger, has said, for example:

> As the science of faith, it [that is, Catholic theology] regards the statements of faith as its object, which it cannot, of its own accord, either produce or *do away with*. It has rather to *serve* them by creating, through methodical thought, a deeper understanding and a more lively personal appropriation of those statements of faith which are received by the Catholic theologian from the Church. The Church, in turn, is consciously bound to the twofold but single witness of Scripture and tradition.... Theology therefore presupposes faith both in the subjective sense of personal willingness to believe on the part of the theologian himself and in the objective sense of the *previously given* statements of faith. In this way, theology is essentially distinct from the so-called *theologia naturalis*, man's natural or philosophical knowledge of God, and is carried out at a *completely new spiritual level*, which is known as the 'supernatural' plane.[2]

The most well-known and important expression of this struc-

2. Ratzinger, 'Theologie III', p. 775; my italics.

tural principle of Catholic theology is the dogma of the infallibility of the pope, to which every Catholic theologian is bound to adhere. Unfortunately, I have already learnt only too well to come to terms with the existence of faculties of Catholic theology at most German universities and can therefore no longer react very strongly against this infringement of the elementary rules of intellectual honesty. All that I can say is – how many Catholic scholars have come to grief on this point!

It is equally obvious at first sight that the thinking of many Lutheran theologians is also totally irrational – for example, Walter Künneth's uncritical appeal to the 'testimony with regard to the resurrection of Jesus'[3] or Karl Barth's proclamation of the virgin birth of Jesus as a dogma with binding force. These theologians also demand that we should sacrifice our intelligence and that we should be prevented from rational thoughts.

For some years now, however, the clarion call has sounded within Protestant theological circles for what Walther von Loewenich called an 'undogmatic Christianity'.[4] To some extent, the whole history of Protestant theology over the past two hundred years can be regarded as an unceasing process of abandoning earlier dogmas and of becoming more and more open to historical and critical thinking. This development reached a climax in such figures as Paul Tillich, Rudolf Bultmann and Friedrich Gogarten.

Many Protestants cherished the hope that these 'modern' theologians would prepare the way for a form of Christian faith which would make it possible for believers to be pious and free at the same time. Others were and still are suspicious of the 'end of dogmatism'.[5] I shall, I think, not be dealing unfairly with the problem if I discuss in detail only the work of those theologians who claim to march under the banner of intellectual honesty. What will emerge from my analysis is, I believe, that their theological thinking only marks the end of Christian dog-

---

3. Künneth, *Glauben an Jesus?*, p. 323, note 15.
4. Loewenich, *Glaube Kirche Theologie*, p. 158 f.
5. Diem, *Dogmatik*, p. 37.

matism as practised up to the present and certainly not the end of Christian dogmatism as such. I shall attempt to show that this is true, in the first place, of Bultmann's and Ebeling's idea of theology, but it can also be extended to cover the theological concept of almost all other present-day Christian thinkers, including not only those who have ceased to be bound to the historical Jesus – namely Paul Tillich[6] and the Swiss Liberal theologians, Fritz Buri, Martin Werner and U. Neuenschwander – but also the 'death of God' theologians, Thomas Altizer and Gabriel Vahanian.

RUDOLF BULTMANN'S CONCEPT OF THEOLOGY

The most striking expression of Rudolf Bultmann's ideas will be found in his extensive programme of demythologization of the Bible, the basis of which is a systematic destruction of the mythology of the New Testament by scientific rationalization. As Bultmann himself has said, 'It is indeed true to say that scientific thought destroys the mythological world-view of the Bible. In the conflict between the objectivizing thought of the myth and the objectivizing thought of modern science, it goes *almost without saying* that the latter will be victorious.'[7]

Bultmann's theological standpoint can be summarized very briefly as follows. Faith becomes no more than a pious and meritorious work if man's understanding and intellect are sacrificed to it. The Christian message is above all an '*intelligible* word ... which does not act by means of magic and does not require either blind subjection as a dogma or the acceptance of absurdities'.[8] 'Faith and lack of faith,' Bultmann has said elsewhere, 'are not a blind, arbitrary decision, but a yes or no expressed with full understanding.'[9]

---

6. Bartley and Weischedel have demonstrated that this is the case with Tillich.

7. Bultmann, 'Zum Problem der Entmythologisierung', p. 184; my italics.

8. Bultmann, *Glauben und Verstehen* I, p. 282; author's italics.

9. Bultmann, 'Neues Testament und Mythologie', p. 46.

IRRATIONALITY IN THEOLOGY

However promising this programme may seem to be for theologians, it is ultimately disappointing. Bultmann also fails, without any convincing reason, to carry critical thought to its ultimate conclusion. He appeals to an authority which cannot be questioned and is guilty of irrational thinking.

What is most remarkable is that he refers to faith again and again as obedience.[10] The word of God, which he prefers to call the *kerygma*, is 'a directive, a *commandment* which must be kept'.[11] It does *not* permit of 'any *discussion*', but 'simply demands faith'.[12] It may not be questioned. It has 'no justification, but demands recognition'.[13] The kerygma is an '*authoritative* address which is handed on by men and which demands faith'.[14]

Bultmann himself has summed up all these statements in an important passage in which he also defines the limits of theology and the kerygma with regard to one another:

It is therefore clear that *this theology is always subject to criticism*, although admittedly to only one criticism, which is, for its part, based on obedience. Otherwise it is true to say that 'the spiritual man judges all things, but is himself to be judged by no one' (1 Cor. ii, 15). *The kerygma, on the other hand, is not subject to any criticism*, because, as an address which demands faith, it cannot be judged from a neutral basis, but requires the renunciation of one's own judgement. But, since the kerygma itself is always expressed only in the conceptuality of human speech, a precise distinction can be made between the kerygma and theology in principle, but not in practice. In other words, it cannot be said unequivocally what the kerygma is, how much and precisely which affirmations it contains.[15]

Theology, then, is not sacrosanct. It may be criticized. But –

---

10. Bultmann, *Glauben und Verstehen* I, pp. 34, 107, 109, 142, 169, 181, 183, 184, 186, 288.; III, p. 27; IV, p. 159, 160; *Theologie des Neuen Testaments*, pp. 315, 318.
11. Bultmann, *Glauben und Verstehen* I, p. 280; my italics.
12. ibid., III, p. 123; my italics.
13. ibid., I, p. 282.
14. ibid., III, p. 124; my italics.
15. ibid., I, p. 186; author's italics; see also *Theologie des Neuen Testaments*, pp. 586–9.

it should be noted – it can only be subjected to the criticism of those who believe and are obedient to faith. A non-Christian, because he is not a 'spiritual man', is not competent to criticize it, since 'theology and the Church are bound to demand *absolutely certain statements*'.[16] The kerygma, however, is completely immune from all criticism. Even a 'spiritual man' may not question it or ask whether it has any rational justification.

Let us be quite clear what this means. To clarify the situation let us contrast the attitude of scientific, rational thinkers with that of Bultmann. Certain basic principles are recognized by all scholars as applying to all their work in the sphere of scientific study. All their premises can always be radically questioned. All their statements must always be open to complete revision. No ultimate authority can be recognized. No debate can ever in principle be closed. Everything that they say is always exposed to the risk of being challenged and even refuted. Bultmann, on the other hand, takes a completely different point of view. According to him, theology may only be criticized by those who believe – he will therefore only permit purely domestic criticism – and the very object of theology, the kerygma, may not be criticized at all.

The question about truth is not asked, then, and the basic assumption is made, at the very outset, that the kerygma is true. The claim made by so many university theologians today, that their faculties are almost the only places left where 'ultimate' questions, especially questions about truth and about the meaning of man's existence, are still asked, is pure nonsense. The practice that is so popular among Protestant theologians, so they claim, that of 'questioning oneself and one's convictions', is purely fictitious. Theology is still, even in the case of Bultmann, pure dogmatism.

The most scandalous aspect of Bultmann's teaching perhaps is that this incontestable kerygma cannot be defined unequivocally – 'it cannot be said unequivocally what the kerygma is'. What Bultmann has involuntarily done is to confirm the fact that, throughout the history of theological study and above all in the

16. Bultmann, *Glauben und Verstehen* I, p. 123; my italics.

present situation, every theologian proclaims something different as the word of God.

This, however, is not all. 'The preaching apostle also belongs to the gospel with his authority, his claim to obedience on the part of the community'.[17] But not only the deceased apostle claims this obedience. According to Bultmann, the essence of the Christian faith consists of this – 'Genuine Christian proclamation is such that it claims to be God's call made through the mouths of men and that it demands faith as authority. Characteristic of the Christian proclamation is the paradox that it is in it that God's call takes place in the words of men'.[18]

The 'eschatological event' of faith, which is identical with this 'paradox' and to which Bultmann is always referring, is simply a way of giving an absolute value to something that is purely relative. What Bultmann has done is to expand the kerygma, which has a changeable content and is admittedly something that has been conditioned and has come about historically, to such an extent that he has made it absolute. This thinking reached catastrophic proportions in the ideas of Bultmann's friend, Gogarten, who did not simply happen to be a fascist.

GERHARD EBELING'S CONCEPT OF THEOLOGY

Gerhard Ebeling also tempts us with the attractive claim of 'intellectual honesty'.[19] In one of his 'Theses for an Introductory Lecture on the Study of Theology', he proclaims with great self-assertion, 'Theology is necessary as a defence of reason against irrationality.'[20] Unlike many theologians who have only attempted 'to eliminate above all disturbing intermediate questions',[21] Ebeling states confidently: 'I want to have the courage to think critically.'[22]

17. ibid., I, p. 179 f.
18. ibid., III, p. 124.
19. Ebeling, *Wort und Glaube*, p. 104 ff.
20. ibid., p. 448.
21. Ebeling, *Das Wesen des christlichen Glaubens*, p. 150.
22. ibid., p. 13.

THE MISERY OF CHRISTIANITY

But, as his remarks about the historical Jesus have already shown, this critical thinking does not appear to extend very far. It is clear that Ebeling agrees with certain affirmations which may not, according to the principles of theology, be too critically questioned. For example, he says that, since the Christian faith is an 'absolute'[23] 'unsurpassable certainty'[24] which excludes 'all doubt',[25] theology, as scientific reflection about this faith, is bound to result in 'statements of a dogmatic character'.[26]

As Ebeling has explained in considerable detail in his long articles on 'theology and philosophy', the point of departure for theology is an 'indisputable, incontestable' datum, the 'proclamation of Jesus Christ', and theology therefore has a 'fundamentally homological and assertory character'. 'Authority' and 'faith' are the characteristics 'of the previously given indisputable datum on which theology is based'.[27] It is also, according to Ebeling, certainly true that our 'understanding of authority is based on the essence of the gospel itself and can even be regarded as identical with the gospel'.[28]

Like Bultmann, Ebeling certainly rejects any attempt to compel faith[29] and equally certainly does not think of authority as 'replacing evidence'.[30] For him, the substance of theology is, on the contrary, 'basically simple' and 'perfectly clear'.[31]

Nevertheless, the evidence of Ebeling's 'event of the word, which reveals itself to the conscience as the power of the indisputable' datum[32] is not accepted by all his fellow-theologians, let alone by thinking non-Christians. He does not, above all, submit his alleged evidence to a thorough examination, but simply presents it quite dogmatically, maintaining that evidence

23. ibid., p. 229 f.
24. Ebeling, *Was heisst Glauben*, p. 17.
25. Ebeling, *Wort Gottes und Tradition*, p. 151.
26. Ebeling, *Theologie und Verkündigung*, p. 11.
27. Ebeling, 'Theologie und Philosophie', pp. 822, 823.
28. Ebeling, *Wort Gottes und Tradition*, p. 171.
29. Ebeling, *Das Wesen des christlichen Glaubens*, p. 142 f.
30. Ebeling, 'Theologie und Philosophie', p. 823.
31. Ebeling, *Das Wesen . . .*, p. 161; see pp. 113, 153, 237, 242, 247; *Wort und Glaube*, p. 448; *Vom Gebet*, p. 84.
32. Ebeling, 'Theologie und Philosophie', p. 824 f.

IRRATIONALITY IN THEOLOGY

is always evidence. Faith, on the other hand, is, for Ebeling, the 'safe assurance that cannot be refuted by any event in the future' and 'existence under the great sign of full consent, which can never result in disappointment'. The word of God, which is based on faith, is, Ebeling insists, a 'word which saves, which can never be held up by anything in its effectiveness, and which is definitive and always valid'.[33]

What kind of irresponsible 'thinking' is this? I could put up with Ebeling's acclamation of the substance of theology as irrefutable, but how he is able to reconcile proclaiming a human word – and, even according to Ebeling, it is only human words that are known to us – as 'always valid' with 'intellectual honesty' is beyond me.

The dogma of papal infallibility is certainly not confined exclusively to Catholic theology – it is an expression of an essential element in all Christian theology, in which the function of man's reason is reduced to what was known, in early Protestant orthodoxy, as the *usus organicus rationis*. Reason serves simply as an *organon*, an instrument which has to assimilate and reproduce the previously given content of revelation quite uncritically.

The close affinity between the theological concept and the positivistic concept of reason is revealed with surprising clarity here. Just as all theology presupposes the truth and authority of the word of God and only subsequently develops them – or, in the extreme case of scholasticism, tries to prove them – so too does reason, cut down to the measure of positivism, fit itself all too easily into previously given relationships.

Since, in positivism, being and obligation, facts and decisions, knowledge and values are all kept strictly separate, norms and aims cannot be rationally debated. Reason is formalized into an instrument which helps man to reach previously given aims (intentional rationality).

Positivism and theology are very similar in that both deprive the orientation of action by norms and aims of its rational basis, motivation and critical function. If norms are not determined by reason, then of necessity they become the victims of irrationality.

33. Ebeling, *Das Wesen* . . ., pp. 235, 170, 236.

They become heteronomous – which is why theology always keeps the will of God in readiness. Reason cut down to the measure of positivism is made complete by revelation.

Every theologian appeals to authoritative tradition. If he has to make a statement about the question of lifelong monogamy, for example, he will not as a rule first rationally consider what is to be said in favour of it today and what is to be said against it, but rather, if he is a Protestant, what the commandment 'thou shalt not commit adultery' means and then what the modern aspects of marriage signify 'in the light of the Bible'. A Catholic theologian would tend to base his arguments on official pronouncements made by the Church rather than directly on the Bible, but otherwise his approach would not be essentially different.

So much, then, for the first structural principle of theology – adherence to authority. Let us now consider very briefly its second principle – what I have called 'maximum content'. The theologians' concept of God is itself the best possible example of this principle. Anselm of Canterbury (d. 1109), for instance, defined God as the being *quo maius cogitari non potest* – 'in comparison with whom nothing greater can be conceived'. God is, according to the theologians, omnipotent, omnipresent, omniscient and so on. Anthropological definitions such as 'You must be perfect, as your heavenly Father is perfect' (Matt. v, 48) follow from these definitions of God with the help of analogies. Flowery excesses such as *complete* surrender to God and to the service of one's neighbour, *unreserved* openness to the future, *unsurpassable* certainty of salvation, *unlimited* forgiveness, *unconditional* obedience and *unrepeatable* event decorate the pages of every theological book and article.

The following passage taken from Gerhard Ebeling's work is a veritable treasure-house of superlatives, which the author clearly uses to silence all possible objections before they can be expressed and which contain a rather unpleasant element of propaganda. It is obvious, Ebeling writes, that

faith can only exist as the certainty of being able to take one's stand on what is *ultimately* valid and on what is true in *the most extreme case*, of

IRRATIONALITY IN THEOLOGY

being able to depend on the one who *undoubtedly* keeps to what he promises and to whom the *last* word is due, of being able to have confidence in what will *without any doubt* be fulfilled, in what cannot be prevented from coming *by anything at all* and against which *no* resistance at all is possible, and in what transcends *everything* in power; of being able therefore to entrust oneself to him, to consent to and to rely on what is in *the most true* sense worthwhile.[34]

Christian theology is so narcissistically preoccupied with itself and so convinced of its own infallibility that it can only be aware of other views within its own pattern of absolutism. Just as the devil cannot get away from God and still has to celebrate a Mass – admittedly a horribly perverted 'black' Mass – so too the supposed atheist can never escape from God and is bound to become the victim of a substitute god.

The criticism of dogmatism directed against theologians always returns as regularly as a boomerang to the thrower and usually in the form of what may be called a 'you too' argument. The pattern of this 'argument' is, briefly, as follows: You want to be critical also and you really think that you can destroy the foundations of Christian dogmatism, but you too have become entangled, without noticing it, in dogmatism. You too are taking unquestionable principles as your point of departure, and you too have ultimately let yourself become involved in a commitment which can no longer be discussed rationally. No one can really do without this and so we theologians cannot be criticized fairly.

Let me give three illustrations of this kind of 'argument'. The well-known theologian at the University of Basle, Karl Barth, replied to an article in which the philosopher Max Bense of Stuttgart gave his reasons for being an atheist ('Warum man Atheist sein muss') with an article entitled 'Denken heisst Nachdenken' – 'Thought is Reflection'. In his article, Barth puts his question to Bense: Should he therefore not be very careful if he aims to call himself an atheist and pass himself off as one? Does not he too ascribe to every thinking being a

---

34. Ebeling, *Das Wesen* . . ., p. 170; my italics.

highest value and a highest dignity only attributable to a God – to the one whom he regards as his God?

Here Barth is guilty of a theologian's misunderstanding of Bense's reference to man as the highest being. He presupposes the view that man is the absolutely highest being, whereas Bense regards man in fact only as the relatively highest being, the highest compared with all the other relative and finite beings that we know. So Barth continues, 'It is therefore irrelevant whether they call it "God", as pagans in the past and more recently have done and still do' and this is why the philosopher 'wishes to attack the Christian faith and deny the one whom he confesses as God in the strength of his special faith and in the name of his special God'. But, Barth argues, the attempts made by Bense and all atheists to do this are made in vain – atheism is quite impracticable. Man belongs to the Christian God 'who is by nature not without man and not against him, but for him, the God of every man, even the man who claims to be an atheist'.[35]

In his book, in which he asks whether atheism is not simply self-deception (*Atheismus – eine Selbsttäuschung?*), the Protestant theologian Gunther Backhaus takes Gerhard Szczesny to task:

He too proposes as science what is less than science. He does not put 'science' forward against 'dogmatism' or 'revelation'. Here 'dogmatism' is contrasted with dogmatism and that is why the struggle is so bitter. Conviction is opposed to conviction.

He continues,

There is really no counterposition to the truth of God which is not, for its part, *dogmatic*. Every counterposition *must*, on the other hand, be dogmatic. Of itself, it necessarily becomes a *counter*-religion. . . . One does *not* want to be religious, but one *must* be religious![36]

The feeble declamations of Eberhard Leppin, a successor and imitator of Friedrich Gogarten, are not essentially different. This Protestant pastor has written a reply to a book by Gerhard Szczesny with the impressive title *Glaubt ihr nicht so bleibt ihr nicht*, in which he says that Szczesny 'uses science not to throw

35. Barth, 'Denken . . .', p. 203 f.
36. Backhaus, *Atheismus* . . ., pp. 59, 61; author's italics.

IRRATIONALITY IN THEOLOGY

light on the truth, but to conceal it' and that 'Szczesny is not aware that his post-Christian philosophy is a decision of unbelief in which the stake is man himself. The truth or falsehood of this decision cannot be proved or refuted with rational arguments'. Leppin regards it as important to understand that there is, between the Christian position and that of atheism, 'an alternative which cannot be decided upon by rational arguments'.[37]

On what are they founded, these Christian demands which make serious reflection and communication impossible and replace them by drivel about 'decisions'? Backhaus says that his view is both 'theologically and empirically' based.[38] It is certainly theological insofar as it is the direct product of a theological way of thinking. It is also, to some extent at least, empirical, since it cannot be disputed that many people have created substitute religions and gods for themselves. But it is not logical. As Max Horkheimer has said:

> Let it be said in answer to those who serve religion with philosophy that the necessity to make a religion out of the absence of religion is a factual, not a logical, necessity. There is no logically compelling reason for setting up any other absolute in the place of the fallen absolute, other gods in the place of the fallen gods or denial in the place of reverence. People might even be able to forget the absence of religion today, but they are too weak to do so.[39]

This weakness is rooted in the frightening state of this world which again and again urges us to seek refuge in the illusions of imaginary consolations. That is why theology can only be criticized successfully if this is done as part of a wider criticism of ideology itself. This in turn can only be successful if this criticism of ideology leads to a democratic practice which will do away with all situations in the world which call for consoling illusions. 'Criticism of heaven thus changes into criticism of earth, *criticism of religion* into *criticism of the law* and *criticism of theology* into *criticism of politics*.'[40]

37. Leppin, *Glaubt ihr nicht so bleibt ihr nicht*, pp. 130, 127, 70.
38. ibid., p. 61.
39. Regius, *Dämmerung*, p. 131 note.
40. Karl Marx, *Zur Kritik der Hegelschen Rechtsphilosophie*, Introduction; author's italics; quoted from Lenk, p. 106.

The Demythologization Programme –
A Romantic Attempt to Vindicate the
Honour of the Christian Faith

The word 'demythologization' is, of course, indissolubly linked with the name of the Professor of New Testament Studies at Marburg University, Rudolf Bultmann. Yet what demythologization involves is certainly not confined to one single theologian. A meaningful assessment of Bultmann's programme of hermeneutics can only be made within the framework of the whole of theology and the whole history of theological studies. As I hope to show in this section of my book, demythologization is really no more than a modern way of playing the same game theologians have been playing professionally for a very long time indeed – the manipulation of authoritative texts so that they can still be put to use today or, to quote from what Franz Overbeck has said about 'writing for the Church', 'organized ambiguity and dishonesty'.[41]

The essence that is common to all Christian theology, then, is also revealed in the demythologization programme, but there are four compelling reasons for devoting special attention to it.

1. The whole of Protestant theology today has been stamped with the questions Bultmann and his disciples have asked and the answers they have given. This is clearly indicated by such catch phrases as the 'generation *post Bultmann natum*' of Gollwitzer,[42] or James Robinson's reference to a 'post-Bultmannian' phase in theology.[43]

2. Catholic theologians have also not been able to ignore Bultmann and have in fact been deeply influenced by his programme of demythologization. One of the most interesting theological works to have been published in recent years is Gotthold Hasenhüttl's book on the Catholic encounter with the theology of Rudolf Bultmann (*Der Glaubensvollzug. Eine Begeg-*

41. Quoted from Nigg, *Franz Overbeck*, p. 101.
42. Gollwitzer, *Post Bultmann Locutum* I, p. 17.
43. James M. Robinson, *A New Quest of the Historical Jesus*.

IRRATIONALITY IN THEOLOGY

nung mit Rudolf Bultmann aus katholischem Glaubensverständnis), in which the author rather pointedly interprets Bultmann's thinking as that of a good Catholic, with the exception of his ideas about Church doctrines, in which he does not think consistently.

3. Unlike the liberal theology of the nineteenth century, which did not penetrate to any great extent beyond the frontiers of the university world, Bultmann's ideas have become widely known to a large public. Popular books such as J. A. T. Robinson's *Honest to God*, mass national rallies like the German Catholic *Kirchentage*, great numbers of *avant garde* young Protestant pastors who go about demythologizing in public, and finally the 'No Other Gospel' movement have all had the effect of popularizing the programme.

4. Although many Christians, not only fundamentalists but also more 'progressive' theologians, condemn Bultmann's theology as opening the way to atheism or, more politely, as heterodoxy, countless others have welcomed it as offering new faith and new hope to Christianity. What I have to say here about demythologization is addressed especially to the latter, because I should like to show them that their new hope and faith are based on an illusion which is the direct result of a desire to cling at all costs to the Church.

My analysis will be guided above all by two main questions:

1. Can the demythologizers justify themselves in the light of the Bible or do they do violence to the biblical texts?

2. What is the result of demythologization? Will the Christian message be made more acceptable to thinking non-Christians by it, or will it not confirm their view that it is both superfluous and dangerous?

THE PROCEDURE: THE 'HERMENEUTICAL' BRAINWASHING OF UNPOPULAR IDEAS AND TEXTS

The demythologization programme thrives on the conviction that the Christian faith and scientific thought are not mutually exclusive. They are, on the contrary, the demythologizers' believe, so able to co-exist that full justice can be done to both. Schleiermacher's famous question – 'Will the knot of history be unravelled thus – Christianity with barbarism and science with unbelief?' is therefore emphatically denied.

As Bultmann himself has stated,[44] this twofold theme is at the basis of all his thinking. On the one hand, he wants to keep in step with modern scientific thought which – 'it almost goes without saying'[45] – destroys the mythology of the Bible. On the other hand, however, he is motivated by the theological concern to proclaim the gospel in the modern age in such a way that it can be believed and understood. Both these themes are so closely interwoven that criticism of biblical mythology is placed at the service of the proclamation of the gospel itself. 'Demythologization removes, by its criticism of the biblical image of the world, the stumbling-block which this world-view necessarily places in the way of modern man. In so doing, it at the same time illuminates the *authentic stumbling-block* which confronts not only modern man, but every man, in the Bible.'[46]

What is Bultmann's procedure, then, for reconciling the irreconcilable contradiction between science and faith? He makes use of a venerable method, much loved by politicians when they want to throw a veil over contradictions – the method of 'interpretation'. Even if the myths contained in the New Testament were to be completely denied as far as their objective conceptual content was concerned, they would not be 'eliminated', but 'interpreted'.[47]

According to Bultmann, the Bible can be 'interpreted' because, although the Bible does undoubtedly contain mythology, it does not *only* contain mythology.[48] The fact that the New Testament also clings obstinately to the real historical figure of the man Jesus of Nazareth is, Bultmann insists, clear evidence that it does not present us with pure mythology, but

44. Bultmann, *Glauben und Verstehen* III, p. 179 f.
45. Bultmann, 'Zum Problem der Entmythologisierung', p. 184.
46. Bultmann, ibid., p. 188; author's italics.
47. See, for example, Bultmann, 'Neues Testament und Mythologie', pp. 24, 26.
48. See, for example, ibid., pp. 22, 26.

IRRATIONALITY IN THEOLOGY

only with historically broken mythology. As he himself says,

> *History and myth are curiously interwoven here.* The historical Jesus, whose father and mother are known (John vi, 42), is said to be at the same time the pre-existent son of God. Beside the historical event of the crucifixion, there is also the resurrection, which is not a historical event. ...Thus the urgent question is *whether the meaning of the mythology of the New Testament is not simply to express the significance of the historical figure of Jesus and his history*, that is, their significance as a saving figure and as a saving event. This might be the meaning of the mythology of the New Testament and its objective conceptual content might have to be sacrificed.[49]

With this theatrical trick, which gives the illusion of solving the problem very neatly, Bultmann describes the essence of his method. The myth is not the matter of the New Testament, but simply an 'interpretament', which is at the same time also dispensable and exchangeable. The real matter of the New Testament, the 'intention' of the myth, is not its 'objective conceptual content', but 'the existential understanding expressed in these concepts'.[50] Everything that the myth says literally is disqualified as inessential. What the myth really aims to do is 'to speak about the reality of man himself'.[51] In a word, 'the myth has to be interpreted not cosmologically, but anthropologically, or even better, existentially.'[52]

This astonishing 'interpretation', which can only delude those who feel obliged both to destroy biblical mythology with criticism and to preserve it with reverence – what else is it but an intellectual's denial of what is essentially contained in the Bible?

Bultmann has put forward three arguments for insisting on an existential interpretation of the New Testament:

1. The most widely differing myths, 'as far as their ideas are concerned, quite unreconciled and even contradicting each other', are juxtaposed in the New Testament. 'For example, the idea of the death of Christ as a sacrifice and a cosmic event and

49. ibid., p. 41; author's italics.
50. ibid., p. 23.
51. Bultmann, *Glauben und Verstehen* IV, p. 134.
52. Bultmann, 'Neues Testament und Mythologie', p. 22.

the interpretation of his person as the Messiah and the second Adam are found side by side. The concept of the *kenosis* of the pre-existent Christ (Phil. ii, 6 ff.) and the account of his miracles, through which he proves himself to be the Messiah, contradict each other. Similarly contradictory are the idea of the virgin birth and the notion of his pre-existence'.[53] Herbert Braun, who has given many quite drastic examples of this exegetical discovery, has come to the conclusion that, since these biblical statements 'cannot be reconciled with each other', they illustrate, 'by their very disparity', that it cannot 'in their case be a question of what they say, in express terms, in contradiction to each other'.[54]

Here, then, a (mythological) necessity has been doctored to become an (existential) virtue. Why should it be concluded from the mutually contradictory statements made by the biblical authors that each of these authors did not take his own ideas seriously? It is far truer to say that the myths are in competition with each other, and that they were also felt to be so later. This is, after all, borne out by the evidence of the history of the editing of the gospels – the fact that scandalous or inadequate statements about Jesus were replaced later by more august pronouncements. The early Church, which was responsible for the New Testament canon – which is therefore an epiphenomenon and irrelevant as far as the meaning of the individual scriptures is concerned – either simply ignored the contradictions or made them harmonize with each other. (This means, in other words, that the contradictions were felt by the early Church to be annoying.)

My point, then, is this – to play these irreconcilable myths off against each other and to attempt to interpret them existentially is clear evidence of a refusal to take the biblical authors themselves seriously. According to the hermeneutical principle followed by Bultmann and his school, an author must be understood better than he has understood himself. To apply this principle here is, in my view, pure cynicism born of an apologe-

53. ibid., p. 23.
54. Braun, *Gesammelte Studien* ..., p. 325.

IRRATIONALITY IN THEOLOGY

tical necessity. It is not without good reason that Franz Overbeck has said that the New Testament needs to be especially protected against the 'malicious and subjective attempts on the part of exegetes on its life'.[55]

2. Bultmann's second reason for interpreting the New Testament existentially is that the process of demythologization was already beginning to take place in the New Testament itself. Paul, he claims, made an initial attempt to demythologize and the unknown author of the fourth gospel carried out a radical demythologization. To what extent is this true?

Bultmann says that 'the decisive step was taken by Paul, who did not see the turning point of the ancient world into the new world in the future, but in the fact that Jesus Christ had come'.[56] He is convinced that the apocalyptic view of the world was in principle overcome by Paul's insistence that the time of salvation had already dawned for the believer with Christ's coming – 'the future was already anticipated here'[57] – because salvation was no longer thought of as supernatural, but as historical.

But this is wrong. To what extent would Paul have wanted to demythologize if he believed that the era of salvation had already begun? As Bultmann himself admits, but deceitfully believes that it is possible to ignore, Paul did not renounce the apocalyptic view of the future at all. He fully expected that a cosmic drama would take place in the near future – that the dead would rise again at the sound of the trumpet, that Christ would descend on a cloud from heaven, that those who believe would fly up on clouds to meet him and that the last judgement would be held (1 Cor. xv; 1 Thess. iv, 13 ff.).

As Franz Overbeck has pointed out emphatically enough in the past and as Ernst Käsemann and his disciple Peter Stuhlmacher have indicated more recently,[58] the whole of Paul's

55. Overbeck, *Christentum und Kultur*, p. 76.
56. Bultmann, *Glauben und Verstehen* IV, p. 154; see also III, p. 89; 'Neues Testament und Mythologie', p. 30.
57. Bultmann, *Glauben und Verstehen* IV, p. 155.
58. Overbeck, *Christentum und Kultur*, p. 53 ff.; Käsemann, *Exegetische Versuche und Besinnungen* II, pp. 23 f., 125 ff., 192 f., 244 ff., Stuhlmacher, p. 203 *ff*.

thinking was shot through with his expectation of the impending end of the world. All his most important theological ideas were determined by this expectation. Even his hasty missionary journeys had an apocalyptical motivation – he wanted to win as many converts as possible to the gospel as quickly as possible, before the second coming of the Lord.

As Overbeck has observed, 'No one who thinks that he is able to share Paul's view has ever really understood him properly. Even those who are opposed to this affirmation involuntarily testify to its truth by the manner in which they distort what he has said in order to make it palatable.'[59] By dismissing considerable parts of Paul's letters as irrelevant, Bultmann is also guilty of cutting the apostle down to his own measure.

Very much the same thing applies to Bultmann's favourite gospel, John's gospel. 'Whereas Paul ... concentrated on the expectation of Christ's coming and the end of this world, John did not emphasize them and insisted on the idea of the present life as given by Jesus himself. For him, Jesus' [first] coming was already a judgement on the world and this judgement was at the same time a separation.' In another article, Bultmann has said, 'For John, Jesus' resurrection, Pentecost and Jesus' *parousia* are one single event and those who already believe have eternal life now.'[60] A neat way of making the ancient cosmological view historical.

As in the case of Paul, so too in the case of the fourth gospel: it is clearly wrong to talk about a New Testament model of demythologization here. Even if it were possible to agree with Bultmann and to explain the existing apocalyptic aspects of John's gospel as elements that were introduced by later editors in the Church in order to achieve harmony in the text, it cannot be denied that the view of the gospel is still mythological. All that the fourth gospel has done is to replace Jewish mythology by gnostic mythology – as Bultmann himself admits, but later chooses to ignore. John fully expected 'that the souls of those who had been saved would gradually rise up, after death, to the

59. Overbeck, *Christentum und Kultur*, p. 54.
60. Bultmann, *Glauben und Verstehen* III, p. 89; IV, p. 155.

IRRATIONALITY IN THEOLOGY

world of light, until this earth eventually became engulfed in darkness and chaos'.[61]

The absurdity of regarding an exchange of elements, which are themselves interchangeable because they are irrational, as the beginning of a process of demythologization within the New Testament itself also emerges in the light of the following consideration.

What is, of course, quite certain is that the New Testament does not only contain mythology, at least if the historical existence of the man Jesus is more probable than his non-existence. But – and every 'but' is important, as all conservative dogmatic theologians and several critical exegetes realize – this real man was at once mythologized and it was only as such that he was important to the authors of the New Testament. Primitive Christianity simply did not recognize a historical Jesus. All that the very early Christians knew was a mythical Christ figure who appeared on earth working miracles. Everything that Paul and John said about Jesus is based on the implicit or explicit assumption that this was the eternal and pre-existent son of God who was, as such, sinless. Christ – the Christ of Paul and John – was not a human individual, but a *macroanthropos*, a heavenly being of cosmic proportions who assumed a human form only temporarily, for a short period while he was on earth. History and myth are not simply 'curiously interwoven' here, as Bultmann has said – they are *inseparably* interlaced with each other.

Primitive Christianity is tied to the ancient world by a thousand threads. The New Testament is tied to Judaism and Hellenism by a thousand threads. As he has himself, rather surprisingly, admitted, Bultmann cuts through them all. Even for the great demythologizer, the Bible has, as it were, 'come down from heaven', and its 'origin, which has to be fathomed historically and critically, obviously does not concern him at this moment'.[62]

It is possible, however, to verify the fact that the early Christian authors really meant what they said by considering the myth of

61. ibid., III, p. 83.   62. ibid., I, p. 100.

Jesus' resurrection from the dead, which is the central myth of the New Testament, simply because they themselves – very fortunately – defended their view strenuously against those who tended to understand the resurrection in the way that Bultmann later recommended. Bultmann, of course, reduced the 'Easter event' to 'visionary experiences' on the part of the disciples, experiences which could be explained historically in the light of the disciples' close personal association with Jesus during his life on earth.[63]

This result of critical research is not disputed by Bultmann, because, as he says, what is said in the New Testament about the resurrection does not in any way imply a second fact in addition to the fact of the crucifixion, but *'faith in the resurrection is nothing more than faith in the crucifixion as a saving event'*.[64]

Did the early Christians really believe this and intend this to be believed by others? I think not. As I have said above, Jesus' resurrection from the dead is defended in the whole of the New Testament against Jewish and gnostic attacks and the view that is so vigorously defended is precisely that which Bultmann rejects. The crucifixion of Jesus only acquires its saving character from the resurrection and the resurrection is regarded *everywhere* in the New Testament as a historical fact to which eyewitnesses bear authentic testimony. Even Bultmann has never disputed that the realistic accounts of the Easter event in the gospels (with the exception, Bultmann claims without much reason, of the gospel of John) maintain this view of the resurrection. Even Paul, the pope of the New Testament, appealed to a great number of witnesses who had seen the risen Lord and could be asked about it afterwards. He stressed too that he had received this list of witnesses from the apostles in Jerusalem (1 Cor. xv, 3–8).

Bultmann, however, criticizes Paul destructively by calling his argument, which was supported by witnesses who were alive and could be questioned, theologically 'fatal'.[65] But it is not fatal to

63. Bultmann, 'Neues Testament und Mythologie', p. 47.
64. ibid., p. 46; author's italics.
65. ibid., pp. 45, 130.

IRRATIONALITY IN THEOLOGY

Paul's, but to Bultmann's argument, because this is further clear evidence of the way in which the meaning of history is corrupted by apologetical interests. The intellectual scruples of Bultmann, which are largely based on existentialism, are completely alien to the predominantly mythological thinking of the apostle to the gentiles. As Wilhelm Kamlah has said, quite penetratingly in my opinion, there is something

> dangerous in saying, quite simply, that we are now able to understand what Paul 'really meant' by, for example, the resurrection. For, as a man whose thinking was mythical, he had no difficulty in thinking about the bodily resurrection of the Lord and of all the dead as if he 'really meant' all this.... We tend to underestimate the difficulties inherent in our own situation if we recognize the mythical structure of primitive Christian thought on the one hand, but also believe, on the other, that Paul 'really' did and 'meant' what we do and mean now.[66]

3. Bultmann's third argument is, in a nutshell, that the 'essence of the myth' itself demands that it should be demythologized. 'The real meaning of the myth is not to provide an objective image of the world. The myth rather expresses man's understanding of himself in his world.'[67] Bultmann is therefore insinuating that the authors of the New Testament were incapable of saying what they really wanted to say. The myths that they used did not adequately serve the real purpose of the New Testament authors and consequently have to be corrected. Although they talked about a 'transcendent power', they did so 'in an inadequate way', by imagining 'the hereafter to be what is distant in space, as heaven above the earth and as hell below it'.[68] A reality which cannot be made objective is thus objectivized.

But Bultmann's reasoning is at fault in two ways here. How can he know the meaning of the reality of the mythology of the Bible if not from the very myths themselves? Yet, as I have

---

66. Kamlah, *Christentum und Geschichtlichkeit*, p. 346.
67. Bultmann, 'Neues Testament und Mythologie', p. 22.
68. Bultmann, 'Zum Problem der Entmythologisierung', p. 183.

shown and as Bultmann himself has admitted, he does not take the myths themselves seriously, but denounces them as irrelevant. Above all, how can he know that any reality at all underlies the mythology of the New Testament after having destroyed its 'objective conceptual content' by rational argument? In boldly asserting that 'myths give an immanent worldly objectivity to the transcendent reality and mythology objectivizes the hereafter into this worldliness',[69] he is making a naïve and unfounded presupposition that there is in fact such a reality.

He admits, however, to this fallacious twofold argument – which he mistakenly accepts as already proved when it is not – in a passage in which he has written about his own programme of demythologization: 'It is *assumed* here that the myth speaks of a reality, but not in an adequate manner. A certain understanding of that reality is similarly *assumed*.'[70]

By concocting the mythology of the New Testament in advance according to his own theological recipe, which is based on his prejudice against objectivization, Bultmann has succeeded in warming up the older allegorical method of interpretation which Philo applied to the Old Testament and Origen adopted for Christianity. This allegorical method is based on the idea that a god – or God – communicates with man in profound riddles and oracles, with the result that everything spoken by the deity must mean something different from what it says literally, in other words, that the obvious, literal meaning conceals a deeper, mysterious meaning. Bultmann quite clearly believes that the New Testament statements have a double meaning, because he has affirmed that 'the mythological statements as a whole contain a deeper meaning which is hidden under the cover of mythology'.[71]

The existential allegorical method allows Bultmann to follow his critical bent and to deny the conceptual content of the New Testament myths on the one hand and, on the other, to claim the authority of the Bible for his own personal 'existentialist'

69. Bultmann, *Glauben und Verstehen* IV, p. 146.
70. ibid., IV, p. 128; my italics.
71. ibid., IV, p. 145 f.

IRRATIONALITY IN THEOLOGY

philosophy. This constant sacrilege committed against the biblical texts is, of course, not something of which only Bultmann is guilty – it is the essential stock-in-trade of all theologians.

The vice was, moreover, already practised in the Old Testament itself. As the history of the handing down of the historical and prophetic books of the Old Testament shows, later editors often changed the traditional words of the texts to suit their own wishes and needs and even altered the original passages to mean exactly the opposite. Let me give an example of this. The historical prophet Isaiah uttered his oracle against the Egyptians and prophesied their downfall (Isa. xviii, 1–6). This negative meaning was not acceptable, however, to a later editor, who simply added another verse to this oracle (Isa. xviii, 7) and the threat became a blessing. In the present version, the Egyptians bring their gifts to Yahweh on Mount Zion. Gerhard von Rad, professor in Old Testament studies at Heidelberg University, has justified such distortions by attributing them to 'an authentic power which is conscious of its authority to change the ancient message if necessary in different historical circumstances'.[72]

Very much the same was done by the authors of the New Testament. In order to prove that Jesus was the promised Messiah, they gave a completely new interpretation to Old Testament texts, without regard for the context or the meaning of the words, and related them directly to Jesus. For example, in order to prove the virgin birth of Jesus, Matthew appealed (Matt. i, 23) to the words of the prophet Isaiah who had said to King Ahaz (Isa. vii, 14): 'Therefore Yahweh himself will give you a sign. Behold, a young woman shall conceive and bear a son, and shall call his name Immanuel'. Although the historical understanding of this verse has been widely disputed among Old Testament scholars, two things are quite certain. Firstly, Isaiah was speaking of a young woman and Matthew of a virgin. The two words were clearly distinguished both in the Greek and in the Hebrew. Secondly, if Isaiah was proclaiming that a sign would be given to King Ahaz, as the text says, then this sign, if

72. Rad, *Theologie des Alten Testaments* II, p. 59.

it were to be at all meaningful, would have to be given while Ahaz was still living. It does therefore look as though the Matthaean idea of a prophecy that was to be fulfilled several centuries later was quite arbitrary.

It would seem that theologians of every period of time are compelled to traffic in mysteries and to cheat themselves and others either cunningly or clumsily. The reason for their chronic misery is not difficult to find. Instead of using their own intelligence and making an independent analysis of the situation, they always rely on the authoritative tradition of the past – 'revelation'. Since this tradition of the past is regarded as in some way normative, it can usually only be adapted to the needs of the present with the help of 'hermeneutical' tricks of various kinds. In this way, theologians lose both the real past and the real present.

THE RESULT (EXPRESSED IN A FRIENDLY WAY): MUCH ADO ABOUT NOTHING

Theologians who, in one way or another, go in for demythologization and the new hermeneutics think of themselves as being very modern indeed. If they quote from Nietzsche, referring to his 'madman', or from Jean Paul's 'The Dead Christ's Speech from the Cosmic System that there is no God'[73] and flirt with atheism, they really imagine that they have their finger on the pulse of the modern age. It is true, of course, that Ebeling made an accurate diagnosis of the situation when he said that atheism 'does not threaten Christians purely from the outside, but has already to a certain extent penetrated into our inmost being through the walls of our hearts like something atmospherical, the influence of which no one can escape'.[74] But as soon as he tries to deprive this atheism, with its atmospheric influence, of its power by explaining it away as a part of

---

73. See, for example, Bornkamm, *Gesammelte Aufsätze* II, p. 245 ff. (Jean Paul); Ebeling, *Das Wesen* . . ., p. 93 ff. (Nietzsche).
74. Ebeling, *Wort und Glaube*, p. 360.

IRRATIONALITY IN THEOLOGY

the Christian teaching about God – what he calls the doctrine of the hidden God[75] – then one is bound to recognize this as pure dreaming beside hermeneutical fireplaces.

The illusions of modern theologians about their real situation are the direct consequence of their faulty vision. They engage in debate, it is true, but almost always exclusively with members of their own profession. Compared with the views of an archreactionary like Walter Künneth, of course, what 'modern' theologians such as Tillich, Braun, Buri, Ebeling and Moltmann are saying and doing at least gives the impression of being in touch with the needs and problems of the present. This impression is further reinforced – and the mind is further confused – by their frequent references to the philosophies of such men as Martin Heidegger, whose mythology of being, it is claimed, embodies all modern thinking.

But what are the factors which make even the demythologized scandal of faith unacceptable to contemporary man?

1. The theology of the demythologizers is no less irrational and no less authoritarian than the theology practised throughout history. It too seeks refuge in a blind commitment which defies rational verification. Its replacement of the word 'God' by other, supposedly more serviceable, concepts such as being, love, fellow-humanity and 'that which concerns us unconditionally' is simply naïve. All that this does is to repress and displace religiosity. The very idea of God and all its substitutes must be given up completely. It is only then that the 'autonomy of contemporary man' will become something more than mere talk.

2. The modern theologians, without exception, have nothing new at all to offer the best representatives of atheistic humanism. As Walter Kaufmann has so shrewdly observed, their method is that of 'conversion by definition'.[76]

Herbert Braun, for example, has defined God as a 'special kind of fellow-humanity'. He does not simply echo the first epistle of John and say 'God is love', but turns this formula the

---

75. As Ebeling did in his lecture on the doctrine of God ('Gotteslehre') in 1964 in Zürich; see also his essay 'Existenz zwischen Gott und Gott'.
76. Kaufmann, *Der Glaube eines Ketzers*, p. 104.

other way round and says 'Love is God'. After having humanized 'God' in this way, he begins to regard 'the atheistic position' as 'irrelevant'. Like so many other theologians, he cannot imagine that it is possible to think differently and asks artlessly: 'Is there really such a thing as an atheist?' After all, Braun believes that 'man as man, man in his fellow-humanity, implies God'.[77]

Long before Herbert Braun, Paul Tillich had enrolled all suitable non-Christians in the past and the present as Christian believers. His conception of the 'latent Church', as opposed to the 'manifest Church', had only one purpose. That was to claim all the really significant ethical and cultural values and achievements of mankind for Christianity, and especially for Protestant Christianity. He made every effort to persuade suitable non-Christians that they were basically Christians, but they would not admit it.

This most brazen form of claiming everything for Christianity is, of course, not new. The apologists of the early Church used the same technique as early as the second century. A typical example is the doctrine of the *Logos spermatikos*, that of the germinal truth. According to this teaching, the divine *Logos* was expressed not only in the words of the Old Testament patriarchs and prophets, but also in the writings of the ancient Greeks, Indians, Persians and Egyptians. The divine truth was, of course, definitively and fully revealed only in Christ, but it was also germinally prefigured in the civilizations of the non-Christian world This is why Justin, the Church Father, was able to call Socrates and Heraclitus Christians. Justin's motto was: 'Everything true that has ever been said is Christian' (*Apologies*, II, 13).

Just as MacIntyre conceded to Tillich a 'verbal triumph over the atheists',[78] Helmut Gollwitzer has also pointed to the practical weaknesses of Braun's position, calling his a Pyrrhic victory. Gollwitzer makes an atheist come forward and ask Braun why

77. Braun, *Gesammelte Studien*..., pp. 341, 298; *Post Bultmann Locutum* I, p. 31 f.; 'Gottes Existenz...', p. 408.
78. MacIntyre, 'Gott und die Theologen', p. 68.

he, Braun, 'does not want to be converted to his way, that is, the atheistic way of expressing himself, as the much more honest and contemporary way', since, Gollwitzer concludes, 'what is involved now is clearly no longer a difference between ways of expressing things'.[79]

Is this really the case? Ought I, then, to affirm that Braun is a latent atheist and that I am a manifest atheist? Apart from the fact that I should prefer to leave the enrolment of members, manifest or latent, to Christians, I feel bound to ask one question – to what extent is Herbert Braun an atheist? The different way of speaking does not simply come about by chance. Braun's thinking also reveals the theologian's characteristic adherence to authority and is therefore fundamentally different from the enlightened atheism that I advocate. One of the 'religious and philosophical assertions' which Braun calls for is, for example, 'the simple fact that man needs the New Testament'.[80] Like all theologians, Braun gives the maximum content to all his statements and in this way surrounds the reality of man with mystification. He conjures up the Christian faith as 'the unrepeatable, unique event and irrepressible insistence of my being addressed, demanded and held in the sense of final validity'.[81]

3. Several modern theologians, including especially Paul Tillich, Fritz Buri and Dorothee Sölle, interpret the biblical mythology symbolically. Apart from the individual differences between their theories, the mythology of the Bible is, for them,

the powerful symbolic expression of man's understanding of his own existence. ... How could we speak about the last things without myths? We should be a poor race of men if this symbolic world were lost to us. We have therefore to be concerned not only with the right interpretation of the biblical myths, but also with their tradition. If it is freed from false claims, the Christian mythology can be of service to us as the expression of man's existential understanding of himself, which is what it really is, and thus bear its own witness to us and

79. Gollwitzer, *Die Existenz Gottes* ..., p. 73, 75.
80. Braun, *Post Bultmann Locutum* I, p. 35.
81. Braun, *Gesammelte Studien*, p. 339.

continue to bear witness through our exegesis. The task and the significance of preaching and worship are characterized by this.[82]

There are several reasons why I am not convinced by this romantic aestheticism:

1. According to the intention of the biblical authors, the myths of the Bible were not symbols. In condemning a literalistic misunderstanding of the biblical mythology – 'this symbolic material is not meant in its real, literal sense'[83] – Tillich is doing as much violence to the mythology of the Bible as Bultmann does with his existential interpretation. Both Tillich and Bultmann disdain to understand the Bible and prefer to interpret it.

2. The biblical mythology has been extinct for a long time now, as the theologians whom I have mentioned shamefully admit by their use of the concept of the 'need for interpretation' which in this context, means breathing the breath of their own life into dead texts. To quote Theodor Adorno:

Now that the existential trifles have been removed from the scene, we are left with the recommendation of religious customs devoid of all religious content. As objects of folk-lore, cultic forms are like empty husks, outlasting the mystery that they once contained. This situation has, however, not been realized, but defended with the help of jargon.[84]

3. As Bartley and Kaufmann have already shown in some detail,[85] Tillich's symbolic interpretation cannot be upheld. Tillich calls the cross of Christ the perfect and objectively true symbol, because it does not make itself into an absolute value, but always refers, self-critically, to something higher. It suitably expresses the unconditional character of the unconditional and at the same time resists being made into a fetish. For this reason, it is true to say that 'Every affirmation of Jesus as the Christ

82. Buri, 'Entmythologisierung . . .', p. 99.
83. Tillich, *Symbol und Wirklichkeit*, p. 4.
84. Adorno, *Jargon der Eigentlichkeit*, p. 24.
85. Kaufmann, *Der Glaube eines Ketzers*, pp. 136–139; Bartley, *The Retreat to Commitment*.

IRRATIONALITY IN THEOLOGY

which does not at the same time include an affirmation of Jesus as the crucified one, is a form of idolatry. The ultimate concern of the Christian is not Jesus, but Christ in Jesus the crucified one.'[86]

The truth of the fascist ideology can also – as Bartley and Kaufmann have also shown – be quite easily proved with the help of these formal criteria. The Führer regarded himself as the instrument of divine providence and sacrificed everything that was in him – including, at the end, himself – to the one absolutely valid aim. By using every possible means to convince the people that the good of the community was more important than the welfare of the individual, he encouraged them to sacrifice their own conditional and finite desires in favour of the unconditional whole. Finally, his soldiers, the men who killed and were killed under the symbol of the swastika, did not, unfortunately, think of exchanging the symbol for the unconditional value to which it referred.

The final conclusion can only be this – the modern theology based on interpreting the Bible existentially and symbolically is not modern and is completely worn out. What really arouses my anger and scandalizes me deeply is that so much of university theology has tried to justify its existence for more than two hundred years by means of apologetic tricks of this kind. Ever since the beginning of the Enlightenment, theologians have tried again and again to reconcile rational thought with the mythology of the Bible. Schleiermacher, for example, in his 'Speeches about Religion to the Educated who Despise it', which he published anonymously in 1799, admitted that 'God and immortality disappeared from the sight of those who doubted' at a very early stage.[87] Instead of coming to an honest conclusion about this, however, he made use of the usual theological sophistry and thus became a leading Father of the nineteenth-century Church.

The strange pride that many Protestants take in the history of

86. Tillich, *Wesen und Wandel des Glaubens*, p. 113 f.
87. Schleiermacher, *Über die Religion*, p. 8.

theology over the past two centuries is not only misplaced – it is also quite ridiculous. Tillich has written:

> It was an expression of Protestant courage when theologians subjected the holy writings of their own church to a critical analysis through the historical method. It appears that no other religion in human history exercised such boldness and took upon itself the same risk. Certainly Islam, orthodox Judaism, and Roman Catholicism did not do so. This courage received its reward, in that Protestantism was able to join the general historical consciousness and was not forced into an isolated and narrow spiritual world without influence in the creative development of spiritual life. Protestantism (except in its fundamentalistic groups) was not driven into that unconscious dishonesty wherein the results of historical research are rejected on the basis of dogmatic prejudice, not on the basis of evidence. ... It became more and more manifest that the Christian assertion that Jesus is the Christ does not contradict the most uncompromising historical honesty.[88]

But among precisely which theologians has this conviction really increased? Those who were quite uncompromisingly historical in their thinking, such as David Friedrich Strauss, the brothers Edgar and Bruno Bauer and Franz Overbeck, eventually renounced faith. The others, who have remained faithful to their profession, have not been quite so uncompromisingly honest, but have read their own ideals into the Bible, as Albert Schweitzer's famous *Geschichte der Leben-Jesu-Forschung* has shown.

But how significant are these later phenomena in comparison with the little known but disturbing fact that almost the whole of the recent destructive historical criticism of the Bible was already anticipated in later classical antiquity by such opponents of Christianity as Porphyry, Celsus and Julian?

The Protestant theologian Adolf von Harnack (d. 1930) had this to say about the fifteen books which Porphyry wrote 'Against the Christians':

---

88. Tillich, *Systematic Theology* II, p. 124

IRRATIONALITY IN THEOLOGY

It is perhaps the richest and most thorough work that has ever been written against Christianity ... *the conflict between the philosophy of religion and Christianity is still taking place today in the sphere where Porphyry placed it, and even today Porphyry has not been refuted.*[89]

One or two illustrations may bring this more vividly to life. Modern biblical criticism has shown that most of the supposed prophecies in the Bible are in fact *vaticinia ex eventu*, that is, 'prophecies' which were not formulated until after the event and which were then given an authority of the past so that the event which had already taken place might be (divinely) justified. Porphyry exposed this fact when he wrote that the Old Testament prophets had 'said nothing about the future, but had simply given an account of the past' – '*non ... futura dixisse, sed narrasse praeterita*'.[90] Porphyry's example in this case was the book of Daniel, which was, it was claimed, written by a prophet called Daniel during the Babylonian exile in the sixth century before Christ, and which, it was believed, foretold the history of the world. In fact, it was written round about the year 165 B.C. at the time of the Maccabean battles, with the aim of consoling the persecuted believers by deluding them into thinking that their martyrdom had been prophesied.

What Porphyry had to say about the New Testament is no less lacking in contemporary interest.[91] He called the evangelists, for example, 'inventors, not narrators' of the events. (I have already discussed this phenomenon, which is well known in modern form criticism, in the section on 'The Impossibility of Knowing the Historical Jesus', as those sayings of Jesus which were invented by the primitive Christian community.) Porphyry was quite perspicacious enough to recognize the inconsistencies in Matthew's and Luke's accounts of Jesus' birth and childhood and the many contradictions in the four accounts of

---

89. Harnack, *Die Mission und Ausbreitung des Christentums*..., p. 353; author's italics.

90. Porphyry, *Fragment* 43, lines 14 f.; Harnack, *Porphyrius*, p. 67.

91. The following quotations from Porphyry: *Fragment* 15, line 1; *Fragments* 11 and 12; *Fragment* 15, line 19; *Fragment* 16, line 1; *Fragment* 15, line 20 f.; *Fragment* 64, line 15; see Harnack, pp. 49 ff., 85.

the Passion were sufficient proof for him that they were legendary. The New Testament authors might have guessed everything or they might have inferred everything from the Old Testament. If, however, they were not even able to give a truthful account of the death of Jesus, then their other narratives were obviously unreliable. Porphyry concluded from the insoluble contradictions of the different accounts of the resurrection that Christians were here too 'telling myths'.

It is obvious, then, that Porphyry was arguing historically, not dogmatically. He disputed the resurrection of Jesus, not on the basis of some 'irreligious' prejudice, but because he regarded the sources as unreliable. Unfortunately, space prevents me from quoting examples of Porphyry's criticism of other parts of the New Testament or from giving any examples at all of Celsus's or Julian's equally up-to-date and destructive polemics against Christianity. The philologist Wilhelm Nestle gave a good, critical account of them, with numerous examples, in his excellent article on the principal objections raised by classical Greek thinkers to Christianity ('Die Haupteinwände des antiken Denkens gegen das Christentum').

It is therefore hardly surprising that these works, which were so destructive to Christianity, were banished by the early Church as soon as it became established as the state Church. The last copies of Porphyry's books were burnt in 448 during the reign of Theodosius II – and, what is more, not only the books themselves were burnt, but also their Christian 'refutations', because they contained too many original quotations!

It is also hardly surprising that modern theologians maintain a solid silence where these ancient authors are concerned. Their names are not mentioned at all, let alone their criticism of Christianity, anywhere in the six hundred pages of Professor Werner Georg Kümmel's history of historical research into the New Testament (*Das Neue Testament. Geschichte der Erforschung seiner Probleme*). According to Kümmel, 'there can be no question of any historical consideration of primitive Christianity ... before the Enlightenment'.[92] Porphyry is also completely

92. Kümmel, *Einleitung in das Neue Testament*, p. 3.

ignored in Professor Hans-Joachim Kraus's parallel history of historical and critical research into the Old Testament (*Geschichte der historisch-kritischen Erforschung des Alten Testaments von der Reformation bis zur Gegenwart*).

3

Post-Christian Perspectives – Religious Freedom

THE problems which Christianity has never succeeded in solving and could, in fact, never solve can only be overcome in an emancipated society, that is, a society which has as its conscious aim the greatest happiness of all its members.

One aspect of society's coming of age will be discussed in this chapter – religious freedom. In considering this question, we can at least get a partial glimpse of what a really human society might look like.

The Concept of Religious Freedom

The human right of religious freedom or freedom of worship implies firstly, freedom from coercion, secondly, equality and thirdly, the guarantee of individual freedom.

In the first place, this means the abolition in principle of what has been practised throughout the history of man – that more powerful people should force their less powerful fellows to submit to their will. As far as religious and philosophical views are concerned, this implies that every human being may confess whatever faith he himself believes to be right or have no religion at all, if this seems to him to be right. He can praise or deny God as he wishes and can do this even if it is contrary to the convictions of the overwhelming majority of his fellow-men. Freedom from religious coercion means, in other words, that the otherwise democratic principle of the majority is not applicable in the case of religion.

In order to eliminate the possibility of even more refined methods of imposing one's will on others from operating, the second category of religious freedom lays down that no privilege or disadvantage of any kind may be attached to open profession of a certain faith or to the profession of no faith at all. This is the only guarantee of the principle of equal rights for all men.

The third and last aspect of religious freedom is the so-called negative freedom, the right of the individual to preserve complete silence about his religious or a-religious views. This is necessary in order to protect the individual in that sphere of his intimate life which is constantly exposed to the danger of manipulation under the present conditions of human society.

The inevitable outcome of democracy in practice is that the principle of democracy should also be expressed in the institutional and ideological separation of the organization of the state from all religious or a-religious groups. It is only if the state maintains strict neutrality and absolute equality with regard to all religious and philosophical views that there can be any guarantee that there will be religious freedom in the state and that the state will serve all its members equally.

These principles have already been laid down, at least partly, in the Constitution of the Federal Republic of West Germany. The court responsible for the Federal Constitution decided recently (14 December 1965) on the following complex of questions:

> By Art. 4 I, Art. 3 III, Art. 33 III GG [Bonn Constitutional Law] as well as by Art. 136 I and IV and Art. 137 I WRV [Weimar Constitution] in connection with Art. 140 GG [Bonn Constitution], the Constitution imposes on the state, as the domicile of all citizens without respect of persons, philosophical and religious neutrality. It forbids the introduction of legal forms leading to the establishment of any state church and the extension of any privileges to particular religious confessions. . . . It follows from this duty to observe religious and confessional neutrality that . . .[1]

Let me quote the articles of the Constitution mentioned in the above passage.

Art. 4 I: Freedom of faith, freedom of conscience and freedom of religious and philosophical confession are inviolable.

---

1. Quoted from Fischer in *Vorgänge*, 1966, p. 1.

Art. 3 III: No one may be discriminated against or privileged because of his sex, his birth, his race, his language, his country of origin, his faith or his religious or philosophical views.

Art. 33 III: The enjoyment of civil and civic rights, admission to public offices and the enjoyment of rights acquired in public service are independent of religious confession. No disadvantage may accrue to anyone because of his membership or non-membership of any religious confession or of any philosophical group.

The articles of the Weimar Constitution, which have been incorporated into the Bonn Constitution by Art. 140 GG of the Bonn Constitution, are as follows:

Art. 136 I: Civil and civic rights and duties are neither conditioned nor limited by the exercise of religious freedom.

Art. 136 IV: No one may be compelled to take part in an action, ceremony or practice of any church or to take any form of religious oath.

Art. 137 I: There is no state church.

An important article, which is not mentioned in the statement by the court responsible for the Constitution which I have quoted above, is Art. 136 III WRV (Weimar Constitution), which guarantees the so-called negative religious freedom: 'No one is obliged to reveal his religious convictions. The authorities have the right to inquire about membership of a religious community only insofar as rights or duties are dependent on this or as a legally instituted statistical survey requires it.'

These clear democratic principles have not yet been fully realized in practice in the Federal Republic of West Germany and the reasons for this are not only contradictions within the Constitution itself, but also laws and practices that are contrary to the Constitution.

The state certainly acts against the ideas of religious and philosophical neutrality and equality expressed in the Constitution by according a number of privileges to certain religious communities, especially the two largest churches. Let me give one notorious example of this.

The apparently democratic argument which is always used to

justify the reduction of non-Christians to an inferior social group is that ninety-seven per cent of the population of West Germany belong to one or other of the Christian churches. This is only apparently democratic because basic human rights cannot ever be measured arithmetically according to 'majorities' and they are there mainly in order to protect the minority. A further reason is that this 'democratic' argument that ninety-seven per cent of the population is Christian is based on an infringement of religious freedom which is normally suppressed because it is so scandalous. It is based, in other words, on the fact of infant baptism.

To what extent is infant baptism contrary to the Constitution? What happens when a child is baptized? A person, not an adult, but a mere child – and human rights apply to every person without regard to his age – is compelled, without being asked whether he consents or not, to take part in a religious action. Even worse than this, he is made, without his consent, the object of a religious act performed by others.

However insignificant the external act may be – at the request of the Christian parents, a religious functionary sprinkles water on a baby's head while reciting religious formulae – the conviction of the person performing the act, what is expressed in the act itself and the legal consequences of that act for the baptized person are very important indeed. According to the opinion of the overwhelming majority of theologians and practising priests and pastors, baptism establishes an indissoluble relationship between God and the baptized child. God calls the child by his name, the Protestant service says, and claims him for his own. Baptism is an irrevocable act of God's grace. The baptized person is imprinted with an indelible seal, so that, according to Catholic canon law – which is, of course, not valid according to civil law – he can never leave the Church. Even though they are less unanimous in their opinions about the impossibility of leaving the Church after baptism, Protestant theologians do not hold a radically different view.

What, then, happens when a child is baptized? People presume to coerce another person into accepting a religious ideology irrevocably for the rest of his life without asking him whether he consents or not – and in this case the act of coercion is all the worse because the victim is a defenceless child. One is inevitably reminded of the Christian Middle Ages and the Church's practice of keeping slaves, who were regarded as belonging to the Church and to God for the whole of their lives, as inalienable property which could not be disposed of by men.

What are the legal consequences of the act of infant baptism? The situation is *de facto* still the same as it was according to the system of the Peace of Augsburg of 1555, which reaffirmed the centuries-old practice that the sovereign ruler of a country should determine the religion of his subjects (*cuius regio, eius religio*) and which also introduced the liberal measure that subjects whose faith was different from that of their prince could emigrate (*privilegium emigrandi*). Nowadays, of course, people are not made Protestants or Catholics as subjects of their sovereign rulers, but as subjects of their parents. In other words, the situation is that of *cuius generatio, eius religio*. There is now, however, evidence of a certain nobility and freedom in that they can always, in accordance with civil law, leave the Church afterwards.

It is, of course, always possible to refer to the law of 1921 concerning the religious education of children in Germany, which is still valid, in an attempt to justify infant baptism.[2] This law lays down that the child comes of age in the religious sense at the age of fourteen and that, until that age, the parents are to exercise their 'parental right' and determine the child's religious education. My fundamental objection to the use of this law to vindicate infant baptism is that it is one of those legal formulations which is contradictory to the constitutional law. Such laws are null and void since the constitutional laws are binding on the 'legislature, the executive and the administration as directly valid law' (Bonn Constitution 1 III). But, quite apart from this, the German law concerning the religious education of children cannot, in my opinion, be quoted in justification of infant bap-

2. The text will be found in Fischer, *Trennung von Staat und Kirche*, p. 323 f.

tism, because, even though a child does not come of age in the religious sense until he is fourteen years old, this does not mean that he does not possess, until he is fourteen, the inalienable human right to religious freedom. This basic human right cannot, however, be adequately expressed while the child is still so young, which is why those who have the legal right and duty to educate the child – in other words, the parents – have to vindicate their right. In any case, the much vaunted right of the parents reaches the limit beyond which it cannot go when it encounters the human right of the child to religious freedom. This basic human right precludes not only the baptism of infants, but also all one-sided religious – or, for that matter, a-religious – indoctrination on the part of the parents.

The Separation of State and Churches

One of the most important privileges enjoyed by the two largest Christian Churches and several other smaller religious communities in West Germany is the right to have taxes collected from their members by the state department of inland revenue. The state places at the disposal of all religious communities which are statutorily recognized as 'public bodies' the lists of all those who are liable to pay taxes, and automatically deducts the church tax together with income tax from their earnings. This church tax is the most important source of revenue for the various religious communities. The two largest Christian 'public bodies', the Evangelical Church and the Roman Catholic Church, together receive more than 2 milliard DM each year from church taxes. This privilege is, of course, guaranteed by the West German Constitution (Art. 137 WRV of the Weimar Constitution in connection with Art. 140 GG of the Bonn Constitution), but it is in flagrant contradiction to the basic human right to religious freedom, in that the state is thereby violating its own principle of religious and philosophical impartiality and equality. It is fundamentally undemocratic even to call religious communities or churches 'public bodies'. In a democracy, religious or philosophical groups can only be organized privately, in civil law, as societies or associations.

This church tax is scandalous enough, but it does, after all, usually affect only those who belong to the churches concerned, in that the churches call on the power of the 'secular arm' to make their members pay up. Another example of close cooperation in Germany between the state and the Churches which is, in my opinion, far more offensive is this: the special disbursements, the so-called 'state disbursements', made to the religious communities. These take the form of gratuitous gifts of money, usually made without any qualification as to how the money is to be used, and payments in kind to various religious communities, which are, naturally enough, almost always the two largest Churches.

According to the published figures[3] of the statistical office of the Federal Republic, these religious communities received 164·579 million DM from the state in 1959. Of this, one hundred and fifty million DM went to the two biggest Churches. The special disbursements made by the federation, the *Länder* and the municipalities are not included in this sum of money. The federal government, for example, gave the Evangelical and the Roman Catholic Churches eighty-three million DM from the state fund for development help in 1962.[4]

According to the analysis published by the canon lawyer, Werner Weber, the disbursements to the Churches can be classified as follows: '(a) expenditure on the maintenance of Church order (episcopal sees and institutions, cathedral chapters, high consistories, local Church offices and superintendents etc.); (b) expenditure on education and the care and payment of the clergy; (c) the upkeep of Church buildings in individual cases; (d) disbursements for the maintenance of the clergy and of worship on the basis of special claims, and (e) disbursements from endowment funds under the control of the state. In addition, there are also the indirect disbursements made by the state for the upkeep of university theological faculties, the training of teachers of

3. Figures taken from Fischer, *Vorgänge*, 1963, p. 109 f.
4. Fischer, *Vorgänge*, 1963, p. 129, note 2.

religion, church musicians and canon lawyers, the provision of religious education in the state schools and the maintenance of pastoral care in the armed forces and in various public institutions.'[5]

These privileges are all directly contradictory to the principle of equality and impartiality and result in the reduction of non-Christians to an inferior social status – to say nothing of the hypocrisy practised by the Churches in accepting these taxes and disbursements. They indulge Sunday after Sunday in sermons lamenting and denouncing the rampant nihilism and growing lack of faith in the world, but are not slow to recognize that the children of the world can be made to pay up.

Their attempts to justify these abuses are pathetic. They regard the money they receive as compensation for the secularization of Church property at the time of the Reformation and of the so-called *Reichsdeputationshauptschluss* of Ratisbon (1803–1810). Those princes who had gone over to the Protestant faith in the sixteenth century had at the same time taken over Church property, such as diocesan, monastic and other foundations, which had hitherto belonged to the Roman Catholic Church and, when the reformers intervened, also accepted financial responsibility for the Church in their territories. The *Reichsdeputationshauptschluss* had also given large tracts of the territory on the right bank of the Rhine, including the free cities of the Empire, to the German princes in compensation for their loss of much of the land on the left bank of the river to Napoleon. At the same time it was decreed that the princes should contribute towards the financial support of the Church.

It is almost inconceivable that the Churches should go back a century and a half in one case and four centuries in the other to the political dissolution of anachronistic Church states in order to justify the reception of money in recompense now. Why, in that case, do they not go back even farther into the past and demand money to compensate for the Carolingian secularizations of the eighth and ninth centuries?

But, in any case, the Weimar Constitution had already laid

5. Weber, 'Staatsleistungen an die Kirche', p. 317.

down, in Art. 138 I, that these state disbursements were to be discontinued and this article has been included in the more recent Bonn Constitution. The legal enactments that are necessary if this statement in the Constitution is to be carried out have not yet been prepared, apparently because many politicians do not regard a clear injunction such as this as binding, especially where the religious and political establishment is threatened.

The settlements which the individual *Länder* of the Federal Republic have made with the Churches cannot seriously be called a 'discontinuation' of the state disbursements. In accordance with a settlement concluded in 1955, the *Land* of Lower Saxony pays both the larger Churches 7·7 million DM in subsidies each year to cover clerical remuneration, and this amount is subject to adjustment to meet rising salaries. What is more, both confessions have received a single allowance of 5·5 million DM each. In 1960, Hessen concluded the most generous settlement of all with the Evangelical Church of the *Land*. Under the terms of this treaty, the Protestants are granted each year a total subsidy of 8 million DM, and there is also a clause in the agreement guaranteeing that this sum will be adjusted according to the rise in clerical remuneration.

So that these privileges, which conform so well to the class structure of our society, might be adequately protected, the state and the Churches went a stage further in violating the West German Constitution, and concluded in 1957 an agreement concerning the pastoral care of members of the armed forces. The forces chaplains are *de facto* officially employed and paid by the state, which is entirely responsible for organizing and financing the pastoral care of its citizens doing military service. This open offence against the principle of neutrality is not covered by any exceptive provision in the Constitution.

The Separation of Universities and Churches

The situation is no different with regard to the theological faculties of German universities. Their continued existence is quite contrary to the Constitution. It is true, of course, that their survival was guaranteed under Art. 149 III of the Weimar Constitution. But since this article, unlike other articles dealing with religious questions in the Weimar Constitution (Arts. 136, 137, 138, 139, 141), was not included in the Bonn Constitution, the 'only possible conclusion,' as the constitutional jurist Erwin Fischer has said, 'is that they [the theological faculties] are no longer acceptable because of the absence of a suitable exceptive provision in the Constitution.'[6]

It cannot be logically concluded that there should be theological faculties at the universities because there is a constitutional guarantee of religious instruction in the schools in accordance with Art. 7 III. It has been argued that the theological faculties fulfil the task of training teachers of religion, but this only forms a very small part of their work – most students of theology at the universities enter the priesthood or the pastorate. What is more, the state would, according to Art. 137 III WRV of the Weimar Constitution taken in connection with Art. 140 GG of the Bonn Constitution, be violating the constitutionally guaranteed inner autonomy of the religious communities if it attempted to determine the training of teachers of religion. As a result of this, pastors and teachers of religion are able to teach religion in schools without having been trained as teachers in accordance with the regulations prescribed by the state. In this context, too, it is interesting to note that religious instruction is given in state schools in some *Länder* of the Federal Republic – Hessen and Bavaria, for example – by members of certain free religious groups who certainly have no free religious faculty at any German university.

In the context of this discussion about the theological faculties, the Catholic theologian Karl Rahner put forward this cunning argument:

> If the state does not want to be so 'neutral' towards the religion of its members that this neutrality is really a form of hostility, because it is hostile to present one definite philosophy among others, then it must let the theological faculties at its universities continue to exist. The state will be acting neutrally by granting this possibility to each one

6. Fischer, *Trennung* . . . p. 252.

of the more important 'religions' in the widest sense. If, for example, 'atheistic humanism' were the considered and professed view of a substantial social group within the state, and this view did not simply exhaust its possibilities purely in denying the other religions and therefore did not lack the inner resources for scientific speculation, then the state would have to establish a 'theological faculty of atheistic humanism' at its universities.[7]

This reasoning does not hold water. The neutrality of the state as far as religion and philosophy are concerned is not an arithmetical matter. This haggling about numbers, in which Rahner wants to involve non-Christians as well, is blatantly contrary to the Constitution.[8] According to Art. 3 III, which I have already quoted, *no one*, no single individual, may be discriminated against or privileged because of his religious or philosophical convictions. The fact that basic human rights cannot be measured arithmetically has recently been borne out by the judgment made by the supreme court of Hessen on prayers in state schools.

I have another objection to Rahner's argument. Is the university a fairground where everyone can peddle any article he likes as long as a sufficient number of people are interested in it? At a university, only scientific disciplines have any right to a place. I have already shown how unscientific the Christian theologies are. It goes without saying that all other theologies – including the 'theology' of atheistic humanism – can be no less unscientific as dogmatic structures.

This does not mean, however, that religion as such should not be the object of scientific speculation and research. To say that religion is a private matter which does not concern the state is not quite precise enough. It would be more correct to say that only the individual's religion is a private matter, but that the objective phenomenon of religion as such is not in any sense a private matter which does not concern the state. This is why I believe that the theological faculties as they exist at present should be abolished and replaced by new departments for the

7. Szczesny, *Die Antwort der Religionen . . .*, p. 295.
8. See Fischer, *Trennung . . .*, p. 88 ff.

historical study of comparative religion in the faculties of philosophy.

A really comprehensive department for the scientific study of comparative religion would include at least the following schools: (1) a school of general and systematic comparative religion, with a chair; (2) a school for the study of Christianity with a professor in New Testament studies and a professor responsible for the history of Christianity; (3) a school for the study of Judaism with a professor in Old Testament studies and a professor responsible for the history of Judaism; (4) a school in Islamic studies, with a chair; (5) a school of Asiatic religions with a professor of Buddhism and a professor of Hinduism; (6) a school, with a professor, for the study of the history of the criticism of religion; (7) a school of religious sociology and psychology, with a chair, and (8) a school for educational theory and practice in the teaching of religion, with a chair.

A comprehensive department for the study of comparative religion such as this, situated within the framework of a critical university, would be able to demonstrate how effective and productive interdisciplinary teaching and research could be. There are many ways in which the work of such a department could be interconnected with that of other departments and faculties – for instance, with those of history, archaeology, classics, ethnology, social and cultural anthropology, philosophy and the history of law and the natural sciences.

Who would in the main follow this new course of studies in comparative religion? Firstly, I imagine, those who aimed to become Christian theologians, who would study principally at their own Church institutions, and secondly those who wished to teach religion. It is, after all, extremely important for religious education, which has hitherto been given in the state schools of West Germany according to the teachings of the largest Christian Churches, to be replaced by instruction in comparative religion.

The prospective teacher of comparative religion ought to be given in the first place a thorough grounding in the whole sphere of study provided by the department and then allowed to specialize to some degree according to his own personal religious or anti-religious interests. In any case, he should be given the opportunity to gain a deep insight into Christianity, Judaism and the history of the criticism of religion. Above all, there should be no exclusive emphasis on purely western studies.

The Separation of Schools and Churches

Schooling is another case where undemocratic principles have penetrated very deeply. On the one hand, the state is neutral with regard to religious and philosophical views. On the other, the whole system of primary and secondary education is under state control and all children between the statutory ages are obliged to receive a full-time education. The result of this should therefore be that schools which are neutral in the matter of religion and philosophy should be the norm. In other words, state schools should in principle be undenominational schools.

There are, however, within the West German educational system frequent infringements of this basic principle. Let me give only one instance. The Constitution of the *Land* Hessen, Art. 56 II, states: 'In all schools in Hessen, the children of all religious denominations and all philosophies are, as a rule, educated in common [in undenominational schools]'.[9] But in the legal agreement which the *Land* Hessen concluded with the Evangelical Church of the *Land* on 10 June 1960, there is an article (15 I) which states quite clearly: 'The public schools are undenominational schools on a Christian basis'.[10]

This blatant infringement of the Constitution has been confirmed by the judgment made by the supreme court of Hessen on school prayers: 'The Constitution of Hessen offers no support for the assumption that the schools of Hessen are undenominational schools'.[11]

It is clear, then, that many of the States' governments and Church leaders in the Federal Republic are quite indifferent to

9. Quoted from Fischer, *Trennung* . . ., p. 331.
10. Quoted from the official *Gesetz- und Verordnungsblatt für das Land Hessen*, 57.
11. Quoted from Fischer, *Vorgänge*, 1965, p. 483.

basic democratic principles. Surely it goes without saying that undenominational state schools cannot be founded either on a Christian or on an atheistic basis, but have, in a community which freely professes the right to religious freedom, to be neutral?

Another infringement of this right, which is, in this case, covered by the Federal Constitution, is the fact that religious instruction in schools is subdivided according to the teachings of the important Churches. Article 7 III of the Constitution guarantees 'religious instruction in accordance with the principles of the religious communities ... as a regular school subject'. The state is thus given a task which should properly speaking be carried out by the religious communities or Churches themselves. Although this 'regular school subject' is optional both for teachers and for pupils – it is an 'obligatory subject on the curriculum of the school, but an optional subject for individual pupils and teachers'[12] – the principle of separation is nonetheless violated.

The only religious instruction which can and should be given in state schools is a scientific and historical study of comparative religion, providing an introduction to the consideration and criticism of all the major world religions. Only teaching of this kind would do justice to the right of children and young people to religious freedom and only this would leave them free and enable them to choose, without being influenced by the limitations and prejudices of their parents, the religion which they themselves found most convincing, or to remain entirely free of religion.

This programme of education in comparative religion, which should be supplemented in the final years of schooling by philosophy, goes much further than the claims of several Protestant educational reformers. The weaknesses of the arrangement that has been followed up to the present have been recognized by, for instance, Gert Otto and Martin Stallmann, professors of practical theology at Mainz and Göttingen. Both these men, who

12. According to the jurist Klein, quoted in Fischer, *Trennung* ..., p. 232.

are concerned with the teaching of religion in schools, would like to see the special and isolated position of religious education largely broken down, the secular character of the schools given more explicit recognition and a form of instruction which was free from 'dogmatic adherence'[13] adopted. Gert Otto would like to do away – very generously – with school prayers, worship and religious services in school, and is in favour of what he calls 'bi-confessional' teaching – a form of instruction which would include both Evangelical and Roman Catholic teachings together. But these propositions can easily be recognized as rather impotent hybrids which introduce no qualitative changes into the present system.

What can I say in conclusion? The simplest and most honourable course for the Churches to take, of course, would be for them to give up their long-established but false positions of power. But it is equally obvious that their liaison with the state and all that they gain from it is more promising and offers more in the way of security than their own God. In the face of this clinging to worldly power, everything that the Churches have to say, with their usual insistence on maximum content, about the Christian's 'unconditional surrender' in faith to God and his renunciation of guarantees here on earth is exposed as empty hypocrisy.

13. Stallmann, *Christentum und Schule*, p. 199.

4

The Christian West – Ideology and Reality

JUST as the people of Israel long ago glorified the barren hill-country of Palestine and called it a 'land flowing with milk and honey', so too is the Christian west praised by the people of God of the New Covenant as the fulfilment of all human desires.

O Christian Rome ... you are a shining beacon of civilization and the whole of Europe and the world are indebted to you for all the inspiration and holiness, wisdom and morality that make their people and their history most sublime and glorious. You are a mother of love; your monuments, your schools and universities are triumphant witnesses to your love, which bears all things, believes all things, hopes all things, endures all things, to become all things for all men; to call all men to the freedom which Christ has given them in order to lead them to that rest and to that peace which makes all nations brothers, and all men everywhere, however different they may be in language and customs, one family and the world one fatherland.[1]

This is Pope Pius XII's eulogy of the Christian west, with its centre in Rome, the Holy City, in his Christmas message of 1941.

The Catholic version of the idea of a Christian west is usually based on a medieval ideal of religious unity, Gothic cathedrals and flourishing culture. The Protestant version tends naturally enough to emphasize aspects of the modern age and to trace all the more recent achievements – modern technology, mathematical and scientific progress and, of course, historical and critical thought – back to origins which are ultimately Christian. In other words, the much discussed secularization of and removal of God from the modern world is regarded as a 'legitimate consequence' of the gospel.

1. Quoted from Hugo Rahner, *Abendland*, p. 19.

But this is a massive distortion of history, as the collection of fossils in the first part of this book has shown. Almost everything that was originally disputed in the bitter struggle against Christianity has subsequently been claimed by the Church as its own.

What was it really like in Europe when Christianity was at the zenith of its power – in other words, in the Middle Ages? When practically nothing could take place unless it was blessed by Holy Mother Church? When the Christian spirit permeated and fashioned everything – the private and the public sphere of life, the family, education, the economy and politics? When the popes were so powerful that they could name and depose emperors and kings at will?

What happened? An endless series of wars ravaged Europe. Popes and bishops appeared in armour as generals leading their troops.

Countless peasants – villeins, who often owned no more than their clothes – had to spend their whole lives in dreary serfdom, cultivating the huge estates of their spiritual and secular feudal lords.

Intellectual life was at a very low ebb. The overwhelming majority of the population could neither read nor write and lived in a state of primitive superstition which was actively encouraged by the Church in the form of relics, amulets, holy water and so on. The universities were dominated by scholasticism, according to which the most convincing and valid argument was that which could be supported by the greatest number of quotations from the Church Fathers and the Bible – a method which was clearly totally unscientific.

Most people suffered from extremely poor physical and psychological health. Illness was regarded as the consequence of sin, which was why the Fourth Lateran Council of 1215 forbade doctors, under pain of excommunication, to treat a sick person who had not confessed his sins. The imposition of hands, exorcism and prayer were the approved methods for Christian doctors. Plagues were fought by means of processions and services of intercession. (It is interesting to note that even in 1829 a pope – Leo XII – forbade vaccination because smallpox was, in his opinion, a punishment from heaven. The rising death-rate from the disease did not trouble him.)

Sexuality was, of course, outlawed and repressed as sinful, and for centuries this resulted in outbreaks of mass psychosis, perversion, sadism and neuroses of a violence hardly known in human history before or since.

All this was enveloped in the smoke and flames rising from the countless fires on which human victims were burnt to ashes to the accompaniment of prayers.

What about the impressively beautiful Romanesque and Gothic cathedrals with their solemn high masses celebrated with courtly splendour? Should they be excepted from the general pattern of medieval life? Not at all. The medieval cathedrals serve the same purpose to the panegyrists of the Christian Middle Ages as the *Autobahnen* to those who still seek to justify some aspects of National Socialism. In both cases, however, what is overlooked is that these show-pieces cannot be isolated from the other aspects of two inhuman systems. Just as the German motorways were, from the very beginning, built with the military aims of the Third Reich in view, so too were the churches and cathedrals of the Middle Ages erected to strengthen the ideological supremacy of the ruling nobility. From the pulpits of these magnificent monuments the subjects of the secular and ecclesiastical princes were exhorted to obedience and humility to God and his lords on earth. From those distant altars, their eyes were turned towards an illusory life beyond death which – provided they were obedient and humble enough – would compensate them for all that they had had to go without and suffer during the misery of their lives here on earth.

Nothing is more characteristic of the Christian west than the fact that men had their tongues cut out in the Middle Ages for defaming God ('blasphemy'), and that they are even now threatened with court proceedings, while the constant defamation of man which is represented by Christianity itself is generally not even recognized as such.

So much for the Catholic ideal of the Christian west. What

about the common Protestant assertion that the 'secularity of the world' is a direct consequence of the Christian faith, explaining, for example, why it is only in the Christian west that technological progress could have been so great?

This argument fails completely when confronted with the absurd inference that Christianity was, for the eighteen or so centuries which preceded the secularization of the world, living continually in total contradiction to its own aims and intentions. It is, after all, a simple and undeniable fact that, during this long period lasting hundreds of years, the Churches did everything but secularize the world. Both the world of nature and human society were believed to be full of occult and sacral powers – they were certainly not freed from the grip of demons and spirits by the Churches. There was deep and widespread belief in spirits and devils throughout the Christian centuries and this belief is still with us today. Those who denied that witches existed were branded as atheists, because faith in God and faith in demons were inextricably interwoven. Those who opposed the monarchy were also condemned as atheists, because faith in God and faith in feudalism were inseparably entwined.

All movements or books which sought to remove God from the world and secularize it in any way were ruthlessly condemned. Giordano Bruno was burnt to death on 2 February 1600. Galileo was forced in 1633 to recant his teaching, which contradicted the biblical image of the world. All the books which taught the new cosmology were placed on the Index of Forbidden Books. It was not until 1822 that the Holy Office in Rome consented to allow the Copernican cosmology to be disseminated among Christians.

Darwin's teaching was rejected vehemently. Even as late as 1925, a trial was held in the State of Tennessee at the instigation of a group of fervent Protestants – the so-called 'ape trial' – in which a teacher was condemned for teaching the theory of evolution at his school. The law on the basis of which he was condemned has not yet been repealed.[2] Pope Pius XII was also

2. See Benz, *Schöpfungsglaube und Endzeiterwartung*, p. 181 ff.

opposed to the theory of the origin of the species (see the encyclical *Humani Generis* of 1950).

Another fact which radically refutes the favourite Protestant argument that Christianity is ultimately responsible for the secularization of the world is the chronic Christian deficiency in the sphere of education. It is certainly true, of course, that schooling and university education originated in the Church. But, although Christian apologists are always claiming this as an honour, the Church cannot really be proud of it. On the contrary – Christianity is directly responsible for the appalling ignorance and lack of education which is one of the most striking aspects of the history of the west. Whereas in pagan Greece and Rome people even at the lowest social level were generally able to read and write,[3] and scientific studies were pursued at the academies, the overwhelming majority of people living in the Christian west have been illiterate throughout the centuries.

The idea of giving a basic education to all people did not even arise in more than fifteen hundred years of Christianity. It was not even envisaged as an ideal worth striving towards, let alone putting into effect. Even today, there are countless Christians living in Italy, Spain and Portugal who can neither read nor write. The Christian west has not produced any real education at all, either for the mass of the people or for the intellectually gifted – if there are good Christian educational institutions today, they are directly or indirectly based on the secular model.

Even the much-praised medieval universities of, for example, Paris and Bologna cannot be used to correct the miserable picture of Christian ignorance as soon as it is remembered that it took Christianity twelve hundred years to produce them.

My contention that Christianity has brutalized men and kept them ignorant, rather than educating them and raising them up, is not based on some bold but false claim made by a handful of outspoken freethinkers, but on a historically demonstrable and bitter fact. This fact is not the result of the chance failure of a long succession of popes who were hostile to learning and limited

3. See Weniger, 'Bildungswesen', p. 1283.

in their vision to provide any suitable education, but of the irreconcilable opposition of faith to rational thought.

One indirect argument against the assertion that the secularity of the modern world is essentially rooted in the Christian faith emerges clearly from the fact, so often overlooked, that there is and has been not only a Christian west but also a Christian east. It is notorious that this Christian east – Egypt, Ethiopia, Syria and Russia – has produced no technology, no mathematics or science and no historical and critical thought. If faith in Jesus Christ had really been the motivating force for the eventual secularization of the world, it should surely have proved its worth in the east as well. Since this has not happened, then we can only conclude – if we at the same time take the other factors mentioned in this chapter into consideration – that it is not because of Christianity, but for other reasons altogether, that the world has become secularized.

The most convincing reason for this argument is that there is and always has been another, non-Christian west as well as the Christian west. In spite of all the human beings and books burnt by believers in their determination to keep the west exclusively Christian, there are at least five other historical streams of culture and thought in Europe, each with a long tradition – the continental Germanic heritage, the tradition of Jewish spirituality, the heritage of Roman and Greek antiquity, the culture of the Arab and Saracen world and the European Enlightenment with its resultant movements such as liberalism and Marxism.

The secularization of the modern world has its roots not in the Christian ideology of the west, but in these traditions. The Greeks and the Romans possessed a quite astonishing knowledge of physics and astronomy and were able to turn this knowledge to good account. The Greek philosophical tradition also produced a number of atheistic thinkers, such as Protagoras, Democritus, Prodicus, Critias, Euhemerus, Trasymachus and Diagoras, among whose writings all the themes discussed in modern atheism will be found.

The culture of the Arabs and Saracens has also had an

important influence on Europe, although the study of this influence has so far been seriously neglected (see Sigrid Hunke's book on the Arabian heritage in the west – *Allahs Sonne über dem Abendland*). Europe not only owes its system of numbers to the Arabs, but also much of its fundamental knowledge of mathematics, astronomy, medicine and even philosophy (the work of Avicenna, for example).

Finally, the much despised Enlightenment performed an invaluable service by helping to further the idea that human reason was supreme and in so doing came into constant conflict with the Churches. It also brought to the fore the concept of humanity which is indispensable nowadays even to many Christians.

Let me conclude with the words written by Karl Marx in the introduction to his *Critique of Hegel's Philosophy of Law*: 'The criticism of religion ends with the doctrine that man is the highest being for men, thus with the categorical imperative to overthrow all relationships in which man is a debased, enslaved, abandoned and despised being, relationships which cannot be better described than by echoing the cry of the Frenchman when he heard about a planned tax on dogs – "Poor dogs! They want to treat you like men!"'[4]

4. Quoted from Marx/Engels, *Über Religion*, p. 38.

Bibliography

The following abbreviations have been used for the titles of journals:

ET = *Evangelische Theologie*
KZ = *Kirche in der Zeit*
RGG = *Religion in Geschichte und Gegenwart*, Tübingen, 1957/65.
TZ = *Theologische Zeitschrift*
ZTK = *Zeitschrift für Theologie und Kirche*

ADORNO, THEODOR W., *Negative Dialektik*, Frankfurt a.M., 1966.
  Eingriffe, Frankfurt a.M., 1966.
  'Erinnerungen an Paul Tillich', in *Werk und Wirken Paul Tillichs*, Stuttgart, 1967.
  Jargon der Eigentlichkeit, Frankfurt a.M., 1964.
  Minima Moralia, Frankfurt a.M., 1964.
  'Offenbarung oder autonome Vernunft', in *Frankfurter Hefte* 13, 1958, pp. 397 ff., 484 ff.
ADORNO, THEODOR W., and others, *The Authoritarian Personality*, New York, 1950.
ADORNO, THEODOR W., and HORKHEIMER, MAX, *Dialektik der Aufklärung*, Amsterdam, 1947.
  Sociologica II, Frankfurt a.M., 1962.
ALBERT, HANS, 'Die Idee der kritischen Vernunft', in Szczesny (ed.), *Club Voltaire* I.
  'Tradition und Kritik', in Szczesny (ed.), *Club Voltaire* II.
ALTHAUS, PAUL, 'Christologie', in RGG.
  Die letzten Dinge, 9th ed., Gütersloh, 1964.
  Die Ethik Martin Luthers, Gütersloh, 1965.
  'Jungfrauengeburt', in RGG.
  Luthers Haltung im Bauernkrieg, Darmstadt, 1962.
  Die Theologie Martin Luthers, Gütersloh, 1962.
ANDERSEN, WILHELM, 'Selbstpreisgabe der Theologie?' in *Deutsches Pfarrerblatt* 62, 1962.

BIBLIOGRAPHY

ANDRESEN, CARL, *Logos und Nomos*, Berlin, 1955.
APPEL, NIKOLAUS, *Kanon und Kirche*, Paderborn, 1964.
AUGUSTIN, HERMANN W., (ed.), *Diskussion zu Bischof Robinsons 'Gott ist anders'*, 2nd ed., Munich, 1965.
BACKHAUS, GUNTHER, *Atheismus – eine Selbsttäuschung?* Munich and Basle, 1962.
BARTH, KARL, 'Denken heisst Nachdenken', in KZ 21, 1966, p. 203 ff.
Die kirchliche Dogmatik, Zürich, I, 1, 8th ed., 1964; II, 2, 5th ed., 1960.
Die protestantische Theologie im 19. Jahrhundert, 3rd ed., Zürich, 1960.
BARTLEY, WILLIAM W., *The Retreat to Commitment*, New York, (*Flucht ins Engagement*, Munich, 1964).
BARTSCH, HANS WERNER, (ed.), *Ehrlich gegenüber Gott*, 2nd ed., Hamburg, 1964.
(ed.) *Kerygma und Mythos*, Hamburg and Bergstedt: I, 4th ed., 1960; II, 1952; III, 2nd ed., 1957.
(ed.) *Post Bultmann Locutum*, II, Hamburg and Bergstedt, 1965.
BASCHWITZ, KURT, *Hexen und Hexenprozesse*, Munich, 1966.
BAUER, WALTER, *Aufsätze und Kleine Schriften*, Tübingen, 1967.
Rechtgläubigkeit und Ketzerei im ältesten Christentum, 2nd ed., Tübingen, 1964.
BÄUMER, RUDOLF, (ed.), *Kein anderes Evangelium*, Wuppertal, 1966.
Bekenntnisschriften der Evangelisch-Lutherischen Kirche, 4th ed., Göttingen, 1959.
BENSE, MAX, 'Warum man Atheist sein muss', in Szczesny (ed.), *Club Voltaire* I.
BENZ, ERNST, *Ecclesia spiritualis*, 1934, reprinted Darmstadt, 1964.
Ideen zu einer Theologie der Religionsgeschichte, Mainz and Wiesbaden, 1961.
Nietzsches Ideen zur Geschichte des Christentums und der Kirche, Leiden, 1956.
Schöpfungsglaube und Endzeiterwartung, Munich, 1965.
BEUMANN, HELMUT, (ed.), *Heidenmission und Kreuzzugsgedanke in der deutschen Ostpolitik des Mittelalters*, Darmstadt, 1963.
BEUTLER, WERNER, 'Toleranz als Staatsprinzip', in *Werkhefte* 16, 1962, pp. 180 ff., 235 ff.
BIENERT, WALTER, (ed.), *Das Christentum und die Juden*, Cologne, 1966.

BLANKE, FRITZ, *Missionsprobleme des Mittelalters und der Neuzeit*, Zürich and Stuttgart, 1966.

BONHOEFFER, DIETRICH, *Widerstand und Ergebung*, 11th ed., Munich, 1962.

BORNKAMM, GÜNTHER, 'Das Ende des Gesetzes. Paulusstudien', in *Gesammelte Aufsätze* I, 3rd ed., Munich, 1961.

'Evangelien', in RGG.

Jesus von Nazareth, 5th ed., Stuttgart, 1960.

'Studien zu Antike und Urchristentum', *Gesammelte Aufsätze* II, 2nd ed., Munich, 1963.

BORNKAMM, HEINRICH, 'Toleranz, II', in RGG.

BRAUN, HERBERT, 'Christentum. Entstehung', in RGG.

'Gottes Existenz und meine Geschichtlichkeit im Neuen Testament', in Dinkler (ed.), *Zeit und Geschichte*.

Gesammelte Studien zum Neuen Testament und seiner Umwelt, Tübingen, 1962.

Post Bultmann Locutum: see Bartsch (ed.), and Symanowski (ed.).

BRÖCKER, WALTER, and BUHR, HEINRICH, *Zur Theologie des Geistes*, Pfullingen, 1960.

BRONDER, DIETRICH, *Christentum in Selbstauflösung*, 2nd ed. Hanover.

BUHR, HEINRICH, *Der Glaube – was ist das?* Pfullingen, 1963.

BULTMANN, RUDOLF, 'Briefwechsel mit Dvoracek zur Eschatologie' in KZ 18, 1963, p. 31 f.

Das Evangelium des Johannes, 17th ed., Göttingen, 1962.

'Zur Frage der Entmythologisierung', in Bartsch (ed.), *Kerygma und Mythos* III.

Geschichte und Eschatologie, Tübingen, 1958.

Die Geschichte der synoptischen Tradition, 5th ed., Göttingen, 1961

Glauben und Verstehen, Tübingen: I, 4th ed., 1961; II, 3rd ed. 1961; III, 1960; IV, 1965.

'Ist die Apokalyptik die Mutter der christlichen Theologie?', in *Apophoreta*, Berlin, 1964.

Jesus, Tübingen, 1961.

Marburger Predigten, Tübingen, 1956.

'Mythos und Mythologie im NT', in RGG.

'Neues Testament und Mythologie', in Bartsch (ed.), *Kerygma und Mythos* I.

'Zum Problem der Entmythologisierung', in Bartsch (ed.), *Kerygma und Mythos* II.

BIBLIOGRAPHY

Theologie des Neuen Testaments, 4th ed., Tübingen, 1961.
Das Urchristentum im Rahmen der antiken Religionen, Hamburg, 1962.
Das Verhältnis der urchristlichen Christusbotschaft zum historischen Jesus, 3rd ed., Heidelberg, 1962.

BURI, FRITZ, 'Entmythologisierung oder Entkerygmatisierung der Theologie', in Bartsch (ed.), *Kerygma und Mythos* II.
'Theologie der Existenz', in Bartsch (ed.), *Kerygma und Mythos* III.
'Theologie und Philosophie', in TZ 8, 1952, p. 116 ff.

CAMPENHAUSEN, HANS VON, *Griechische Kirchenväter*, 3rd ed., Stuttgart, 1961.
Lateinische Kirchenväter, Stuttgart, 1960.

CARMICHAEL, JOEL, *The Death of Jesus*, Penguin Books, 1966 (*Leben und Tod des Jesus von Nazareth*, 2nd ed., Munich, 1965).

COMFORT, ALEX *Sex in Society*, London, 1963 (*Der aufgeklärte Eros*, Munich, 1963.)

CONZELMANN, HANS, 'Entmythologisierung', in Schultz (ed.), *Theologie für Nichttheologen* I.
'Heidenchristentum', in RGG.
'Jesus Christus', in RGG.
'Randbemerkungen zur Lage im "Neuen Testament"', in ET 22, 1962, p. 225 ff.
'Wo steht die Kirche?', in *Blätter für deutsche und internationale Politik* 10, 1965, p. 1014 ff.

DESCHNER, KARLHEINZ, *Abermals krähte der Hahn* (Eine kritische Kirchengeschichte von den Anfängen bis zu Pius XII), 2nd ed., Stuttgart, 1964.
(ed.) *Das Jahrhundert der Barbarei*, Munich, 1966.
(ed.) *Jesusbilder in theologischer Sicht*, Munich, 1966.
Mit Gott und den Faschisten, Stuttgart, 1965.

DIBELIUS, MARTIN, *Die Formgeschichte des Evangeliums*, 4th ed., Tübingen, 1961.

DIEM, HERMANN, *Dogmatik*, Munich, 1955.

DINKLER, ERICH, *Bibelautorität und Bibelkritik*, Tübingen, 1950.
'Weltbild III', in RGG.
(ed.) *Zeit und Geschichte*, Tübingen, 1964.

DOBSCHÜTZ, ERNST VON, 'Christentum und Sklaverei', in *Realenzyklopädie fürpr otestantische Theologie und Kirche* 18, 3rd ed., Leipzig, 1906.

EBELING, GERHARD, 'Die Botschaft von Gott an das Zeitalter des Atheismus', in *Monatsschrift für Pastoraltheologie* 52, 1963, p. 8 ff.

'Die Evidenz des Ethischen und die Theologie', in ZTK 57, 1960, p. 318 ff.

'Existenz zwischen Gott und Gott', in ZTK 62, 1965, p. 86 ff.

Vom Gebet, Tübingen, 1963.

'Geist und Buchstabe', in RGG.

Die Geschichtlichkeit der Kirche und ihrer Verkündigung als theologisches Problem, Tübingen, 1954.

'Der Grund christlicher Theologie', in ZTK 58, 1961, p. 227 ff.

'Hauptprobleme der protestantischen Theologie in der Gegenwart', in ZTK 58, 1961, p. 123 ff.

'Hermeneutik', in RGG.

'Hermeneutische Theologie?', in KZ 20, 1965, p. 484 ff.

'Theologie', in RGG.

'Theologie und Philosophie, in RGG.

Theologie und Verkündigung, Tübingen, 1962.

'Tradition', in RGG.

'Verantworten des Glaubens in Begegnung mit dem Denken M. Heideggers', in ZTK 58, 1961, Beiheft 2, p. 119 ff.

Was heisst Glauben?, Tübingen, 1958.

Das Wesen des christlichen Glaubens, Tübingen, 1961.

Wort und Glaube, 2nd ed., Tübingen, 1962.

Wort Gottes und Tradition, Göttingen, 1964.

ECKERT, WILLEHAD P., LEVINSON, NATHAN, and STÖHR, MARTIN (eds.), *Antijudaismus im Neuen Testament?*, Munich, 1967.

ERDMANN, CARL, *Die Entstehung des Kreuzzugsgedankens*, 1935, reprinted Darmstadt, 1965.

ERLER, ADALBERT, 'Inquisition', in RGG.

ERLINGHAGEN, KARL, *Katholisches Bildungsdefizit in Deutschland*, Freiburg, Basle and Vienna, 1965.

FISCHER, ERWIN, 'Das Bundesverfassungsgericht über Staat und Kirche', in *Vorgänge* 4, 1965, p. 351 ff.

'Die Entscheidungen über Schulgebet und Religionsunterricht', in *Vorgänge* 4, 1965, p. 457 ff.

'Die Kirchensteuerentscheidungen', in *Vorgänge* 5, 1966, p. 1 ff.

'Religionsunterricht', in *Vorgänge* 4, 1965, p. 283 f.

'Schulgebet in Hessen', in *Vorgänge* 4, 1965, p. 342 f.

'Staat und Kirche nach dem Grundgesetz', in *Vorgänge* 4, 1965, p. 178 ff.

Trennung von Staat und Kirche, Munich, 1964.

FLAKE, OTTO, *Der letzte Gott*, Hamburg, 1961.

FLATTEN, HEINRICH, *Fort mit der Kirchensteuer?* Cologne, 1964.

FLECHTHEIM, OSSIP K., *Eine Welt oder keine?* Frankfurt a.M., 1964.

FRIES, HEINRICH, *Ärgernis und Widerspruch*, Würzburg, 1965.

FUCHS, ERNST, *Gesammelte Aufsätze* I, Tübingen, 1959.

Gesammelte Aufsätze II, Tübingen, 1960.

Gesammelte Aufsätze III, Tübingen, 1965.

'Zum Rechtsstreit über das "Schulgebet" in der hessischen Gemeinschaftsschule' (duplicated manuscript), Marburg, February 1966.

'Theologie oder Ideologie', in *Theologische Literaturzeitung* 88, 1963, p. 257 ff.

GAMM, HANS-JOCHEN, *Judentumskunde*, 2nd ed., Munich and Recklinghausen, 1960.

GEIGER, THEODOR, *Ideologie und Wahrheit*, Stuttgart and Vienna, 1953.

'Gesetz zu dem Vertrag des Landes Hessen mit den Evangelischen Landeskirchen in Hessen', in *Gesetz- und Verordnungsblatt für das Land Hessen* 10, 1960, p. 54 ff.

GEYER, HANS GEORG, 'Theologie des Nihilismus', in ET 23, 1963, p. 86 ff.

GIGON, OLOF, *Die antike Kultur und das Christentum*, Gütersloh, 1966.

GILG, ARNOLD, *Weg und Bedeutung der altkirchlichen Christologie*, 2nd ed., Munich, 1961.

GLASER, HERMANN, *Eros in der Politik*, Cologne, 1967.

GOGARTEN, FRIEDRICH, *Entmythologisierung und Kirche*, 3rd ed., Stuttgart, 1958.

GOLLWITZER, HELMUT, *Die Christen und die Atomwaffen*, Munich, 1957.

Die Existenz Gottes im Bekenntnis des Glaubens, 4th ed., Munich, 1964.

'Der Glaube an Jesus Christus und der sogenannte historische Jesus', in H. Ristow, K. Matthiae (eds.), *Der historische Jesus und der kerygmatische Christus*.

Post Bultmann Locutum, see Bartsch and Symanowski (ed.).

Die marxistische Religionskritik und der christliche Glaube, Munich and Hamburg, 1965.

GOLLWITZER, HELMUT, and WEISCHEDEL, WILHELM, *Denken und Glauben*, Stuttgart, 1965.

GOTTSCHICK, JOHANNES, 'Ehe, christliche', in *Realenzyklopädie für protestantische Theologie und Kirche* 5, 3rd ed., Leipzig, 1898.

GRASS, HANS, *Ostergeschehen und Osterberichte*, 2nd ed., Göttingen, 1962.

'Der theologische Pluralismus und die Wahrheitsfrage', in KZ 20, 1965, p. 146 ff.

GRÄSSER, ERICH, 'Die antijüdische Polemik im Johannesevangeliun', in *New Testament Studies* 11, 1964-5, p. 74 ff.

GRUNDMANN, HERBERT, *Religiöse Bewegung im Mittelalter*, 2nd ed., Darmstadt, 1961.

Ketzergeschichte des Mittelalters, Göttingen, 1963.

'Kreuzzüge', in RGG.

HABERMAS, JÜRGEN, 'Erkenntnis und Interesse', in Rudolf Sinz (ed.), *Zur Ideologie und Ideologiekritik*, Freiburg i.Br., 1967.

Zur Logik der Sozialwissenchaften, Tübingen, 1967, Supplement 5 of the *Philosophische Rundschau*.

Theorie und Praxis, Neuwied and Berlin, 1963.

'Analytische Wissenschaftstheorie und Dialektik', in Max Horkheimer (ed.), *Zeugnisse*, Frankfurt a.M., 1963.

HAENSSLER, ERNST, *Der liberale Protestantismus auf Irrwegen*, Bern, 1954.

Theologie – ein Fremdkörper in der Universität der Gegenwart, Bern, 1960.

HANSEN, JOSEPH, *Quellen und Untersuchungen zur Geschichte des Hexenwahns und der Hexenverfolgung im Mittelalter*, 1901, reprinted Hildesheim, 1963.

HARENBERG, WERNER, *Jesus und die Kirchen*, Stuttgart and Berlin, 1966.

HARNACK, ADOLF VON, *Kritik des Neuen Testaments*, Leipzig, 1911.

Die Mission und Ausbreitung des Christentums in den ersten drei Jahrhunderten, Leipzig, 1902.

(ed.) *Porphyrius 'Gegen die Christen'*, 15 vols., Berlin, 1916.

HARVEY, A. VAN, and OGDEN, SCHUBERT M., 'Wie neu ist die "Neue Frage nach dem historischen Jesus"?', in ZTK 59, 1962, p. 46 ff.

HASENHÜTTL, GOTTHOLD, *Der Glaubensvollzug*, Essen, 1963.

HEER, FRIEDRICH, *Gottes erste Liebe*, Munich and Esslingen, 1967.

Mittelalter, Zürich, 1964.

BIBLIOGRAPHY

HEER, FRIEDRICH, and SZCZESNY, GERHARD, *Glaube und Unglaube*, Munich, 1960.

Heilige Schrift des Alten und des Neuen Testaments, Die, Zürich, 1959.

HESSISCHER STAATSGERICHTSHOF, 'Das Urteil über das Schuilgebet an den hessischen Schulen', in *Vorgänge* 4, 1965, p. 476 ff.

HEUSSI, KARL, *Kompendium der Kirchengeschichte*, 12th ed., Tübingen, 1960.

HIRSCHAUER, GERD, *Der Katholizismus vor dem Risiko der Freiheit*, Munich, 1966.

HOLL, KARL, 'Die Missionsmethode der alten und die der mittelalterlichen Kirche', in *Gesammelte Aufsätze zue Kirchengeschichte* III, Tübingen, 1928.

HOPPE, MAX, 'Fragen eines deutschen Buddhisten an das "christliche Abendland"', in Kurt Hutten and Siegfried von Kortzfleisch (eds.), *Asien missioniert im Abendland*, Stuttgart, 1962.

HORKHEIMER, MAX, 'Erinnerungen an Paul Tillich' and 'Letzte Spur von Theologie – Paul Tillichs Vermächtnis', in *Werk und Wirken Paul Tillichs*, Stuttgart, 1967.

Zur Kritik der instrumentellen Vernunft, Frankfurt a.M., 1967. See also under Adorno and Regius.

HUCK, ALBERT, and LIETZMANN, HANS, *Synopse der ersten drei Evangelien*, 9th ed., Tübingen, 1950.

HUNKE, SIGRID, *Allahs Sonne über dem Abendland*, Stuttgart, 1962.

HUSS, HERMANN, and SCHRÖDER, ANDREAS (eds.), *Antisemitismus*, Frankfurt a.M., 1965.

HUTTEN, KURT, *Seher Grübler Enthusiasten*, 9th ed., Stuttgart, 1964.

INSTITUT FÜR SOZIALFORSCHUNG, *Soziologische Exkurse*, 2nd ed., Frankfurt a.M., 1956.

JASPERS, KARL, 'Wahrheit und Unheil der Bultmannschen Entmythologisierung', in Bartsch (ed.), *Kerygma und Mythos* III.

JEDIN, HUBERT, *Kleine Konziliengeschichte*, 6th ed., Freiburg i.Br., 1963.

JEREMIAS, JOACHIM, *Die Gleichnisse Jesu*, 6th ed., Göttingen, 1962.

JÜNGEL, EBERHARD, *Paulus und Jesus*, 2nd ed., Tübingen, 1964.

JUNGK, ROBERT, and MUNDT, HANS JOSEF (eds.), *Modelle für eine neue Welt*, Munich, 1964 ff.

KÄHLER, MARTIN, *Der sogenannte historische Jesus und der geschichtliche, biblische Christus*, edited by E. Wolf, 3rd ed., Munich, 1961.

KAMEN, HENRY, *Intoleranz und Toleranz zwischen Reformation und Aufklärung*, Munich, 1967.

KAMLAH, WILHELM, *Christentum und Geschichtlichkeit*, 2nd ed., Stuttgart and Cologne, 1951.

KÄSEMANN, ERNST, *Jesu letzter Wille nach Johannes 17*, Tübingen, 1966.

'Konsequente Traditionsgeschichte?', in ZTK 62, 1965, p. 137 ff.

Exegetische Versuche und Besinnungen, Göttingen: I, 2nd ed., 1960; II, 1964.

KÄSTNER, ERICH, 'Über das Verbrennen von Büchern', in Szczesny (ed.), *Club Voltaire* I, Munich, 1963.

KAUFMANN, WALTER, *Der Glaube eines Ketzers*, Munich, 1965.

KITTEL, GERHARD, and FRIEDRICH, GERHARD, *Theologisches Wörterbuch zum Neuen Testament*, Stuttgart, 1933 ff.

KLEIN, GÜNTER, *Wunderglaube und Neues Testament*, Wuppertal and Barmen, 1960.

KLOHR, OLOF, *Naturwissenschaft, Religion und Kirche*, Berlin, 1958.

(ed.) *Religion und Atheismus heute*, Berlin, 1966.

KNIGHT, MARGARET, 'Erziehung ohne Religion', in Szczesny (ed.), *Club Voltaire* I.

KNOLL, AUGUST M., *Katholische Kirche und scholastisches Naturrecht*, Vienna, Frankfurt, Zürich, 1962.

Zins und Gnade, Neuwied and Berlin, 1967.

KÖNIG, B. EMIL, *Ausgeburten des Menschenwahns im Spiegel der Hexenprozesse und der Autodafés*, Berlin-Schöneberg, n.d.

KÖSTER, HELMUT, 'Häretiker im Urchristentum', in RGG.

'Häretiker im Urchristentum als theologisches Problem', in Dinkler (ed.), *Zeit und Geschichte*.

KRAUS, HANS-JOACHIM, *Geschichte der historisch-kritischen Erforschung des Alten Testaments von der Reformation bis zur Gegenwart*, Neukirchen, 1956.

'Kirche und Synagoge', in *Das Judentum in Geschichte und Gegenwart*, Hamburg, 1961.

KRECK, WALTER, 'Die Frage nach dem historischen Jesus als dogmatisches Problem', in ET 22, 1962, p. 460 ff.

KÜHNER, HANS, *Index Romanus*, Nuremberg, 1963.

Neues Papstlexikon, Frankfurt and Hamburg, 1965.

Tabus der Kirchengeschichte, 2nd ed., Nuremberg, 1965.

KÜMMEL, WERNER GEORG, *Einleitung in das Neue Testament*, 12th ed., Heidelberg, 1963.

'Jesusforschung seit 1950', in *Theologische Rundschau* 31, 1965-6, pp. 15 ff., 289 ff.

'Judenchristentum, I.', in RGG.
Das Neue Testament, Munich, 1958.
'Sittlichkeit, V', in RGG.
'Urchristentum', in RGG.
KÜNNETH, WALTER, *Glauben an Jesus?* 2nd ed., Hamburg, 1963.
Von Gott reden? Wuppertal, 1965.
KUPISCH, KARL, *Kirche und soziale Frage im 19. Jahrhundert*, Zürich, 1963.
LAS CASAS, BARTOLOMÉ DE, *Kurzgefasster Bericht von der Verwüstung der Westindischen Länder*, Frankfurt a.M., 1966.
LEESE, KURT, *Die Religionskrisis des Abendlandes und die religiöse Lage der Gegenwart*, Hamburg, 1948.
LENIN, VLADIMIR ILYICH, *Über die Religion*, 6th ed., Berlin, 1965.
LENK, KURT (ed.), *Ideologie. Ideologiekritik und Wissenssoziologie*, 2nd ed., Neuwied and Berlin, 1964.
LEPPIN, EBERHARD, *Glaubt ihr nicht so bleibt ihr nicht*, Tübingen, 1966.
LOEWENICH, WALTHER VON, *Die Geschichte der Kirche*, 5th ed, Witten, 1957.
Glaube Kirche Theologie, Witten, 1958.
Der moderne Katholizismus, Witten, 1955.
LÖGSTRUP, KNUD EILER, *Die ethische Forderung*, Tübingen, 1959.
LOOFS, FRIEDRICH and ALAND, KURT, *Leitfaden zum Studium der Dogmengeschichte*, 6th ed., Tübingen, 1959.
LÖWITH, KARL, 'Die philosophische Kritik der christlichen Religion im 19. Jahrhundert', in *Theologische Rundschau* 5, 1933, pp. 131 ff., 201 ff.
'Nietzsches antichristliche Bergpredigt', in Szczesny (ed.), *Club Voltaire* I.
LUDWIG, GERHARD, *Massenmord im Weltgeschehen*, Stuttgart, 1951.
MACHOVEC, MILAN, *Marxismus und dialektische Theologie*, Zürich, 1965.
MACINTYRE, ALASDAIR, 'Gott und die Theologen', in Augustin, H. W. (ed.), *Diskussion zu Bischof Robinsons 'Gott ist anders'*.
MARSCH, WOLF-DIETER, 'Ehe', in RGG.
'Frau', in RGG.
MARX, KARL, and ENGELS, FRIEDRICH, *Über Religion* (ed. Institut für Marxismus-Leninismus), Berlin, 1958.
MARXSEN, WILLI, *Anfangsprobleme der Christologie*, Gütersloh, 1960.

MAUTHNER, FRITZ, *Der Atheismus und seine Geschichte im Abendland*, 1920, reprinted Hildesheim, 1963.

MITSCHERLICH, ALEXANDER, 'Thesen zu einer Diskussion über Atheismus', in Szczesny (ed.), *Club Voltaire* I.

MORUS (pseudonym for Richard Lewinsohn), *Eine Weltgeschichte der Sexualität*, Hamburg, 1966.

MÜLLER, HANS (ed.), *Katholische Kirche und Nationalsozialismus*, Munich, 1965.

MÜLLER-LAUTER, WOLFGANG, 'Zarathustras Schatten haben lange Beine', in ET 23, 1963, p. 193 ff.

MÜLLER-SCHWEFE, HANS-RUDOLF, *Der Standort der Theologie in unserer Zeit*, 2nd ed., Göttingen, 1961.

NESTLE, WILHELM, 'Die Haupteinwände des antiken Denkens gegen das Christentum', in *Archiv für Religionswissenschaft* 37, Leipzig and Berlin, 1941–2.

Die Krisis des Christentums, Stuttgart, 1947.

NEUSÜSS, ARNHELM, 'Ideologische Aspekte der Diskussion über Utopie', unpublished manuscript, Marburg, 1965.

NIGG, WALTER, *Das Buch der Ketzer*, 4th ed., Zürich and Stuttgart, 1962.

Franz Overbeck, Munich, 1931.

Das ewige Reich, 2nd ed., Zürich, 1954.

NOLLER, GERHARD, 'Philosophische und christliche Theologie', in ET 22, 1962, p. 650 ff.

Novum Testamentum Graece, ed. Von Eberhard, Nestle and Aland, Kurt, 24th ed., Stuttgart, 1960.

OTTO, GERT, 'Zur Frage der Repräsentanz des Christlichen in der Schule der Gegenwart', in KZ 22, 1967, p. 517 ff.

'Religionsunterricht und politische Situation', in *Denken – Glauben – Handeln. Almanach auf das fünfzigste Jahr des Furche Verlags*, Hamburg, 1966.

Schule Religionsunterricht Kirche, 2nd ed., Göttingen, 1964.

OVERBECK, FRANZ, *Christentum und Kultur*, 2nd ed., Darmstadt, 1963.

Über die Christlichkeit unserer heutigen Theologie, 3rd ed., Darmstadt, 1963.

Selbstbekenntnisse, Frankfurt a.M., 1966.

'Über das Verhältnis der alten Kirche zue Sklaverei im römischen Reiche', in *Studien zur Geschichte der alten Kirche*, Darmstadt, 1965.

BIBLIOGRAPHY

PANNENBERG, WOLFHART, *Grundzüge der Christologie*, Gütersloh, 1964.

'Heilsgeschehen und Geschichte', in *Kerygma und Dogma* 5, 1959, p. 218 ff., 259 ff.

(ed.) *Offenbarung als Geschichte*, 2nd ed., Göttingen, 1963.

PETRY, GERHARD, 'Das Ende der Theologie?' in KZ 18, 1963, p. 14 ff.

PFANNMÜLLER, GUSTAV, *Jesus im Urteil der Jahrhunderte*, Leipzig and Berlin, 1908.

PFISTER, OSKAR, *Calvins Eingreifen in die Hexer- und Hexenprozesse von Peney 1545 nach seiner Bedeutung für Geschichte und Gegenwart*, Zürich, 1947.

Das Christentum und die Angst, Zürich, 1944.

PICHT, GEORG, *Die deutsche Bildungskatastrophe*, Munich, 1965.

PLESSNER, HELMUT, *Die verspätete Nation*, 4th ed., Stuttgart, 1966.

PORPHYRY, see Harnack (ed.).

PZILLAS, FREIDRICH, *Die Lebenskräfte des Christentums*, Bad Godesberg, 1960.

RAD, GERHARD VON, *Theologie des Alten Testaments*, Munich: I, 4th ed., 1962; II, 3rd ed., 1962.

RAHNER, HUGO, *Abendland*, Freiburg, Basle and Vienna, 1966.

RATZINGER, JOSEPH, 'Theologie, III, Katholische Theologie', in RGG.

REGIUS, HEINRICH (Pseudonym for Max Horkheimer), *Dämmerung*, Zürich, 1934.

REICKE, SIEGFRIED, 'Kirchengut und Säkularisation', in RGG.

RISTOW, HELMUT, and MATTHIAE, KARL (eds.), *Der historische Jesus und der kerygmatische Christus*, 2nd ed., Berlin, 1961.

ROBINSON, JAMES M., *A New Quest of the Historical Jesus*, London, 1959 (*Kerygma und historischer Jesus*, Zürich and Stuttgart, 1960).

ROBINSON, JOHN A. T., *Christian Morals Today*, London, 1964 (*Christliche Moral heute*, Munich, 1964).

Honest to God, London, 1963 (*Gott ist anders*, Munich, 1963).

The New Reformation?, London, 1965 (*Eine neue Reformation?* Munich, 1965).

ROSSA, KURT, *Todesstrafen*, Oldenburg and Hamburg, 1966.

RUSSELL, BERTRAND, *Why I am not a Christian*, London, 1957 (*Warum ich kein Christ bin*, 2nd ed., Munich, 1963.)

SCHEUNER, ULRICH, 'Kirche und Staat' and 'Staatkirche', in RGG.

SCHLEIERMACHER, FRIEDRICH, *Über die Religion*, Hamburg, 1961.

SCHMIDT, KURT DIETRICH, *Grundriss der Kirchengeschichte*, 4th ed., Göttingen, 1963.

SCHREY, HEINZ-HORST, 'Theologie II, Evangelische Theologie', in RGG.

SCHULTZ, HANS JÜRGEN (ed.), *Juden Christen Deutsche*, 3rd ed., Stuttgart, Olten and Freiburg i.Br., 1963.

(ed.) *Theologie für Nichttheologen*, (first series), Stuttgart, 1963.

SCHWEITZER, ALBERT, *Geschichte der Leben-Jesu-Forschung*, 7th ed., Munich and Hamburg, 1966.

SEEBERG, REINHOLD, 'Luthers Anschauung von dem Geschlechtsleben und der Ehe und ihre geschichtliche Stellung', in *Luther-Jahrbuch* 4, 1925.

SÖLLE, DOROTHEE, *Stellvertretung*, Stuttgart, 1965.

SPEICHER, GÜNTER, *Doch sie können ihn nicht töten*, Düsseldorf and Vienna, 1966.

STALLMANN, MARTIN, *Christentum und Schule*, Stuttgart, 1958.

STAUFFER, ETHELBERT, *Jerusalem und Rom im Zeitalter Jesu Christi*, Berne, 1957.

Jesus, Berne, 1957.

STEPHAN, GERHARD, 'Der Streit um den historischen Jesus innerhalb der Bultmannschule', in KZ 20, 1965, p. 492 ff.

STRECKER, GEORG, *Der Weg der Gerechtigkeit*, Göttingen, 1962.

STUHLMACHER, PETER, *Gerechtigkeit Gottes bei Paulus*, Göttingen, 1965.

SYMANOWSKI, HORST (ed.), *Post Bultmann Locutum*, I, Hamburg and Bergstedt, 1965.

SZCZESNY, GERHARD (ed.), *Die Antwort der Religionen auf 31 Fragen*, Gütersloh, 1965.

(ed.). *Club Voltaire*, Munich; I, 1963; II, 1965; III, 1967.

'Das Gespräch zwischen "Glaube" und "Unglaube"', in *Vorgänge* 4, 1965, p. 203 ff.

Die Zukunft des Unglaubens, Munich, 1960. See also under Heer, Friedrich.

TAYLOR, G. RATTRAY, *Sex in History*, London, 1953 (*Wandlungen der Sexualität*, Düsseldorf and Cologne, 1957).

Theologiestudium, Munich, 1965.

THIELICKE, HELMUT, *Über die Angst des heutigen Theologiestudenten vor dem geistlichen Amt*, Tübingen, 1967.

TILLICH, PAUL, *On the Boundary*, London, 1967 (*Auf der Grenze*, 2nd ed., Munich and Hamburg, 1965).

Symbol und Wirklichkeit, Göttingen, n.d.

Systematic Theology, London, Vol. I, 1933; Vol. II, 1955; Vol. III,

1957 (*Systematische Theologie*, Stuttgart: I, 2nd ed., 1956; II, 1958; III, 1966),
Wesen und Wandel des Glaubens, Berlin, 1961.

TOPITSCH, ERNST, 'Hegel und das Dritte Reich', in *Der Monat* 18, 1966.
Sozialphilosophie zwischen Ideologie und Wissenschaft, Neuwied, 1961.
Vom Ursprung und Ende der Metaphysik, Vienna, 1958.

ULONSKA, HERBERT, 'Ketzer und Zeuge', in KZ 20, 1965, p. 535 ff.

VAN DER LEEUW, GERARDUS, *Die Bilanz des Christentums*, Zürich, 1947.
Phänomenologie der Religion, 2nd ed., Tübingen, 1956.

VIERING, FRITZ (ed.), *Die Bedeutung der Auferstehungsbotschaft für den Glauben an Jesus Christus*, Gütersloh, 1966.

WEBER, WERNER, 'Staatsleistungen an die Kirche', in RGG.

WEEBER, RUDOLF, 'Kirchensteuer', in RGG.

WEIN, HERMANN, 'Zum Rationalismus-Irrationalismus-Streit der deutschen Gegenwart', in Szczesny (ed.), *Club Voltaire* I.

WEISCHEDEL, WILHELM, 'Philosophische Theologie im Schatten des Nihilismus', in ET 22, 1962, p. 233 ff.
'Paul Tillichs philosophische Theologie', in *Der Spannungsbogen. Festgabe für Paul Tillich zum 75. Geburtstag*, Stuttgart, 1961. See also under Gollwitzer, Helmut.

WENDLAND, HEINZ-DIETRICH, 'Sklaverei und Christentum', in RGG.

WENIGER, ERICH, 'Bildungswesen', in RGG.

WERNER, MARTIN, *Die Entstehung des christlichen Dogmas*, Stuttgart, 1959.

WITTE, JOHANNES, 'Sklaverei und Christentum', in RGG, 1st and 2nd eds.

WOLF, ERNST, 'Zur gegenwärtigen Lage der evangelischen Theologie in Deutschland', in *Der evangelische Erzieher* 18, 1966, p. 161 ff.

WYNEKEN, GUSTAV, *Abschied vom Christentum*, 2nd ed., Munich, 1964.

ZAHRNT, HEINZ, *Es begann mit Jesus von Nazareth*, Stuttgart, 1960.
Die Sache mit Gott, Munich, 1966.

ZSCHARNACK, LEOPOLD, 'Frau, II', in RGG, 1st ed.

ZURHELLEN-PFLEIDERER, ELISE, 'Frau, III', in RGG, 2nd ed.

Glossary

Apologetics: the defence of the Christian faith
Christology: teaching about Jesus Christ
Epiphany: the appearance of God
Eschatology: teaching about the last things
Exegesis: explanation, interpretation, especially of the Bible
Exorcism: the driving out of demons and devils
Hermeneutics: interpretation, the doctrine of understanding
Incarnation: (Christ's) becoming man
Kenosis: Christ's emptying of himself when he became man
Kerygma: the essential message of the gospel
Mariology: teaching about Mary
Pancritical: subjecting everything to total criticism and asking oneself every question
Parousia: the second coming of Christ
Pre-existence: the heavenly existence of Christ before his birth as man
Syncretic religion: mixed religion

MORE ABOUT PENGUINS
AND PELICANS

Penguinews, which appears every month, contains details of all the new books issued by Penguins as they are published. From time to time it is supplemented by *Penguins in Print*, which is a complete list of all books published by Penguins which are in print. (There are well over three thousand of these.)

A specimen copy of *Penguinews* will be sent to you free on request, and you can become a subscriber for the price of the postage. For a year's issues (including the complete lists) please send 30p if you live in the United Kingdom, or 60p if you live elsewhere. Just write to Dept EP, Penguin Books Ltd, Harmondsworth, Middlesex, enclosing a cheque or postal order, and your name will be added to the mailing list.

Some other books published by Penguins are described on the following pages.

Note: *Penguinews* and *Penguins in Print* are not available in the U.S.A. or Canada

Radical Theology and the Death of God

THOMAS J. J. ALTIZER AND
WILLIAM HAMILTON

'... God has died in our time, in our history, in our existence.' What does it mean to say that God is dead? Is it any more than a warning against all idols, all divinities fashioned out of human need, human ideologies? Does it perhaps not just mean that 'existence is not an appropriate word to ascribe to God, that therefore he cannot be said to exist, and he is in that sense dead'? It means this and more.

In this collection Thomas Altizer and William Hamilton provide both an introduction to and an exposition of Radical Theology. The Death-of-God radical theologians have no God, no faith in God, and affirm both the death of God and of all the forms of theism. They attempt to set an atheist point of view within the spectrum of Christian possibilities; their aim being to strive for a whole new way of theological understanding.

Penguin Classics

NIETZSCHE

Translated by R. J. Hollingdale

Twilight of the Idols
The Anti-Christ

Twilight of the Idols, which was written by Nietzsche (1844–1900) in 1888, the year before he went mad, briefly summarizes his views on almost the whole range of his philosophical interests. It remarkably fulfils his ambition to 'say in ten sentences what everyone else says in a book – what everyone else *does not* say in a book'. *The Anti-Christ*, written immediately afterwards, is his longest and least restrained polemic against Christianity and Christian morals, and is expressed in his most vivid and forceful style. The two books in this volume are linked by a special commentary with Nietzsche's other works.

Thus Spoke Zarathustra

No modern philosopher has been more completely misquoted and misrepresented than Friedrich Nietzsche. His phrase, 'God is dead', his insistence that the meaning of life is to be found in purely human terms, and his doctrine of the Superman and the will to power were all later seized upon and unrecognizably twisted by, among others, Nazi intellectuals. This new translation of *Thus Spoke Zarathustra*, a spiritual odyssey through the modern world, is therefore of supreme value to us in judging for ourselves a brilliantly original thinker who has had a powerful influence upon such twentieth-century writers as Shaw, Mann, Sartre, and Camus.

The Way of Transcendence

Christian Faith Without Belief in God

ALISTAIR KEE

'Ours is an age of faith, but not belief.'

Men wish to be committed, but for more and more people belief in God has become impossible. It is Alistair Kee's contention that 'the future of Christianity is not viable unless we can find a way of presenting it which includes the old doctrine of God, but does not demand belief in God as a prior condition of becoming a Christian'.

The Way of Transcendence excitingly breaks through the impasse between conservative theology (outdated in the modern age) and radical theology (which scarcely remains theology). Among contemporary theologians Alistair Kee sees Van Buren, whatever his virtues, as reductionist and positivist; the 'Death of God' movement as nostalgia in radical costume; and such thinkers as Robinson and Macquarrie, for whom belief in God is finally unavoidable, as victims of wish-fulfilment.

We are left with the need for a secular faith which, without excluding God, can enshrine Christian teaching in a secular code.

It is this proposition which makes Alistair Kee's book one of the most impressive Christian works to have appeared since Bultmann.

The Psychology of Moral Behaviour

DEREK WRIGHT

It is by no means true that a sheltered 'moral' upbringing, with lots of early nights and Sunday school, produces the most honest, guilt-free people; neither is altruism the most helpful of qualities.

In *The Psychology of Moral Behaviour* Derek Wright, of the Department of Psychology at the University of Leicester, introduces the reader to the psychological study of moral behaviour, and in particular to the empirical approach within it. The author takes various theoretical perspectives and examines the following subjects in the light of them.

Why some people find it easier to resist temptation than others, and the psychological effects of doing something wrong; what kinds of adult behaviour induce what kinds of behaviour in children; delinquency; altruism; moral insight and ideology; different types of character; religion; education and morality.

The author emphasizes the difficulty of discussing this subject without being biassed by personal beliefs, e.g. Western moral ideas, and sets out to do so along the strictest scientific lines.

Marxism and Christianity

ALASDAIR MACINTYRE

'Christianity is the grandmother of Bolshevism' – Oswald Spengler

Aspiring to be both a Christian and a Marxist – or at least as much of each as was compatible with allegiance to the other – the author was twenty-three when he wrote this book. He argues that Marxism shares in good measure both the content and functions of Christianity and does so because it inherits them from Christianity. He details the religious attitudes and modes of belief that appear in Marxism, both as it developed historically from the philosophies of Hegel and Feuerbach and as it has been carried on by its latter-day interpreters, from Rosa Luxemburg and Trotsky to Kautsky and Lukacs. He shows also how Marxism, no less than Christianity, is subject to the historical relativity that affects all ideologies.

Professor MacIntyre is now in the Department of the History of Ideas at Brandeis University. He has thoroughly revised and elaborated this book in the light of post-Stalinist developments.

'A significant contribution to a fundamental human argument' – *Journal of Theological Studies*.

NOT FOR SALE IN THE U.S.A. OR CANADA

In the Penguin African Library

The Discarded People

An Account of African Resettlement in South Africa

COSMAS DESMOND

One aspect of South African *apartheid* is the resettlement of Africans in Bantu 'homelands'. What this pretty concept entails and has entailed for about 1,000,000 black people – in human suffering, poverty and starvation – is here described by a Christian priest.

Early in 1968 the black population – tenants and parishioners – were arbitrarily removed from the author's mission in Natal and 'resettled' on an unprepared stretch of veld twenty miles away. This first-hand experience of a brutality which recalls Hitler or Stalin set Father Desmond off on a journey of inquiry through the Republic.

The Discarded People factually records what he found – thousands of families uprooted (with fire and force, where necessary) and dumped on bleak, barren sites which offer little hope of food, shelter, work or even water.

Like the television programmes based upon it, this is a book to shock and disgust. As Nadine Gordimer writes in her foreword: 'The physical conditions of life described in this book are such an appalling desolation that one is almost unable to think beyond bread and latrines.'